OUT OF REACH

THE POETRY OF PHILIP LARKIN

Also by Andrew Swarbrick

The Art of Oliver Goldsmith (*editor*)

Philip Larkin: *The Whitsun Weddings* **and** *The Less Deceived*

T. S. Eliot: Selected Poems

Out of Reach

The Poetry of Philip Larkin

ANDREW SWARBRICK

First published in Great Britain 1995 by
MACMILLAN PRESS LTD
Houndmills, Basingstoke, Hampshire RG21 6XS
and London
Companies and representatives
throughout the world

A catalogue record for this book is available from the British
Library.

ISBN 0–333–59661–7

First published in the United States of America 1997 by
ST. MARTIN'S PRESS, INC.,
Scholarly and Reference Division,
175 Fifth Avenue, New York, N.Y. 10010

ISBN 0–312–17452–7

This book is printed on paper suitable for recycling and made from fully
managed and sustained forest sources.

10 9 8 7 6 5 4 3 2
05 04 03 02 01 00 99 98 97

Printed in Malaysia

For Anne, Tom, Jo and William

Contents

Preface

This book has been written in the conviction that Philip Larkin's poetry is important to us. It aims to present Larkin as more adventurous and challenging than we are used to recognising, and to rebut both the old charges of genteel parochialism and the new charges of ideological incorrectness. Although it takes account of recent biographical material, it is not simply an interpretation of the poems by way of the life. Indeed, as this study shows, the relationship between the two is in Larkin's case especially problematic. The focus of this study is on the poems and the rhetorical strategies which make them, in John Bayley's words, 'both wholly accessible and completely mysterious' (in the *London Review of Books*, 5–18 May 1983).

The book is organised around Larkin's separately published collections for the benefit of readers unfamiliar with the *Collected Poems*. Nevertheless, since this is a study of the whole poetic *oeuvre* (with some attention given to his two novels, *Jill* and *A Girl in Winter*), wide reference is made to poems not collected by Larkin in his four volumes. In these cases, references are given to Anthony Thwaite's edition of the *Collected Poems*. I have also been able to include previously unpublished material from Larkin's manuscript notebooks.

My earlier guide to Larkin in the Master Guide series published by Macmillan offered an explicatory account of some of his poems, and students in search of a basic introduction are directed there; I have taken the liberty, in the interim, of changing my mind on some points of interpretation. My hope is that this present book will prove of interest to the general reader and to the specialist alike.

I am grateful to the literary executors and Trustees of the Philip Larkin Estate for permission to consult and publish material lodged in the Philip Larkin Archive at the University of Hull Brynmor Jones Library, and to publish an extract from Larkin's correspondence with Barbara Pym. I owe particular debts to the Hull University Archivist, Brian Dyson; to Andrew Motion and Anthony Thwaite for commenting on a draft version of this book; to Stephen Regan who, as an anonymous reader, made many valuable suggestions during its preparation; to the staff of the Bodleian Library, Oxford, especially in the Department of Western Manuscripts; to the staff of Oxford Central Library; and to Susan Ward for bibliographical assistance. All errors remain my own.

Part of the first chapter appeared as 'Larkin: First and Final Drafts', *Poetry Review*, vol. 83, no. 4 (Winter 1993/94) pp. 50–53.

ANDREW SWARBRICK

Acknowledgements

The author and publishers wish to thank the following for permission to use copyright material:

Carcanet Press Ltd for excerpts from 'Rejoinder to a Critic', 'Limited Achievement' and 'Remembering the Thirties' by Donald Davie from *Collected Poems*, 1990.

Jonathan Clowes Ltd on behalf of the author and Random House UK Ltd for an excerpt from 'Something Nasty in the Bookshop' by Kingsley Amis, reprinted as 'A Bookshop Idyll' in *Collected Poems 1944–79*, Hutchinson, 1979. Copyright © 1956 Kingsley Amis.

Faber & Faber Ltd and Farrar Straus and Giroux, Inc. for excerpts from 'Party Politics', 'Ugly Sister', 'Love, we must part now', 'Blizzard', 'Waiting for breakfast', 'An April Sunday brings the snow', 'Modesties', 'To Failure', 'Strangers', 'Best Society', 'Oils', 'Fiction and the Reading Public', 'Water', 'A Study of Reading Habits', 'The Whitsun Weddings', 'Home is so Sad', 'Talking in Bed', 'Love', 'Dockery and Son', 'An Arundel Tomb', 'The Large Cool Store', 'Reference Back', 'Toads Revisited', 'The Old Fools', 'The Building', 'Money', 'High Windows', 'This Be The Verse', 'Vers de Société', 'MCMXIV', 'The Dance', 'The Life with a Hole in it', 'Sad Steps', 'Show Saturday', 'The Explosion', 'Aubade', 'Love Again', 'The Winter Palace' and 'Continuing to Live' from *Collected Poems* by Philip Larkin. Copyright © 1988, 1989 by the Estate of Philip Larkin.

The Marvell Press for excerpts from 'Born Yesterday', 'Dry-Point', 'Deceptions', 'Next, Please', 'Poetry of Departures', 'Toads', 'Spring' and 'Wires' from *The Less Deceived* by Philip Larkin.

Quotations from Larkin's unpublished manuscripts held in the Philip Larkin Archive at the Brynmor Jones University Library, University of Hull, may not be reproduced without permission from the Estate of Philip Larkin.

Every effort has been made to trace all the copyright-holders, but if any have been inadvertently overlooked the publishers will be pleased to make the necessary arrangement at the first opportunity.

1
Philip Larkin

The few visitors to Philip Larkin's top-floor flat in 32 Pearson Park, Hull, where Larkin lived for eighteen years, might have noticed in the bathroom a montage 'juxtaposing Blake's "Union of Body And Soul" with a Punch-type cartoon of the front and back legs of a pantomime horse pulling in opposite directions against one another and captioned "Ah, at last I've found you!"'.[1] For an intensely private man, Larkin was strangely willing to offer public portraits of himself, however self-parodyingly laconic. The most public revelations of his self-protecting privacy are, of course, the poems. The pursed-up bachelor in 'Spring', the cynically debunking revenant of 'I Remember, I Remember', the sniggering agnostic of 'Church Going', the rootless, childless, provincial librarian, the nostalgic elegist: Larkin's poems seem to come to us very appealingly as the expression of a personality disclosing itself with self-deprecating honesty. Just how much lay hidden behind the disclosures and how self-revealing those masks were has been thoroughly explored by Andrew Motion in his biography of Larkin. This study is not so much interested in the 'personality' of Larkin as in the rhetorical constructions of his poems and the ways in which they aspire to things 'out of reach'. In Larkin's case, this meant a yearning for metaphysical absolutes, for states of being imagined, as it were, beyond the reach of language. He once told an interviewer, 'One longs for infinity and absence, the beauty of somewhere you're not'.[2] His poems are attempts to occupy the imaginative space of 'somewhere you're not' and are ultimately concerned with existential questions of identity, choice and chance, isolation and communality.

On this showing, Larkin is a more adventurous, challenging and provocatively 'modern' writer than his critics, and some of his admirers, have been prepared to concede. The moments of most intense assent in Larkin, his own 'enormous yes', come with the vocabulary of nullity: nowhere, absences, oblivion, the 'dear

1

translucent bergs:/ Silence and space' ('Age'). The terror of death is matched by the yearning for annihilation, the fear of non-existence by the desire for anonymity. The ultimate aspiration is for 'unfenced existence', and in Larkin's work elemental presences take on a metaphysical significance, suggesting everything that is consolingly non-self, the other. Thus, 'Myxomatosis' is an existentialist statement about life as meaningless endurance, and 'Nothing To Be Said' a ludic saying something out of nothing. It should come as no surprise that in his book on Samuel Beckett, Christopher Ricks invoked Larkin.[3]

Larkin's bathroom collage identifies the abiding conflicts from which his poetry emerged, the visionary integration of the spiritual and the corporeal mockingly juxtaposed with the comic disintegration of the pantomime horse. As Motion has remarked, every impulse in Larkin was met and matched by its opposite and the collage reveals the fundamental collision in Larkin which determined the nature of his work. In his poetry we find expressed a lifelong argument between the artist and the philistine, between aspiring aestheticism (here represented by Blake) and the iconoclastic mockery of the cartoon. Larkin's work is very far removed from 'genteel bellyaching' and provincial unadventurousness. It emerges from the delicate negotiation of two powerful forces in Larkin: the passionate desire to live a life devoted to writing, and the iconoclastic fury of having that desire thwarted. The result is an art suspicious of its own claims, resisting its own rhetorical persuasiveness. (D. J. Enright early noted of Larkin that 'he doesn't altogether trust poetry, not even his own',[4] and another critic wrote an essay on Larkin entitled 'Against Imagination'[5]). In Larkin we find exemplified the Yeatsian choice between perfection of the work or perfection of the life. His writing is driven by a sense of failure in both. It is in these terms that this book sets out to answer two questions, one related to the beginning of Larkin's career, the other to the end. How did Larkin develop from the derivatively romantic poet and aspiring novelist of the 1940s to the creator of *The Less Deceived* and *The Whitsun Weddings*? And how are we to explain the uncreative silence by which Larkin was so tormented in the last decade of his life? As Motion's biography indicates, the answers lie in the work itself as much as in the life.

Philip Larkin was born on 9 August 1922, the second child of Sydney and Eva Larkin. His father was the City Treasurer in Coventry and Larkin grew up in comfortable material circumstances; Andrew Motion has described the other, less comfortable circumstances of Larkin's childhood.[6] During his lifetime, Larkin was careful in public to pay tribute to his parents whilst conceding that there had been difficulties: '. . . I wouldn't want it thought that I didn't like my parents. I did like them. But at the same time they were rather awkward people and not very good at being happy. And these things rub off'.[7] When an old schoolfriend, Noel Hughes, wrote in the celebratory *Larkin at Sixty* of Larkin's 'intimidating' and 'solemn' home, Larkin was outraged by the apparent treachery.[8] But a note in his manuscript notebook, dated May 1949, suggests another story: 'In our family/ Love was disgusting as lavatory,/ And not as necessary'.[9] Childhood was far from a 'forgotten boredom' and its tensions, oppressions and inadequacies helped shape not only Larkin's attitude to marriage, but all his attitudes to solitariness and communality.

At school, Larkin seems to have won friendship by his powers of mockingly mimicking his schoolmasters. His stammer contributed to his self-consciousness. Years later, Larkin described for himself (in an unpublished autobiographical fragment) the effect of his stammer:

> Therefore, when I conjure up a vision of myself in boyhood . . . He is giggling into his sleeve, or round a book . . . twisting and doubling up and grimacing with mimicry, red in the face with effort to get his words out before his companion can divine them. The words! already they are as important as the sense. Jerkingly, they come gasping out . . . uttered in the strangled, high-pitched nasal voice of a seaside marionette.[10]

The mimicry will later be translated into the ventriloquisms of Larkin's poems, their caricaturing of attitudes and social location in a representative phrase or cliché. But as described above, the stammer, traces of which remained with him throughout his life, plays a more intriguing role, contributing both to feelings of self-disgust and the determination to outwit. Words were another thing almost out of reach.

It is during Larkin's undergraduate years at Oxford, between 1940 and 1943, that the cleavage in him between the aesthete and the philistine becomes apparent. He continued to write poems as he had as a schoolboy, largely accomplished pastiches of Auden, gathered into bound typescript collections, some of them with self-conscious prefaces. His attitudes to writing and his passionate devotion to the idea of himself as an artist can be gauged from his extensive correspondence with his schoolfriend Jim Sutton, who studied at the Ashmolean in Oxford before serving abroad during the war. The discipleship to D. H. Lawrence, the high-minded art-for-art's-sake attitudes, the cultivation of artistic inspiration: these reveal a vulnerably aspiring Larkin unknown to most of his later readership, and to his friends of that time. Kingsley Amis remembers 'an almost aggressively normal undergraduate of the non-high-brow, non-sherry-sipping sort, hard-swearing, hard-belching . . . I have since thought that some of this was a little strained and over-done, as if to repel any attempt at intimacy'.[11] This also suggests Larkin's resolve – some would say ruthlessness – to present different aspects of himself to gratify different people. What drew Larkin and Amis together was their passion for jazz. Jazz was their art and it contributed significantly to Larkin's thinking about his own writing. The friendship with Amis was important to Larkin's work in helping to subvert his aestheticism by a debunking iconoclasm, a mock-philistine mockery of pretentiousness. As Andrew Motion has shown, Larkin's first novel *Jill* emerges from the irreverent prose fantasies Larkin concocted with Amis, and with this came an altogether more subversive attitude to writing, culminating in the librarian's iconoclastic 'Books are a load of crap'. Larkin himself later commented on the general war-time atmosphere of deprivation which dominated his time at Oxford. 'This was not the Oxford of Michael Fane and his fine bindings, or Charles Ryder and his plovers' eggs . . . At an age when self-importance would have been normal, events cut us ruthlessly down to size.'[12]

Declared unfit for active war-service (because of poor eyesight), Larkin moved in November 1943 to Wellington in Shropshire as sole librarian in the Public Library. The job gave him little joy, but it left him time to write, his energies being largely devoted to completing *Jill*. It was in Wellington that Larkin met Ruth Bowman and began a relationship that was to dominate the next few years of his life and which is sublimated in the romantic postures and disaffections of *The North Ship*. His father's death in 1948 added to Larkin's gloom and by this time his romantic attachments had been further complicated by his relationship with Monica Jones, a lecturer in the English Department at Leicester University, where Larkin had been appointed Assistant Librarian in 1946.

Larkin had arrived at Leicester with a minor reputation as a novelist after the publication of *Jill* in 1946, and it was as a novelist that he was determined to make his literary career. *Jill* had been published, eventually, by the Fortune Press, an idiosyncratic venture run by R.A. Caton. He had published *Poetry from Oxford in Wartime* which had included a few of Larkin's poems and subsequently published Larkin's first collection, *The North Ship*, in 1945. Larkin's second novel, *A Girl in Winter*, was placed with the much more prestigious Faber imprint and published in 1947. But the next few years only served to intensify Larkin's sense of failure, and with it the resentments and sense of betrayal by his artistic ambitions. He wrote substantial drafts of two novels without completing either, and failed to find a publisher for a second collection of poems putatively entitled *In the Grip of Light*.

The breakthrough, personal and creative, came in 1950 when Larkin severed his domestic and romantic entanglements by moving as Sub-Librarian to Queen's University, Belfast. The sense of estrangement he experienced there was crucial in clarifying the arguments in his work about the conception of his own identity, and it was in Belfast that he found his most productive writing conditions. He also met Winifred Arnott, then a trainee librarian, who figures in a number of poems written at this time. As this study shows, it is around 1950 that Larkin began to develop those strategies in his poems which remained central to his particular achievement.

The publication in 1955 of *The Less Deceived* by the Marvell Press near Hull coincided with Larkin's own move to Hull University as Librarian. It was here that he was to spend the remainder of his life, publishing poems with parsimonious care (two further volumes in two decades) to become what Donald Davie called the 'unofficial laureate of post-1945 England'.[13]

The Whitsun Weddings, which appeared in 1964, brought him a remarkable measure of popular esteem and an intensifying pressure to protect the privacy which nurtured his poems and which they talked about so publicly. He won the Queen's Gold Medal for Poetry in 1965. *The North Ship* was re-issued in 1966. *High Windows* followed in 1974 and made Larkin a national monument. His selection of occasional prose was published in 1983 as *Required Writing* and his jazz reviews as *All What Jazz* (in 1970). Together, they give a fragmented and calculated impression of Larkin's poetic credo, one constructed for easy public consumption to perpetuate the impression of an anti-modernist, accessible, empirical, middlebrow unambitiousness: 'This is my essential criticism of modernism, whether perpetrated by Parker, Pound or Picasso: it helps us neither to enjoy nor endure'.[14] That he never read foreign literature is belied, for example, by references in his interviews to Ashbery and Frank O'Hara, his review of Henry de Montherlant (whose 'Happiness writes white' he was fond of quoting) and borrowings in his poetry from French Symbolist sources. But the public mask shielded the privacies of his work, at least for a time, and helped determine the way it was read and received.

This public face was at its most provocative when Larkin compiled *The Oxford Book of Twentieth Century English Verse*, published in 1973. Offering only a cursory rationale, it advanced the work of little-known poets in an effort to show a kind of affecting amateurism surviving the invasions of modernism into a native English tradition. It declared a public ancestry for Larkin, one defiantly unambitious and insular. After 1974, Larkin published even less than formerly, sometimes to oblige commissions, and then subsided into public silence. His personal life grew more distressing, his sense of failure and isolation more profound. He died on 2 December 1985: as he had predicted, at the same age as his father.

Anthony Thwaite assembled a *Collected Poems* in 1988, gathering fugitive published poems, printing some of the longer fragments from Larkin's manuscript notebooks and making a selection from the unpublished poems Larkin wrote before *The North Ship* and *The Less Deceived*. It suddenly offered a rather different impression of Larkin from the one he had carefully cultivated. He was revealed as having written much more than had been assumed, with nearly eighty unfamiliar poems appearing in addition to the newly published juvenilia. Thwaite's chronological arrangement (with the earliest work appended), though it met with hostility from reviewers who thought Larkin's own ordering of poems should have been preserved, allowed otherwise buried patterns to surface. Newly visible were the relatively productive periods and phases of particular preoccupations. It also allowed readers to see at what point the familiar Larkin began to emerge. In his review of the *Collected Poems*, Blake Morrison noted of 'If, My Darling', 'It's the first poem in which Larkin shows signs of dramatizing himself... Once he could wear his defeat like an overcoat, not hide beneath it, Larkin was away'. Morrison summarised his general impression thus: 'what we have should be enough to ensure that Larkin will never again be patronized as a dried-up toad squatting on modernism, but be seen as an original, obsessive, deep-feeling poet who consistently refused the consolations of conventional belief'.[15]

But Morrison's judgement proved optimistic. The publication of Larkin's *Selected Letters* in 1992 met with widespread consternation. The volume was accused of revealing an intemperate, foul-mouthed misogynist and racist bigot whose 'gouts of bile' (as Larkin himself admitted) passed for political opinion. Larkin's most hostile critics seized on these revelations as the values underpinning the whole of Larkin's work and reputation, the sewer, as Tom Paulin put it (fearing the worst of Thwaite's editorial cuts) underneath the national monument. Affronted in the letters by 'a steady stream of casual obscenity, throwaway derogatory remarks about women, and arrogant disdain for those of different skin colour or nationality', Professor Lisa Jardine reassured *Guardian* readers that, in the interests of pluralism, 'we don't tend to teach Larkin much now in my Department'.[16] Later, Bryan Appleyard offered a portrait of Larkin's 'repellent, smelly, inadequate masculinity', parading him as 'a drab symptom of a peculiar contemporary national impulse to refuse all ambition'.[17] There was more general dismay at the unrelieved intensity of Larkin's misery, the inconsolable desolation conveyed in some of his letters. There was a feeling, too, that without a biographical context, the letters left Larkin perilously exposed (though it was odd of some reviewers to find this culpable whilst simultaneously pointing to the nakedness).

The very earliest criticism of Larkin's work had condemned its 'tenderly nursed sense of defeat'; now the life was to be conflated with the work, as if Larkin's writing, even in the letters, was a simple reflex of personality. As this study shows, the relationship between Larkin's life and work is highly problematic and teasingly oblique. Andrew Motion's biography, published shortly after the letters, revealed more of Larkin's deviousness, not only in his relationships with women, but in the strategies by which he presented himself to the world. There is now a danger of our taking the poems less seriously than the letters, though it is a danger Larkin courted. Ian Hamilton pointed out that the Larkin 'revealed' in the letters had been before us all the time in the poems, 'but these were usually so well judged, as dramas or confessions, that we could speak also of a Larkinesque "persona" – a self-projection that might in part be a disguise'. Because of the performative element in the poems, they hover between autobiographical confession and the contrivances of personae. 'We knew he was "fucked up" because he told us so, in poem after poem, but the Larkin we admired *was* "supposed to . . . find it funny or not to care", or at any rate to have the gift of transmuting daily glooms into great haunting statements about love and death – ours as well as his'.[18] Hamilton returns us to the problem of Larkin's 'masks' and ventriloquisms, and the rhetorical strategies which make his poems simultaneously self-revealing and self-protective.

An important source of evidence for the formation of these 'masks' remained private throughout Larkin's lifetime. He lodged his first manuscript workbook (covering the period 1944 to 1950) in the British Library in 1965. But only recently have the remaining seven manuscript notebooks been made available as part of the Philip Larkin Archive in the Brynmor Jones Library at Hull University. The notebooks and other private papers help us to draw the shape of Larkin's career. They also reveal aspects of Larkin's writing practices which the rest of this book will examine in more detail.

What the papers confirm (we should have known it from the poems) is that we fail completely to understand Larkin unless we understand how passionately – ambitiously – he wanted to be a writer. That the writer he envisaged himself becoming was a novelist is, by a tormenting irony, what ultimately determined the shape of his career as a poet. The poems written in the mid-1950s by which he first became widely known are despairing confrontations with his sense of failure as a writer. These confrontations involved the reappraisal of himself and his ways of working from which evolved the poetic identity he made familiar to us.

For all the complaints in the letters about dry periods, his earliest poems written as a schoolboy and undergraduate came all too easily. Anthony Thwaite's *Collected Poems* offered a total of seventy poems written between 1938 and 1945 (including the contents of *The North Ship*), of which twenty-two were printed for the first time. This represents a fair selection of those now available in typescript in the archive. Later, Larkin liked it to be thought that he wrote very little at Oxford, but the record shows otherwise. Between 1939 and July 1942, Larkin regularly typed up and bound a total of seven booklets of poems: September 1939 (7 poems); March 1940 (12 poems); June 1940 (9 poems); August 1940 (17 poems); April 1941 (a selection of 35 poems); January 1942 (7 poems) and July 1942 (13 poems). They are the postures of a young man intent on lyrical melancholy and reliant entirely on poetic inspiration and bardic mannerisms, attitudes very far removed from the grudging pawkiness of Bryan Appleyard's portrait. Along with the letters of this period, they reveal a Larkin romantically aspiring, precocious, precious and, as in his Foreword to 'Chosen Poems, 1941', pompous:

> They exemplify, to my mind, the natural and to some extent inevitable ossification of a 'boyish gift' with the passing of time, shown by the gradual disappearance of spontaneous verse forms and natural energy, and the accompanying depersonalization which characterises the later poems. These latter (still speaking from the stand-point of the psychologist) are nearer the poems of a novelist than the poems of a poet.[19]

Gratifyingly, his later hand has added: *'You hope'*. In these poems, Larkin gives full rein to the aesthete in him, an aspect of himself which later spawned its opposite, that mocking philistinism with which his romanticism remained in lifelong creative conflict.

The Larkin workbooks further disclose a generally neglected feature of Larkin's earliest poems. As Stephen Regan has emphasised, they were conditioned by the context of war, a context all but invisible in Larkin's selection of poems for *The North Ship*.[20] The manuscripts show that Larkin wrote a number of poems quite directly concerned with the war. 'Leave', written between April and July 1942, laconically narrates a serviceman's homecoming. Its conclusion anticipates much of the later Larkin:

> Hilda combed her hair
> In their pink double room;
> He heard the doom
> Of 'Alone at last, dear'.
>
> He had momentary schemes
> Of pretending to sleep
> Then gave up hope –
> She lay in his arms.
>
> . . . [Larkin's ellipsis]
>
> The next day dawned fine
> But soon filled with clouds
> Like dirty great birds:
> It began to rain.

> He lay all morning in bed
> With a hard face;
> She did odd jobs in the house
> Sullenly, as she always did.[21]

Another typescript poem, 'Planes Passing', expresses, as Larkin's letters did, the oppressiveness of the war:

> The guns
> Tap the slack drumhead of the sky
> Where separate bombers crawl,
> Leaving soft trails of sound.
> Time has run into the ground,
> And the past squats upon the earth
> Searching its fur for fleas.
>
> Is life drinking, will it ever lift
> Its head from drinking, and move
> Delicately in an undreamt direction?
> Or have these threads
> Drawn and redrawn in the flesh of night
> Sewn a dead parcel to be stuffed and stink
> Under history's stairs?
>
> The guns give an immediate answer.[22]

The second stanza's opening image anticipates the close of 'Wedding-Wind' (written in 1946), and the rhetorically plaintive phrasing generally recalls the 1930s idiom not so much of Auden as of Stephen Spender's 'Ultima Ratio Regum' (1939): 'The guns spell money's ultimate reason/ In letters of lead on the spring hillside'. 'July miniatures' (included in the July 1942 booklet) offers a simple description:

> Near one of the farms, sunk in the sloping fields,
> A bunch of soldiers (on tactical exercise)
> Lounge smoking at a gate: they are very still;
> Watching two men in shirtsleeves stacking the hay crop;
> Above, unnoticed in the sunless skies,
> A plane banks in a long descending circle
> Preparing to land at the aerodrome, over the hill.[23]

The manuscripts suggest that Larkin wrote quite spontaneously, with only light alterations, attempting to capture the 'sudden vision – lasting a second or less' he described in a 1940 letter. But by the late 1940s, Larkin's work had reached a crisis. Many of these early collections bear the marks of later self-laceration: 'Coiled dogshit', 'trash', 'grrr', 'Tripey', 'Likewise tripish', 'now we get to the real rubbish', 'O a lovely slop of dung, this'. Visible here is that philistine impulse, seen at its most intolerable in some of the letters to Amis and Robert Conquest, but which represented the other, essential side of Larkin's creative conflict.

Larkin addressed this dialectic directly in the autobiographical sketches he wrote for himself as a student at Oxford. Of a contemporary, he wrote:

> Like the rest of us, he had come to Oxford from a grammar school, with a Hopkins in his trunk with notes on sprung-rhythm on the flyleaf, and a sincere appreciation of the beautiful. Like us, too, he had decided it was sham, and had decided to drink. And drink he did.[24]

An annotation anxiously adds: 'Not "it", but his appreciation of it'. A little later, he acknowledges the restorative influence of Bruce Montgomery in the same terms:

> Under his immediate influence, I suddenly revolted against all the things I had previously worshipped – poetry, Lawrence, psychoanalysis, seriousness, the creative life, and so forth. It was like being back in the fourth form again.[25]

In the late 1940s, Larkin wrote in his notebook thirteen pages of self-diagnostic autobiography. It begins:

> There are many writers whose work is utterly without interest except for the pages they spent on themselves. I can think of at least one modern writer who struggled desperately to write short stories and novels but only began to make his way when he hit on a trick of dramatising his own life. That is one of the hints I have taken that brings me to this page.

After lamenting the rise and fall of his ambition to live by writing – 'literary failure is the most shaming and dispiriting of failures. I admit sex runs it pretty close' – he launches into a tortuous sentence driven by fury:

> . . . I don't feel that the most resounding sexual victories could eradicate the half-dozen unfinished novels, the hangdog grin and the familiar question that progresses from *What are you writing now?* through *Are you writing anything now?* to *You write, don't you?* and, finally, to silence, and the indissoluble conviction that with a little more industry, a little less self-indulgence, some tiny incalculable adjustment of forces already at one's command, one would have managed to trap in indestructible terms life as one had lived it, and to win the fame and money without which every life, from time to time, seems simply a degrading and farcical waste of time.[26]

By 1950, Larkin had taken the hint about 'dramatising' himself further. He wrote a thirteen-page Shavian dialogue called 'Round the Point' which opens with 'Geraint' tearing up his work. It is really an essay cast in the form of dialogue, an essay about what Larkin's writing adds up to. Like Larkin, Geraint asks what has happened to the literary promise that had produced a book five years ago (Larkin had by now published his two novels, in 1946 and 1947):

> I've done it once. Why can't I do it again? Five years: the difference between twenty-three and twenty-eight, between success and failure, creation and stagnation. . . But to have got reviews and money and praise when I was a young ass of twenty-three, and not to be able to do it now, fills me with the bitterest, the deepest, the most acrid and corroding depression.[27]

Geraint believes in art for art's sake, the writer as 'feminine: his attitude to life is passive. He is recording-wax, or litmus paper . . . the writer transfixes life for what it is in imaginative terms'. His inquisitor, 'Miller', believes on the contrary that the writer must first and foremost cajole the reader's interest, that the successful writer needs not talent but 'Stupidity. Complacency. Insensitivity'. He dismisses Eliot's dictum about the suffering and the creating mind. 'Real' experience and 'aesthetic' experience are not the same, he argues. Writing is a matter of 'discovering what one writes best' and can only happen when 'you let writing take its place among the things you can't do anything about'.

Through Geraint and Miller, Larkin is thinly dramatising the cleavage in himself between the aesthete and the philistine, between writing as willed self-expression and writing as fortuitous and arbitrary, the product of forces beyond the writer's control. At the end, 'They grin at each other, not altogether pleasantly'. In Larkin, they remained in conflict for some time, but it's clear that it is Miller's view which henceforth will prevail: 'A writer's development is a slow approximation to his fated position'.

As Thwaite notes, after 1949 Larkin began to work intensively at his drafts.[28] The seven newly available notebooks confirm the meticulousness with which he now revised, taking over from the novels an attitude to writing as process. Typically, a poem grows over a long period of revisions and frequent abandonments, some of them permanent (Thwaite includes a few of these in the *Collected Poems* and mentions others in his Introduction). Occasionally, a rhyme-scheme is jotted down, but only rarely a note of the intended structure. Larkin seems to have relied on an exhaustive process of refinement, returning repeatedly to the origin of a poem and writing it out again and again so as to let it evolve from whatever instinct first prodded the poem into being. Only at a very late stage does a poem go to typescript, still subject to amendments. The manuscript of 'Here', for example, ends:

> Here is unforced existence:
> Facing the sun, untalkative, out of reach.[29]

Occasionally, a prose note is written in an effort to clarify the direction of a poem. Drafts of 'Dockery and Son', for example, are interrupted by the note: 'Where do these innate ideas come from, that take half a lifetime to realise, by which time it's too late to do anything about them'.[30] Littering the manuscript pages are doodles, sometimes pornographic, frequently of stylised faces and diagrammatic shapes, as if sublimating the effort of the poems to make careful patterns. (The other recurrent marginalia is Larkin's autographed signature, rehearsed over and over again.)

But it is the dramatising tactic of 'Round the Point' which now takes on most significance in the context of Larkin's subsequent poetic practice. His poetry after 1950 slowly begins to incorporate the force which most threatened it: self-mockery. As he tormentedly abandoned his two putative novels, so his poems take over their dialogic, multivocal idioms. Instead of trying to express 'himself' lyrically, Larkin constructs ventriloquisms, playfully self-revealing masks, just as his letters ingratiate themselves by returning with interest the attitudes and inclinations of the addressee. Their misogyny and bigotry were not a pretence. But they belong to the complex and ambiguous attitudes to sexual desire explored in his poems, attitudes bound up with his feeling profoundly threatened by anything which might claim time and effort he could otherwise devote to his writing. Many of the fragments in the notebooks are arguments with himself about selfishness and selflessness. Their progress was so manifestly difficult because for Larkin these were existential rather than ideological problems. In the end, his most romantic aspiration was for a kind of sublime anonymity.

Mikhail Bakhtin wrote that 'The writer is a person who knows how to work language while remaining outside of it; he has the gift of indirect speech'. Larkin's poems tantalise us by their devious rhetoric which hovers between self-disclosure and self-concealment. The later notebooks show how intensively they work for the 'grace' conferred by 'candour'. Sometimes, they struggle to integrate contradictory feelings, as in 'An Arundel Tomb'. In his biography, Andrew Motion interprets a manuscript annotation at the end of the draft – 'Love isn't stronger than death just because statues hold hands for 600 years' – as a private recognition of the futility of the statue's symbol, a gesture akin to Larkin's defacements of his earlier poetry. But in fact the annotation is written at a point during the revision process and thus stands, less reprovingly, as a prose note to indicate the direction of the poem's conclusion. The subsequent drafts show Larkin trying to incorporate his iconoclastic with his romantic feelings:

> Time has transfigured them into
> Untruth. The stone fidelity
> They hardly meant is all that we
> Are left of them, as if to prove
> Our least accredited instinct true
> And what survives of us is love.

This is crossed through and followed by:

> Time has transfigured them into
> Untruth: the stone fidelity
> They hardly meant is all that we

> Are told, as if thereby they prove
> Our first half-hope, half-instinct true,
> And what survives of us is love.[31]

The workbooks confirm how far away Larkin's poems are from being convulsive expressions of 'personality'. The process of re-drafting works to refine an idiom behind which an elusive identity is effacing itself into anonymity, by projecting at one extreme a voice immediately identifiable as a social type, and at the other working to achieve the sublime anonymity of epigram. The former is evident in 'Lines on a Young Lady's Photograph Album', which first began:

> At last you yielded up the album, which,
> Once opened, sent me distracted like a strange chime
> So many days struck at the same

This gradually becomes:

> At last you yielded up the album, which,
> Once open, sent me distracted. You at all ages
> Flying at me from the thick black pages
> Was a gratuity too rich;
> I choked on such nutritious images.[32]

The next and final version completes this gradual construction of the dirty old man who will pinch a bathing photo.

The drafts of 'Dockery and Son' work in the opposite direction, towards epigram. A version of the final stanza reads:

> And how we got it; when we turn, they rear
> Like sandclouds, blocking the way back, bodying
> For Dockery a son, for me nothing,
> Nothing with all a son's harsh here-and-now.
> Life is first boredom, then fear.
> Whether we use it or not it goes,
> Twisting us to the element we chose,
> And we are dead before we quite see how.

A few days later, the son's harsh 'here-and-now' has become 'patronage', but the ending remained a problem as Larkin worked towards an impersonal fatalism. The final manuscript version runs:

Life is first boredom, then fear.
Whether or not we use it, it goes,
Leaving what we without knowing it chose,
And age, and then the bitter end of age.[33]

In the margin, Larkin has drawn a hangman figure.

At their most obvious, the notebooks confirm how much Larkin wrote compared with what he published. Here, too, is that indecisiveness and evasiveness which characterised his career: to publish was to dare to finish a poem, and to live with its reproving finality. The drafts of Larkin's poems represent in miniature the shape of his whole career, slowly pushing themselves against the silence, a silence which was, in the end, victorious.

2
The Early Poems

Someone said once that the great thing is not to be different from other people, but to be different from yourself.

Philip Larkin[1]

Larkin's *Collected Poems* comes to a chronological end with a poem called 'Party Politics'. It is the last poem Larkin published in his lifetime, and probably the last he ever completed. It consists of two alternately rhymed quatrains and adopts the ironic tone of other social satires such as 'Vers de Société'. In this poem, the speaker complains ruefully that at parties he always seems short of a drink and no tactic guarantees a full glass. It ends:

> You may get drunk, or dry half-hours may pass.
> It seems to turn on where you are. Or who.[2]

The sting-in-the-tail ending suddenly lifts the poem beyond lugubrious comedy into rarefied questions of identity and chance. Questions of who we are, of our capacity to change our lot, of whether we determine our circumstances or are determined by them are amongst the fundamental preoccupations of Larkin's poetry. 'To be different from yourself' was one of Philip Larkin's most compelling and romantic longings. From his very earliest writings, and particularly in his private letters, it is apparent that Larkin scrutinised his own personality with a quite remarkable degree of introspection: remarkable, that is, if we accept at face value the bluff, no-nonsense persona of Larkin's later interviews and some of the portraits of him offered by both his admirers and critics. As a young man, Larkin was intensely preoccupied with his own identity as a writer and fiercely committed to his conception of himself as an artist.

His early work can best be read as attempts to define his own idiom and artistic identity, attempts which involve contradictory impulses: on the one hand, to cultivate his personality as a source of artistic expression; on the other, to escape personality altogether. These poems, and many of their successors, in effect extend that gift for mimicry recalled by his contemporaries.[3] As we shall see, the novels too are constructed from ventriloquisms. At the time, Larkin felt inhibited by his 'fatal gift for pastiche'[4] and anxiously examined his personality in the pursuit of self-expression. But by a consummate paradox, Larkin only establishes his artistic identity when he starts to make use of ironically self-revealing 'masks', when his gift for mimicry is transmuted into the slightly modulating poetic 'voices' which speak within and between his poems. He eventually constructs, or 'finds', his identity by searching for anonymity.

Larkin's first book of poems, *The North Ship*, was published in 1945, and when it was re-issued in 1966 Larkin added an explanatory Introduction to describe briefly the evolution of these youthful poems. 'Looking back', wrote Larkin, 'I find in the poems not one abandoned self but several – the ex-schoolboy, for whom Auden was the only alternative to "old-fashioned" poetry; the undergraduate, whose work a friend affably characterised as "Dylan Thomas, but you've a sentimentality that's all your own"; and the immediately post-Oxford self, isolated in Shropshire with a complete Yeats stolen from the local girls' school. This search for a style was merely one aspect of a general immaturity'.[5] In 1943, in his final year at Oxford, Larkin attended an English Club meeting at which the poet Vernon Watkins 'swamped us with Yeats . . . As a result I spent the next three years trying to write like Yeats, not because I liked his personality or understood his ideas but out of infatuation with his music . . . it is a particularly potent music, pervasive as garlic, and has ruined many a better talent'.[6] (This was the Yeats represented by a 1933 edition.) Finally, 'When reaction came, it was undramatic, complete and permanent. In early 1946 I had some new digs in which the bedroom faced east, so that the sun woke me inconveniently early. I used to read', and the volume he happened to have to hand was *Chosen Poems of Thomas Hardy*. As a demonstration of his 'conversion' to Hardy, Larkin added in the 1966 reprint of *The North Ship* the poem 'Waiting for breakfast', written in December 1947 and which, it is asserted, 'though not noticeably better than the rest, shows the Celtic fever abated and the patient sleeping soundly'.[7]

This Introduction, in effect an essay in disavowal, has come to stand as the 'official' history of Larkin's poetic development. It is an apparently untroubled history of youthful enthusiasms, followed by addiction to Yeats, followed by conversion to the restorative influence of Thomas Hardy. But the history perpetrated by Larkin himself suppresses a much more tumultuous history of experimentation, self-doubt and failure. There is a widespread tendency to hear in *The Less Deceived* the true 'voice' of Larkin and to regard the poems written before about 1950 as deserving merely the indulgence of juvenilia. This is precisely what Larkin's Introduction to *The North Ship* encourages us to do. But now, with the posthumous publication of Larkin's *Collected Poems*, another Larkin emerges, one who is comparatively prolific and altogether more manifestly romantic than the 'Parnassian Ron Glum' (Andrew Motion's phrase) of *The Less Deceived* and beyond. This 'proto-Larkin' did not simply disappear, as Larkin wanted us to believe. His whole career can be read as the often unresolved conflict between a romantic, aspiring Larkin and the empirical, ironic Larkin, between the aesthete and the philistine.

The true ancestry of *The Less Deceived*, it is now clear, involves four transitional periods. The first is the adolescent schoolboy and undergraduate, modelling himself on Auden, Dylan Thomas and a devotion to D. H. Lawrence. This first period is then modified in 1943 by the addiction, via Vernon Watkins, to Yeats. *The North Ship* mainly comprises poems written in 1943–44 during this second period and was followed later in 1947 by an unpublished collection of poems called *In the Grip of Light*, most of which were written between March 1945 and December 1946. The third period begins with a fallow phase between 1947 and 1949, but January 1950 sees the start of a much more productive year. The poems written between January 1950 and February 1951 form the bulk of the next published collection (with only four poems surviving from *In the Grip of Light*), *XX Poems*, privately printed in 1951. The fourth period, between 1951 and 1954, sees the writing of those poems which, added to thirteen poems retained from *XX Poems*, went to make up *The Less Deceived*, published in 1955.

Within this brief chronology are buried not only the poems which Larkin chose not to publish in his volumes or which he failed to publish, but the two novels (*Jill* and *A Girl in Winter*, published in 1946 and 1947), and those personal circumstances which contributed to the development of his poetry during these years. Moreover, this chronology matches very closely the major events of his life at this time, first as an undergraduate at Oxford between 1940 and 1943; then as a librarian at Wellington, Shropshire, between

1943 and 1946; then his second post as a librarian at University College, Leicester between 1946 and 1950; and finally the period between 1950 and 1955 when he worked as Sub-Librarian at Queen's University, Belfast. As Andrew Motion has shown, the poems written during each of these phases closely reflect Larkin's changing personal circumstances.

The earliest of these 'abandoned selves' is the adolescent schoolboy and Oxford undergraduate. The poems of this period selected by Anthony Thwaite for the *Collected Poems* reveal a specific debt to W. H. Auden, a vague appropriation of Dylan Thomas and a profound devotion to D. H. Lawrence. Larkin has recorded how his father's library gave him access to the novels of Aldous Huxley, Katherine Mansfield and D. H. Lawrence, novelists considered daring and experimental in the 1930s. As a schoolboy growing up in a thoroughly conventional household, Larkin relished the challenging unorthodoxy of these writers (his love of jazz expressed the same suppressed iconoclasm) and found in the work of Auden an exciting model. 'I wrote ceaselessly, however; now verse, which I sewed up into little books, now prose, a thousand words a night after homework', recalled Larkin in 1959.[8]

Auden has been called 'the first poet writing in English who felt at home in the twentieth century',[9] and it is clear that the young Larkin was thrilled by Auden's modernity. 'Auden rose like a sun', Larkin wrote in 1943. 'It is impossible to convey the intensity of the delight felt by a . . . mind reared on "Drake's Drum", "Westminster Bridge" and "Ode to a Nightingale", when a poet is found speaking a language thrilling and beautiful, and describing things so near to everyday life that their once-removedness strikes like a strange cymbal'.[10] The Auden thus revered was the Auden of *Poems, The Orators* and *Look, Stranger!* and it is the pre-war Auden to which Larkin remained loyal, as in his review of Auden in 1960 which isolates Auden's first decade as preserving 'almost all we value . . . the wide-angled rhetoric, the seamless lyricism, the sudden gripping dramatizations . . . He was, of course, the first "modern poet", in that he could employ modern perspectives unselfconsciously. . .'.[11]

Larkin's youthful imitations of Auden, slavish as they are, show his gift for mimicry. What he takes from Auden is the collision between private fantasy and social obligation, and the expression of personal desire in terms of a private mythology. There is the same sense of individual (and privileged) isolation and, at the same time, 'moments of impersonal erotic intensity'.[12] Specific imitations of

Auden's rhythms and phrasing are easily visible. Larkin's 'New Year Poem', for example, written at the end of 1940, echoes very closely Auden's 'Spain' (1937), and there are many other such instances.[13] At a more profound level, though, Auden seems to have encouraged Larkin to mythologise his personal dilemmas. An early poem asks '"What was the rock my gliding childhood struck,/ And what bright unreal path has led me here?"'[14] and throughout this period, Larkin's poems seem to grapple with unnamed and unspecified anxieties. 'A Writer' (published in 1941 in an Oxford University magazine) ends: 'It was a gift that he possessed alone:/ To look the world directly in the face;/ The face he did not see to be his own'.[15] Even in these vague and mannered poems, the pre-occupation with identity is evident. Ambitious as they are, they seem to have served something of a therapeutic purpose. For it is possible to see in them a somewhat disembodied eroticism taken over from Auden. A poem written in 1940, the year Larkin went up to Oxford, describes a parting as 'no single act/ Scenery-shifting for the next' and ponders 'the consequence/ Of never seeing this, nor saying/ What, remembered, still seems glowing/ As all of you'.[16] And a letter written in the same year reveals the eighteen-year-old Larkin's poetic intentions:

> But I'm against this poetry-as-a-craft business . . . Poetry (at any rate in my case) is like trying to remember a tune you've forgotten. All corrections are attempts to get nearer to the forgotten tune. A poem is written because the poet gets a sudden vision – lasting one second or less – and he attempts to express the whole of which the vision is a part. Or he attempts to express the vision . . . I am juggling with sounds and associations which will best express the original vision. It is done quite intuitively and esoterically. That is why a poet never thinks of his reader. Why should he? The reader doesn't come into the poem at all.
>
> As for the vision itself, it's got something to do with sex. I don't know what, & I don't particularly want to know. It's not surprising because obviously two creative forces will be in alliance . . . I should think poetry & sex are very closely connected.[17]

In fact, Larkin's writing undergoes its most profound development at the moment when it does think of the reader. Moreover, this reliance on 'intuition' is later supplanted by a much more calculated process of drafting.

Auden authorised Larkin's use of contemporary idiom and imagery in his poems; Dylan Thomas interested him in 'juggling with sounds and associations'. D. H. Lawrence gave him his ambition and image of the writer's relationship with his society. 'To me, Lawrence is what Shakespeare was to Keats and all the other buggers',[18] and Larkin's early letters to his friend J. B. Sutton constantly express an agonised devotion, agonised because of his conviction of inferiority to Lawrence. 'Having read Lawrence, I know what shit is, and won't write it: on the other hand, I can't write anything else. Hence a state of deadlock'.[19] But his reading of Lawrence allowed Larkin to think of his writing as expressions of otherwise repressed emotions and impulses, the Lawrence of *Apocalypse*:

> What we want is to destroy our false, inorganic connections, especially those related to money, and re-establish the living organic connections, with the cosmos, the sun and the earth, with mankind and nation and family. Start with the sun, and the rest will slowly, slowly happen.[20]

An unpublished essay on jazz written by Larkin in 1943 resembles strikingly Lawrence's formulation and suggests something of Larkin's attitude at this time to his own art:

> Jazz is the closest description of the unconscious we have ... The decay of ritual in everything from religion to the lighting of the fire is resulting in the insulation of the unconscious ... Jazz is the new art of the unconscious, and is therefore improvised, for it cannot call upon consciousness to express its own divorce from consciousness.[21]

Here again, art is conceived of as the improvised expression of the unconscious, those 'visions' referred to earlier. The subsequent immersion in Yeats is allied to the romanticism of Lawrence which Larkin absorbed. In many ways, Larkin's work develops from the argument with himself about these formative romantic commitments. His work deals so much with failure because the romantic conception of himself as an artist seemed later to have failed him, and the anger, particularly of his later work, can be traced back to his sense of having been betrayed by his early aspirations. Furthermore, the later Larkin who responds so intensely to elemental presences of light, water and space and who wants to overthrow the 'inorganic connections' of work (in, for example, 'Toads') and money (in 'Money') has his roots here, in the passionate advocacy of Lawrence.[22]

The usual critical approach to Larkin's early poetry (and only with the posthumous *Collected Poems* was a selection of poems written before *The North Ship* made widely available) is to examine it for signs of the later Larkin, or to accept that the poet of *The Less Deceived* emerged by just the complete 'conversion' announced by Larkin in his Introduction to *The North Ship*. Hence, there is a tendency to overlook its most immediate circumstances which contribute to its opaqueness and sense of threat. *The North Ship* was published in 1945 and collected poems written between 1942 and 1944. The earliest poems in the *Collected Poems* date from 1938. Larkin's first poems are, quite precisely, wartime poems. Stephen Regan has offered a fresh perspective by returning Larkin's work to its historical context and reading in the poems the wartime circumstances of their composition. Larkin himself later commented: '. . . one had to live through the forties at one's most impressionable time and . . . a lot of poems I wrote . . . were very much of the age'.[23] Regan suggests that the uncertain events of 1939–45 induced in Larkin's writing a kind of poetry favoured by a wartime poetry-reading public, 'mellifluous, mystifying and resolutely apolitical',[24] as opposed to the earlier Audenesque phase. He notes how, as well as explicit references to military conflict, frequent images of night and darkness and the general sense of fears and constraints 'evoke the uncertainties of wartime Britain'. He concludes, 'The insecurities of wartime Britain helped shape a poetry of restricted choices, quietistic moods and disappointed ideals, but in a more positive way produced a poetry of tenacious survival and vigilant awareness'.[25]

Larkin's own account of the genesis of *The North Ship* makes an intoxication with Yeats crucial. The immediate influence, however, seems to have been Vernon Watkins himself, not in his poetry ('which I don't like an awful lot'[26]), but as an exemplar of the poetic personality. Watkins devoted his life entirely to his writing and Larkin remained impressed by this self-sacrificing pursuit of art. For Larkin, Watkins was living proof of the determination to perfect the work rather than the life.[27] As for Yeats, however 'pervasive' his influence might have been, references to him in the published letters of that time are scant. To J. B. Sutton in April 1943: 'When you come back, you must read a little Yeats: he is very good'.[28] In October 1944: 'I continue reading D. H. L.'s letters with great admiration and delight, also Yeats's poems. They are my two constants at the moment'.[29] At the same time, Larkin appeared to be casting around for a new direction with no mention of Yeats: 'Also I have absorbed (I think) the literature of my early days – Auden, Isherwood & Lawrence. I still read them occasionally, but on the whole I think that only the husks remain for me – the rest I have sucked in ... For something new must be found'.[30] In fact, in his private journal for 1943 Larkin upbraids himself for his 'frantic, neurotic, strained, tense imitations of Yeats's poems'.[31] The Yeatsian manner, so evident in *The North Ship*, represents Larkin's ambition to write impassioned lyrics rather than a specific devotion to Yeats. But it is a slavish adoption of a manner, not, as later, a deliberate manipulation of a mask. The Yeatsian manner was eventually modified almost out of recognition, but not the impulse which first led Larkin to adopt Yeats.[32]

As well as technical borrowings, then, *The North Ship* adopts a Yeatsian attitude. The underlying and unresolved (and unfocused) conflict in *The North Ship* is the Yeatsian choice: 'perfection of the life, or of the work' (Yeats, 'The Choice'). Poem IX urges, 'Let me become an instrument sharply stringed/ For all things to strike music as they please', but asks 'How to recall such music, when the street/ Darkens?' At the same time, this conflict is localised in terms of love and isolation, or community and solitariness. Poem after poem retreats from love to lovelessness, from images of light and heat to darkness and coldness. Poem XIX, called 'Ugly Sister', summarises the conditions which *The North Ship* poems elaborate:

> Since I was not bewitched in adolescence
> And brought to love,
> I will attend to the trees and their gracious silence,
> To winds that move.

Solitary contemplation of elemental presences remains in Larkin's work as an antidote to, or attribute of, lovelessness.

The Yeats absorbed by Larkin was, his Introduction tells us, the early Yeats, not the Yeats of 'the harsher last poems'.[33] Though the idioms Larkin borrows belong largely to the period of Yeats's *The Tower*, it is the *fin de siècle*, misty Celtic twilight Yeats whom Larkin adopts in attitude. *The North Ship* is full of melancholy partings, melancholy introspection and melancholy impotence. Even when the poems try for a more abrasive energy, they lose their way in inflated imagery. Poem XXIV, for example, begins with brisk intentions:

> Love, we must part now: do not let it be
> Calamitous and bitter. In the past
> There has been too much moonlight and self-pity . . .

but ends in the strained imagery of the lovers' parting being like two ships travelling in different directions, 'wind-mastered'. For all the romantic aspiration of *The North Ship*, the imagery of the wind which so dominates these poems suggests an imagination pre-occupied by chance and arbitrariness.

The title-poem, a sequence of five short poems, attempts a kind of Yeatsian allegory. The 'north ship' travels 'Into an unforgiving sea/ Under a fire-spilling star', and the sequence develops around images of coldness and erotic love, an emblematic version of Keats's 'La Belle Dame Sans Merci'. As the ship sails inexorably northwards, so fear gathers into the image of the female lover:

> And beyond all doubt I know
> A girl is standing there
> Who will take no lovers
> Till she winds me in her hair.

The sequence ends with a drunken boatswain singing 'A woman has ten claws' and this fear of sexual commitment and romantic involvement will find itself expressed in different ways throughout Larkin's career. The poem's dreamy evocation of remote coldness merging with sexual fear suggests how Larkin used the Yeatsian model as a way of externalising and mythologising his own psychology. (As an undergraduate, Larkin for a while kept a record of his dreams as a means of psychoanalysing himself.[34]) Later, he would continue to articulate his internal dilemmas, but in a very different rhetoric of strategically constructed attitudes and personae.

There is little to rescue from *The North Ship*. It is clear that Larkin himself, twenty years later, preferred to have the volume quietly forgotten, agreeing to its re-publication by Faber and Faber only to forestall its re-issue by the Fortune Press in the wake of the success of *The Whitsun Weddings*: 'With regard to the republication of the poems, I am still undecided about this. They are such complete rubbish, for the most part, that I am just twice as unwilling to have two editions in print as I am to have one. . .'.[35] The Introduction Larkin wrote is calculatedly downbeat: 'Then, as now, I could never contemplate it without a twinge, faint or powerful, of shame compounded with disappointment. Some of this was caused by the contents. . .'.[36] The general impression of *The North Ship* has been aptly summarised by Andrew Motion as a collection of poems

> . . . almost all languorously drooping in their rhythms and uninventively romantic in their references. They frequently borrow direct from Yeats, and general resemblances abound. Their mood is invariably gloomy without justification, their time of day dawn or dusk, their weather cold, rainy and windy, and their symbolic details monotonous: water, stars, ice, ships, candles, dreams, hands and beds occur with extraordinary frequency and no distinguishing features. . . [37]

The poem written in 1947 and added in expiation by Larkin in 1966, 'Waiting for breakfast', strikes an immediate contrast, though it possesses its own kind of romanticism and returns to precisely the same preoccupations as the rest of *The North Ship*: the relationship between life and art.

Uncovering the buried history of Larkin's work prior to *The Less Deceived* shows how the particular concern with identity evident there has its antecedents in circumstances more troubling than Larkin's Introduction to *The North Ship* cared to admit. The first period of Larkin's poetry, up to 1943, belongs to Auden. The second, between 1943 and 1946, belongs to Yeats and is represented in *The North Ship*. The third, Larkin would have us believe, belongs to Hardy and directly proceeds to *The Less Deceived*. But there is actually a hiatus between 1946 and 1950. *Jill* was published in 1946 and *A Girl in Winter* in 1947; at the end of 1947, Larkin put together the failed collection *In the Grip of Light*. Nearly all the poems printed in 1951 as *XX Poems* were written between January 1950 and February 1951. To compile *The Less Deceived*, Larkin plundered *XX Poems*, and so the real genesis of *The Less Deceived* poems belongs to 1950–51, not entirely to the reading of Hardy early in 1946. In an interview published in 1964, Larkin said of this period, 'I wrote a great many sedulous and worthless Yeats-y poems, and later on far inferior Dylan Thomas poems . . . and this went on for years and years. It wasn't until about 1948 or 9 that I began to write differently, but it wasn't as any conscious reaction'.[38] This contrasts markedly with the 'undramatic, complete and permanent' reaction to Hardy described in the Introduction.

The *Collected Poems* shows that only nine poems were written between 1947 and 1949. These would seem to be the years of crisis which the elevation of the 1946 reading of Hardy seems designed to obscure. There are other reasons, too, for thinking that the 'conversion' to Hardy was in truth an altogether slower, more tentative process, and very far from 'complete'. As Motion concludes: 'Larkin did not simply swap Yeats for Hardy early in his career. The aspect of his personality to which Yeats originally appealed has been radically modified in his maturity – but it has endured, and much of his best work takes the form of a dialectic between the attitudes and qualities of his two mentors.'[39]

One reason for the comparative silence of 1947–9 is Larkin's frustrated immersion in the attempt to write a third novel. Whatever the reasons for its failure, the significance for the rest of Larkin's work of its abandonment cannot be over-emphasised. *The Less Deceived* emerges quite precisely out of the failed novelist (reinforced by the failure to publish the *In the Grip of Light* collection). Larkin's novels offer revealing insight into the identity of Larkin the poet, for it was as a novelist that he first conceived of himself.

Letters written to his friend James Sutton when he was an undergraduate reveal Larkin as passionately committed to a writer's vocation: 'if I don't become some kind of a good writer I shall turn from life in disgust as being totally false, and feelings as being quite untrustworthy'.[40] The young Larkin was an old-fashioned aesthete: 'art is as near religion as one can get' and 'Do you hear any disparaging talk about "Art for Art's sake"? It annoys me. For what other sake can art possibly be undertaken? Let them tell me that'.[41] At the same time, a less exalted Larkin sometimes comes into view, one more cautious and self-doubting: 'Art is awfully *wrong*, you know. Art is born of, and should generate, delight in life. But the delight it generates is purely *vicarious*, – i.e. it's fake'.[42] Later, Hardy helped Larkin come to recognise the 'fakeness' of a false artistic ego, and the note of scepticism here will harden into Larkin's attitude of mocking philistinism. But for the youthful Larkin, poetry derived from inspiration. He distinguished poetry from the novel in terms defiantly romantic, and which made the writing of poetry private, intense and uncertain. Doubting his powers as a novelist, reliant on 'inspiration' for poems, Larkin was vulnerable to any circumstance which might have threatened his identity as a writer.

It was during his time as a librarian in Wellington, Shropshire, that Larkin met Ruth Bowman, a schoolgirl in Wellington. Their involvement, from 1945 to 1950, marks a period of personal and creative turmoil for Larkin. The relationship brought with it, for him, a disturbing recognition of incapacities in his own personality. 'It is rather a disturbing experience', he wrote in 1945, 'to have someone utterly dependent on you, it puts one's least thoughts and actions under a microscope (at any rate, to oneself) and short-circuits one's processes ... And it worries me also to find that I am a long way off being capable of any emotion as simple as what is called love'.[43] The death of his father in 1948 was deeply distressing for Larkin and might have precipitated a doomed engagement to Ruth Bowman. 'I can't say I welcome the thought of marriage ... I suspect all my isolationist feelings as possibly harmful and certainly rather despicable.'[44] By 1949, living with his widowed mother in Leicester, Larkin had reached a point of failure both with his third novel and with his fiancée: 'I have given up my novel & Ruth has given up me, not seeing, as you might say, any future in it. Nor do I! Therefore I am living a disagreeable life at this remnant of a home, with a general sense of being buggered up, & a generally despicable character'.[45] But the relationship tottered on until the end of July 1950 when, finally, the break occurs. 'I have not got engaged. Despite my fine feelings, when it really comes down to terms ... something unmeltable and immoveable rises up in me – something infantile, cowardly, regressive ... I'm a romantic bastard. Remote things seem desirable. Bring them close, and I start shitting myself.'[46] The major reason for the failure of the relationship, it would seem, was the threat Larkin perceived to his writing, a suspicion 'that in my character there is an antipathy between "art" and "life" ... I find, myself, that this letting-in of a second person spells death to perception and the desire to express, as well as the ability'.[47] The engagement to Ruth Bowman (and the domestic trials of looking after his bereaved mother) threw Larkin's personal and artistic life into turmoil and, however dishonourably and with whatever sense of shame, highlighted for him the need to preserve his independence and to risk, even welcome, emotional isolation.

Much of the disillusionment of *The Less Deceived* derives from this period. But many of its themes and, more importantly, aspects of its technique can be traced back to Larkin's two novels. Like *The North Ship* and the poems of this period, the novels revolve around love and isolation, fulfilment and disappointment, choice and chance. *Jill* tells the story of John Kemp, a provincial grammar-school boy at Oxford who, overwhelmed by feelings of social inferiority, constructs a fantasy sister, 'Jill', to whom he writes letters and whose diary he invents. Then he meets the living embodiment of 'Jill', Gillian, to whom he feels a proprietorial attraction. After his clumsy advances, he ends the novel humiliated. Disgraced and ill, he muses:

> Somewhere, in dreams, perhaps, on some other level, they had interlocked and he had had his own way as completely as in life he had been denied it. And this dream showed that love died, whether fulfilled or unfulfilled. He grew confused whether she had accepted him or not, since the result was the same: and as this confusion increased, it spread to fulfilment or unfulfilment, which merged and became inseparable. The difference between them vanished.

This is followed by a passage describing the trees thrashing in the wind outside before we return to John's thoughts. If there was no difference between any opposites, 'Was he not freed, for the rest of his life, from choice?' He watches the trees outside. 'What control could he hope to have over the maddened surface of things?'[48]

The novel is ultimately unsatisfactory because Larkin cannot decide whether he is writing a psychological portrait in the manner of Katherine Mansfield or a documentary social comedy in the manner of Kingsley Amis. *A Girl in Winter* (originally planned as *The Kingdom of Winter*) is more successful in pursuing a coherent strategy as a psychological study. Its central character is Katherine Lind, a European girl exiled in England during the war. The novel reconstructs her pre-war adolescent association with an English family whom she had visited after a pen-friend correspondence with the boy, Robin Fennel. Amidst confusing gestures and responses, her first visit had ended in an unsatisfactory advance from Robin. Now, some years later, she has just heard again from him, and the novel tells the story of the day she is due to meet him. It ends with her indifferently submitting to his seduction and, like *Jill*, gathers imaginative force with images drawn from *The North Ship*:

There was the snow, and her watch ticking. So many snow-
flakes, so many seconds. As time passed they seemed to mingle in
their minds, heaping up into a vast shape that might be a burial
mound, or the cliff of an iceberg whose summit is out of sight.
Into its shadow dreams crowded, full of conceptions and
stirrings of cold, as if icefloes were moving down a lightless
channel of water. They were going in orderly slow procession,
moving from darkness further into darkness, allowing no
suggestion that their order should be broken, or that one day,
however many years distant, the darkness would begin to give
place to light.

Yet their passage was not saddening. Unsatisfied dreams rose
and fell about them, crying out against their implacability, but in
the end glad that such order, such destiny, existed. Against this
knowledge, the heart, the will, and all that made for protest, could
at last sleep.[49]

In terms of themes and imagery, resemblances to Larkin's poetry of
the period abound. But the novels are more significant to Larkin's
development in another way. Both novels are constructed from
ventriloquisms. In *Jill*, John Kemp begins by writing letters to his
'sister', but then constructs her identity by writing 'her' diary. And
the fundamental motive in creating 'Jill' is, by presenting himself as
urbane and sophisticated, to alter his own identity. The process
begins with the letters, then with a narrative account of 'Jill', and concludes with a diary: a development in authorial status from 'real'
first-person address, to third-person narrative and finally to first-person identification. The process refines itself into perfect ventriloquism. Katherine, the 'girl in winter', begins where John Kemp's
creation ended. Although Larkin casts the novel as third-person narrative, it is written from Katherine's centre of consciousness. The
novel in effect sustains John's creation of 'Jill': it is to Larkin what
'Jill's' diaries were to John. And Katherine herself is not so much a
character as a rhetorical device by which Larkin can dramatise his
poetic images and structures of irony (her foreignness gives the perspective of an outsider, the situation typical of Larkin's poems).
Though there are clear technical and structural differences between
the novels, their most crucial feature in terms of Larkin's poetic
development is the way in which his own attitudes and dilemmas are
dramatised by invented 'voices'. The poems by which he became
known represent not so much his 'finding a voice' as an extension of

his novelistic technique of using 'masks' and personae to dramatise his fundamental preoccupation with choice and identity.

Furthermore, the creative history of *Jill* shows that it began very specifically as a kind of facetious ventriloquism. Whilst an undergraduate, Larkin wrote a series of spoof schoolgirl lesbian stories as part of a running gag with Kingsley Amis. He invented the autobiography of 'Brunette Coleman' and went on to write 'her' lesbian narratives pseudonymously (*Trouble at Willow Gables* and *Michaelmas Term at St Bride's*) and a sequence of six poems (*Sugar and Spice*) of which two have survived in the *Collected Poems*: 'Femmes Damnées' and 'The School in August'.[50] Herein lies the construction of personae which evolves into John Kemp's 'Jill' and, finally, a poetic technique which released Larkin from a romantically conceived lyrical consciousness. Andrew Motion describes the psychological importance of 'Brunette Coleman' to Larkin and suggests as well that the whole enterprise demonstrates 'a robustly ironical attitude to art which Larkin's next few years, dominated by his reading of Yeats, would test severely'.[51] In these sexually experimental, fantasy-life creations, then, lie not only a technique which was to become fundamental to Larkin's poetic development, but an attitude of philistine mockery which Larkin's art had eventually to absorb.

What, then, of Larkin's early-morning reading of Hardy, so precisely specified as his creative turning-point and putatively 'proven' by the addition to *The North Ship* of 'Waiting for breakfast'? Larkin moved to new digs in Wellington in January 1946. It is hardly to be expected that a new 'influence' would be immediately evident, though Larkin's Introduction implies this. Hardy's influence, never a technical one, was profound and permanent. Nevertheless, it is only gradually apparent and not in itself sufficient to account for so momentous a change as Larkin describes.

Of the period between 1946 and 1950, Larkin is almost silent. He seems to have been determined to portray all his earlier publications as matters of casual accident and personal disappointment. 'After finishing my first books, say by 1945, I thought I had come to an end. I couldn't write another novel, I published nothing. Then in 1950 I went to Belfast, and things reawoke somehow.'[52] The 'reawakening' is associated with *XX Poems* in which the origins of *The Less Deceived* are visible. In between comes failure: to complete a third novel, to publish *In the Grip of Light* and to get married.

In the Grip of Light mainly comprises poems written between March 1945 and December 1946. The first poem written in 1946 is 'Dying Day', later to appear as 'Going' in both *XX Poems* and *The Less Deceived*. It is a symbolist evocation of mortal dread, of emptiness and impotence. Subsequent poems analyse his feelings in the same Yeatsian terms of light and dark. Like *The North Ship* poems, they attitudinise: they remain the poems of a writer setting out to be 'poetic'. Nothing suggests the influence of Thomas Hardy. But there is an attempt in these poems to overcome the emotional bleakness of *The North Ship*. 'Thaw', for example, turns the snow and ice of *The North Ship* and *A Girl in Winter* to 'sovereign waters . . . causing to fall/ From patient memory forestfuls of grief'[53]. More famously, 'Wedding-Wind' (written in September 1946) depicts the wind not entirely as an image of indifference and arbitrariness (though it appears so again in later poems such as 'Talking in Bed') but as an ambivalent expression of joy. Larkin's title, *In the Grip of Light*, was intended 'to sum up the state of being alive',[54] and in March 1946 Larkin wrote to Sutton: 'the only quality that makes art durable & famous is the quality of generating delight in the state of living'.[55] Evident too is an occasional shift away from the dense poeticisms of *The North Ship* to an idiom approaching conversational speech, as in 'Two Guitar Pieces', 'Träumerai' and 'Waiting for breakfast'.[56] This last was intended by Larkin to show, after the Yeatsian addictions in *The North Ship*, 'the Celtic fever abated and the patient sleeping soundly'.[57] (Interestingly, Larkin did not select it for *In the Grip of Light*.) What it actually shows is an intensifying conflict in Larkin between 'life' and 'art', and between the 'aesthete' and the 'philistine'.

The poem is set in an hotel, the speaker gloomy after spending the night with his lover. The first stanza is calculatedly flat, shorn of any figurative language save the 'loaded' sky 'Sunk' with mist, so as to embody the blankness of 'Featureless morning, featureless night'. But the second stanza brims with poeticisms by converting the attitude and vision of the first into 'Misjudgment'. Far from being 'featureless', the stones 'slept', the mist 'Wandered absolvingly past', the electric lights were 'Pin-points of undisturbed excitement' and the coming day spills

> My world back after a year, my lost lost world
> Like a cropping deer strayed near my path again,
> Bewaring the mind's least clutch. Turning, I kissed her,
> Easily for sheer joy tipping the balance to love.

And what is this 'lost world', recovered 'after a year'? The *Collected Poems* shows a gap of almost precisely a year between this and the preceding poem, 'Thaw'. The return of 'my lost lost world', the 'cropping deer strayed near my path again', is the rediscovery of a poetic impulse after a year's silence.

But the antithesis between the unembellished empiricism of the first stanza and its poeticised transformation in the second remains unresolved in the conclusion. For in turning to kiss the girl, the speaker reckons to have offended this 'tender visiting'. Like 'Wedding-Wind', the poem ends in a series of questions which posit the choice between 'life' – the real girl who belongs to the real world of stanza one – and the Muse who might be 'jealous of her':

> Will you refuse to come till I have sent
> Her terribly away, importantly live
> Part invalid, part baby, and part saint?

The first stanza represents the world without the Muse, the second a world transfigured by anticipation, metaphor and simile. One represents the empirical, unillusioned, documentary Larkin; the other the aspiring aesthete. Larkin's most successful poetry was to find ways of assimilating these identities; for the moment, they remain antithetical. The poem knows not whether to choose the Muse or the girl; neither does it know whether to choose ordinariness or exaltedness. 'Waiting for breakfast', designed to show the conclusion of an aberrant period, actually confirms conflicts which were to remain with Larkin throughout his career.

Larkin's determination to use his writing to 'generate delight in the state of living' collapsed shortly after writing 'Waiting for breakfast'. On 3 February 1948, he heard that Faber had rejected *In the Grip of Light*. His father died on 26 March 1948, and Larkin spent the next two years living with his widowed mother. Eventually, he abandoned his plans for a third novel. Only seven poems were written between March 1948 and the end of 1949. And yet it is here, in the poems written out of profound depression and failure, that we find the true genesis of *The Less Deceived*. In his Introduction to *The North Ship*, Larkin perpetrated a misconception. 'He made it sound as though he had instantly swapped extravagance for good sense, vagueness for precision, imaginary worlds for real ones . . . putting on a stylish and amusing display of candour, he managed to keep certain things hidden.'[58] Amongst those things hidden is that

Hardy's importance to Larkin could only be fully absorbed by him when he was faced with suffering that was first-hand rather than vicarious.

In later years, Larkin's admiration for Hardy was expressed precisely in terms of Hardy's attitude to suffering: 'first, he thought it was "true" ("Tragedy is true guise, Comedy lies"); secondly, it could be demonstrated that Hardy associated sensitivity to suffering and awareness of the causes of pain with superior spiritual character'.[59] By 1962, Hardy's poetry had come to represent for Larkin an existential condition:

> Not till his first wife had died could Hardy's love poetry for her be written, and then it was mixed with a flood of regret and remorse for what he had lost. This kind of paradox is inseparable from poetic creation, and indeed from life altogether. At times it almost appears a sort of basic insincerity in human affection. At others it seems a flaw built deeply into the working of the emotions, creating an inevitable bias in life towards unhappiness. Indeed, it was itself part of Hardy's subject-matter . . . [60]

The fatalistic acceptance of suffering as an unavoidable condition of life and art has its roots in the period following the death of Larkin's father. What Hardy taught him was not a technique, but an attitude to writing, one described by Leslie Stephen and noted approvingly by Hardy: 'The ultimate aim of the poet should be to touch our hearts by showing his own, and not to exhibit his learning, or his fine taste, or his skill in mimicking the notes of his predecessors'.[61] Hardy allowed Larkin to write from his own feelings in a language that could assimilate the demotic and poetic.

> He's not a transcendental writer, he's not a Yeats, he's not an Eliot; his subjects are men, the life of men, time and the passing of time, love and the fading of love . . . When I came to Hardy it was with the sense of relief that I didn't have to try to jack myself up to a concept of poetry that lay outside my own life – this is perhaps what I felt Yeats was trying to make me do. One could simply relapse back into one's own life and write from it. Hardy taught one to feel rather than to write . . . and he taught one as well to have confidence in what one felt.[62]

In a way, Hardy stopped Larkin from being an aesthete.

The 'feelings' out of which Larkin wrote are expressed with a new naturalness and clarity in the poems following the death of his father. They articulate feelings of indecisiveness, sterility and stasis familiar from *The North Ship*, but instead of using a figurative language of symbolism and psychologically expressive imagery, these poems begin to use a language of direct discourse with the reader. They explain rather than declaim.

In turning away from Yeats as a model for his poetry, Larkin was modifying the Yeatsian commitment to the poetic symbol as the fundamental means of poetic expression. Yeats's symbolism, which he developed into a highly complex system of meaning, sought expression by finding correspondences between objects and states of mind, between the observable world and an unseen reality apprehended by an inner consciousness. Yeats maintained that a 'continuous indefinable symbolism' is 'the substance of all style' (*The Symbolism of Poetry*, 1900). The most powerful symbols cannot be rationally explained; their power has the power of myth and subconscious meaning. The symbolist writer explores occult truths and uses the connotative, associative and aural attributes of language in order to suggest rather than state. The symbol evokes unseen worlds. In Yeats's earlier poems, the poet is absorbed in his own feelings, lifted into an exalted state of mind which is signalled by rhetorically ornate expression, the 'music' which so intoxicated Larkin. The poet's tone is hieratic, like a visionary penetrating ultimate truths. As Larkin said, Yeats forced him to 'try and jack myself up' to a poetry of rapt intensity and heightened emotion. By contrast, the effect of Hardy's technique is one of naturalism, of a particular man in particular circumstances speaking to his fellow man. His poetry honours contingency. Hardy's poetic language is familiar and, if not ordinary, then positively laboured rather than ornate. And where Yeats is priestly, Hardy is humble, striving to achieve plainness rather than oratory, chastened by experience rather than exalted by it. The special achievement of Larkin is, eventually, to have developed an idiom in which the influences of both Yeats and Hardy are integrated.

Written in April 1948, 'An April Sunday brings the snow' was the first poem Larkin wrote after the death of his father, a short elegy in his memory.[63] There is no flourishing of poeticisms, no mention of the Muse, no mythologised psychology. Instead, the imagery develops from the poem's contingent circumstances and, rather than relying on the ornate metaphors of the earlier poetry, this elegy works by a simple metonymy, whereby his father's life is identified with the jam he made before he died:[64]

> Which now you will not sit and eat.
> Behind the glass, under the cellophane,
> Remains your final summer – sweet
> And meaningless, and not to come again.

The quiet, conversational cadences, the unforced contemporaneity of 'cellophane', the address from a specific 'I' (the poet clearing the cupboards of his father's jam) to 'you' (the dead father) are amongst the features which mark the poem as a significant stylistic development. Behind it lie Hardy's poems of bereavement: it is Hardy's pathos which silently juxtaposes the preservation of fruit in the jam with the loss of the father's life.

Larkin seems to have written nothing else until the following year. The few poems of 1949 are obsessed with failure, artistic aridity and self-disgust. One poem begins 'I am washed upon a rock/ In an endless girding sea'; another, entitled 'Neurotics', describes a life where 'day by day/ You drag your feet, clay-thick with misery'. 'On Being Twenty-six' and 'To Failure' are grim confessions of despair. The first looks back on the 'pristine drive' which has now exhausted itself in mediocrity but leaves a tormented memory of 'states/ Long since dispersed' and a choice between 'Nothing, and paradise'. 'To Failure' expresses failure as a ghostly malevolence: 'You have been here some time'. These poems are written out of the very condition which threatens them: the etiolation of artistic power. But therein lies the direction Larkin's work was to take, away from impassioned, bardic intensity to a flatter, more mutedly natural mode of expression. This acceptance of plainness is evident in the very language of these poems. 'Modesties' announces this new aesthetic:

> Words as plain as hen-birds' wings
> Do not lie,
> Do not over-broider things –
> Are too shy.[65]

This unemphatic, chastened discretion might slowly 'achieve a flower, although/ No one sees'. This plainness is evident in the conversational use of pronouns, a repetition in these poems of the direct address of 'An April Sunday brings the snow'. 'To Failure' dramatises the conflict between 'my life' and 'you', failure personified. 'Neurotics' uses 'you' in an even more casual way ('No one gives you a thought, as day by day/ You drag your feet ... No one pretends/ To want to help you now') where 'you' could mean 'me'. 'To Failure' is especially notable for its use of a technique Larkin was to exploit effectively throughout his career. It begins:

> You do not come dramatically, with dragons
> That rear up with my life between their paws
> And dash me butchered down beside the wagons,
> The horses panicking; nor as a clause
> Clearly set out to warn what can be lost,
> What out-of-pocket charges must be borne,
> Expenses met ...

'Failure' is figured metonymically, and the poem uses the language of different modes of discourse: here, of fantasy-violence and of legalistic administration. Once again, Larkin's gift for mimicry begins to take his poetry in new directions, towards irony and satire.

'I wrote my first good poem when I was 26', said Larkin in an interview in 1973 (without identifying the poem).[66] Peter Ferguson has suggested the reference is to 'At Grass', which a writer in *The Times Educational Supplement* for 13 July 1956 said (presumably quoting Larkin) grew out of a newsreel film about a retired racehorse which Larkin saw in 1948 (when Larkin was 26). Andrew Motion dates things differently, with Larkin seeing the film on 3 January 1950 and writing the poem the same day (the day given as its completion date in the *Collected Poems*). Whatever the confusion over dates, the publishing history of the poem suggests the importance Larkin attached to it, using it to conclude three volumes (*XX Poems*, *The Less Deceived* and the Fantasy Press pamphlet published in 1954) and making the manuscript drafts available for publication in the celebratory issue of *Phoenix* in 1973. As a later chapter shows, 'At Grass', like all the other poems of this time, deals with the loss of fame and power. But this time, the poem finds consolation in the diminution of power and positively embraces anonymity rather than fame. 'At Grass' occupies a crucial position, marking as it does the moment in Larkin's writing when creativity flows from an acceptance of deprivation. Gradually, deprivation is seen to be not only the natural condition of things, but to foster its own creative yearning for an absolute nullity. The dichotomies of 'Nothing, and paradise' merge: 'nothing' becomes 'paradise'. Larkin was entirely serious when he remarked, famously, 'Deprivation is for me what daffodils were for Wordsworth.'[67] By 1950, deprivation had become inspiration: he wrote to James Sutton, '. . . some things you will not get because you want them so much . . . I can write poems now & again *because I want to write novels so badly*' [Larkin's stress].[68] Larkin was not being merely sentimental when he said in a 1982 interview: 'I didn't choose poetry: poetry chose me'.[69] If his poems are shot through with fatalistic defeatism, it is partly because their creative origins lie in the fatalistic acceptance of their role as surrogate novels.

'At Grass' marks the start of a remarkably fruitful period after the aridity of 1947–9. Larkin's creativity returned once his poetry had accepted the language of prose. *XX Poems*, the collection privately printed in 1951, carried over only four poems from *In the Grip of Light*; all the others (apart from 'Modesties') were written between January 1950 and February 1951, and eleven of these (with the addition of two of the *In the Grip of Light* poems) appeared in *The Less Deceived*. When, on 16 September 1950, he left Leicester for Belfast, he was to find that 'things reawoke somehow'. Disentangling himself from the claims of his mother and his romantic difficulties with Ruth Bowman, Larkin could begin to retreat into solitariness and his own anonymity. On the boat from Liverpool to Belfast, Larkin roughed out an unfinished poem called 'Single to Belfast'. It acknowledges 'a simple hae-morrhage of grief/ For what I abandon' on a journey 'To unknown from lost', but the 'unknown' was a literal and imaginative site he was happy to inhabit.[70] Shortly after arriving in Belfast, Larkin wrote 'Wires' and 'Absences', the one imagining existential containment and confinement, the other a sublime annihilation of selfhood: 'Such attics cleared of me! Such absences!'

But the prevailing mood of *XX Poems* and the unpublished poems of 1950–1 remains gloomy. In writing from his own life, Larkin was committed to writing about failure: failure in love, failure as a writer and, ultimately, the failure of life in the face of death. The failure of love is lamented, or accepted, in a number of poems: one asks 'Who called love conquering,/ When its sweet flower/ So easily dries. . .?'; another, 'Since the majority of me', deals with the thwart-ing of affection. 'Marriages' describes singleness bleakly as 'intelli-gent rancour,/ An integrity of self-hatred'.[71] The 'integrity' thus preserved as the precondition of writing remains, nevertheless, the object of further bitterness. The failure to consolidate the modest success of *Jill* and *A Girl in Winter* with a third novel, together with the recognition of the Yeatsian enthusiasm as something of an aberration, are registered in the poems as the collapse of literary ambition. 'The Literary World' talks of 'Five years of an irresistible force meeting an/immoveable object right in your belly', and 'Fiction and the Reading Public', a precursor of 'A Study of Reading Habits', mocks the kind of literature which gratifies its readership by peddling illusions.[72] 'The Spirit Wooed' recollects nostalgically a time when 'I believed in you' and writing was a matter of certainty. 'My only crime// Was holding you too dear' and the 'spirit' 'daily came less near'.[73] What looks like a poem about the loss of love is in fact another address to the absent Muse. At this period (and indeed throughout his life), Larkin still conceived of the poetry he wanted to write as reliant on 'inspiration'. 'Maturity' sums up the general sense of angry disappointment ('This pantomime/ Of compensating act and counter-act,/ Defeat and counterfeit') which in 'Next, Please', 'To put one brick upon another' and 'The local snivels through the fields' hardens into a sense of mortality's futility: 'All we have done not mattering'.[74] And if, later, a generation of readers came to recognise itself in Larkin's poems, the personal failures of which he writes can be seen as representing the historical circumstances of British society in the years of slow and difficult reconstruction after the end of the Second World War. A nation's loss of imperial power parallels Larkin's lament for his loss of creative power.

A few poems written in 1950–1 express Larkin's sense of 'foreignness' in Belfast. These poems take up, some of them obliquely, the theme of identity and represent the beginning of a major development in Larkin's argument with himself about isolation and community, self and society, an internal debate which was to become such a major feature of his later collections. In 'Strangers', the issue is unfocused but its basic terms emerge and advance the use of Katherine Lind's foreignness in *A Girl in Winter*. Strangers, the poem begins, keep their distance and do not demand attention; as a corollary, 'to live there, among strangers,/ Calls for teashop behaviours. . .'

> Keeping the soul unjostled,
> The pocket unpicked,
> The fancies lurid,
> And the treasure buried.[75]

The sequence of images fails to cohere, but they suggest how being an outsider leaves the speaker free to preserve himself. That his fancies remain 'lurid' and the 'treasure buried' (his imagination and inner self) legitimises his isolation, and the distance between self and others is what preserves the self's knowledge of itself, a 'treasure' that can only be a treasure for as long as it is 'buried'. The formalities of social intercourse – 'teashop behaviours' – preserve this creative distance. This same self-recognition by self-preservation is evident in 'Arrival', whose setting is 'the new city' where 'the past dries in a wind'. The speaker asks to 'lie down, under/ A wide-branched indifference' and to 'let the cluttered-up houses/ Keep their thick lives to themselves'. In this way, mutual ignorance, of stranger with stranger, 'Seems a kind of innocence' which is preserved until 'my own life impound it'.[76] Ignorance is 'innocence', but once the new becomes absorbed in the personality, both are contaminated. The poem begins to articulate what 'Absences', written at about the same time, symbolically pictures: that this 'innocence' can only be preserved in a kind of paradise of pristine self-annihilation. 'The March Past', a poem prompted by watching a Belfast procession, shows why an escape from personality is so desirable. The sudden noise and bustle of the marching 'cut short/ Memory, intention, thought' and for a moment, in this suspended pause, the speaker experienced 'a sudden flock of visions'. But what then came back to mind was 'a blind// Astonishing remorse for things now ended', things which 'should be deep,/ Rarely exhumable'.[77] Clearly, guilt is one reason for the personality to want to forget itself.

The arguments about solitude revolve around contradictions. Solitude preserves the artist's creative integrity, but most of all the speaker of these poems wants not to express himself, but escape himself. Herein lies the ultimate romantic yearning in Larkin that is perceptible throughout his career: a desire not so much for transcendence as for a sublime self-forgetting. 'Beneath it all, desire of oblivion runs' ('Wants', written in 1950). But the only oblivion conceivable is death, which even these early poems wrestle with as an existential absurdity: life is 'A style of dying only' ('Arrival'). Later in his career, Larkin will write poems that stop just short of inarticulacy in their imagining an ultimate 'other', the ultimate non-self. So, Larkin's poems about the individual and society are bound up with these existential questions and only occasionally will they win their way to hard-won integrations of self and others.

The process begins when Larkin comes to accept the artist not as separate, but as ordinary, an ordinariness which, however 'dull', is uniquely precious:

> If that is what a skilled,
> Vigilant, flexible,
> Unemphasised, enthralled
> Catching of happiness is called.

> ('Born Yesterday')

With this comes a recognition that exclusion from society, remaining as an observer behind the window-pane where Larkin's speakers are so often situated, allows the artist to memorialise and honour the life of a community ('those she has least use for see her best' – 'Spring'), to identify its collective delusions and, occasionally, to celebrate its bonds. It is from his self-imposed role as internal exile that Larkin's later poetry emerges, from the gap between self and others, a disjunction embodied in his use of dramatised personae. When Larkin's poems look beyond society, to elemental presences, they yearn not just for an escape from society, but from selfhood. Solitude allows him self-recognition; paradoxically that self-recognition confirms the existential prison of selfhood which is simultaneously individual and universal. In his lifelong contemplation of identity, these are the antitheses Larkin's poems occasionally manage to synthesise.

Usually seen merely as a precursor of 'Vers de Société', 'Best Society', probably written in 1951, rehearses some of the fundamental contradictions Larkin was to spend the rest of his poetic career trying to resolve. The title refers to Wordsworth's lines (in *The Prelude*, Book II) celebrating the childhood experience of 'Solitude,/ More active, even, than "best society"'. Solitude, Larkin's poem says, is more difficult to get the more it is desired. But it is also undesirable, not really because it is thought 'Our virtues are all social', but because our individuality can only be defined in terms of difference from and similarity to others:

> for what
> You are alone has, to achieve
> The rank of fact, to be expressed
> In terms of others . . .

Solitude allows one to define oneself, but self-definition can only be relative (or else transformed into absolutes by 'oblivion' and ultimate 'absence'). So identity emerges by its relationship with and separateness from other identities. But however thus defined, it is only in solitude that the self can truly know itself. Larkin's writing, even at its most ironical and satirical, becomes an attempt to define himself. The attempt starts in his youth when, as a dandyish aesthete, Larkin expesses identity as an egocentric, lyrical 'I'. But it shifts, with difficulty (apparent in the coyness of the quotation below), to the perception of self through others so as to achieve a sublime anonymity. Failure becomes triumph; vacancy is all:

> Once more
> Uncontradicting solitude
> Supports me on its giant palm;
> And like a sea-anemone
> Or simple snail, there cautiously
> Unfolds, emerges, what I am.[78]

3

The Less Deceived

The *Untitled Poems* which Larkin sent to George Hartley for the Marvell Press early in 1955 contained thirteen poems carried over from Larkin's *XX Poems* which had been privately printed in Belfast in 1951. Clearly, these were the poems in which he had most confidence (only two poems survive from *In the Grip of Light* to reappear in both *XX Poems* and *The Less Deceived*: they are 'Going' and 'Wedding-Wind') and which he regarded as correctives to the excesses of *The North Ship*. Apart from the two *In the Grip of Light* poems, every poem in *The Less Deceived* was completed after December 1949: that is, they represent the poems he wrote just prior to and following his move to Belfast. The burial of *The North Ship* and *In the Grip of Light* was all but complete.

Hartley wanted another title and Larkin shifted 'The Less Deceived' from a poem (now entitled 'Deceptions') to the title-page. Its source is to be found in Shakespeare's *Hamlet*: in his vicious mock-madness, Hamlet toys with Ophelia's love for him, claiming firstly, 'I did love you once' and moments later, 'I loved you not'. Ophelia's reply is stunned: 'I was the more deceived' (*Hamlet*, III.i.). The title might well have had a private significance for Larkin[1], but on a more general level it clearly signals an attitude of wary suspiciousness and worldly scepticism, particularly in personal relationships. In offering the title, Larkin explained to Hartley:

> I especially didn't want an 'ambiguous' title, or one that made any claims to policy or belief: this (*The Less Deceived*) would however give a certain amount of sad-eyed (and clear-eyed) realism, and if they [i.e. readers] did pick up the context they might grasp my fundamentally passive attitude to poetry (and life too, I suppose) which believes that the agent is always more deceived than the patient, because action comes from desire, and we all know that desire comes from wanting something we haven't got, which may not make us any happier when we have it. On the

other hand suffering – well, there is positively no deception about that. No one *imagines* their suffering.[2]

The immediate context is the poem 'Deceptions', but Larkin's explanation clearly has a bearing on the whole collection. It is worth remembering, particularly following Larkin's remarks about the importance of Hardy to him, that these poems emerge from personal experience – of the disappointments of love, of the desire for fame and escape from the drudgery of ordinary routine, of weighing up the cost of emotional commitment in relation to individual freedom. 'My poems are nothing if not personal', Larkin commented.[3]

Perhaps the most obviously 'personal' poems (though not necessarily 'confessional') in *The Less Deceived* are those dealing with romantic involvement. Of these, the earliest is 'Wedding-Wind' which was completed in September 1946 when Larkin was involved with Ruth Bowman. It is one of the very few occasions in the whole of Larkin's work when he clearly writes as another character: it's worth recalling that in 1946 Larkin regarded himself primarily as a novelist. The poem imagines the feelings of a farmer's wife on the day after her wedding. James Booth dismisses it as 'somewhat artificial, recalling the midland pastoral atmosphere of early D. H. Lawrence, with added touches from Dylan Thomas. External images of nature are forced to do duty for internal emotional insights . . .'.[4] Certainly, there's more than a touch of Dylan Thomas in the opening with its stop-start syntax ('And . . . And . . . That . . .'), self-conscious verbal music and ecstatic mood. But the poem is notable for its attempted identification with a character far removed from Larkin's youthful experience, and the expression of ambiguous feelings. The wind which has blown throughout her wedding day and night is associated by the woman with her happiness, a 'bodying-forth . . . Of joy'. But the wind is used by the poet here, as elsewhere, as an ambivalent symbol: the horses are made restless in the night and now 'All's ravelled' by the wind's 'Hunting and thrashing'. The final image, of cattle kneeling to drink water, expresses the woman's gratitude and sense of blessedness, of her conviction of essential unity between herself and the natural world which makes her love not only personal but a universal principle of life. But this affirmation is framed by a vulnerable rhetorical question ('Can even death dry up . . . ?'). And although the poem portrays the woman's exultant joy, there is beyond her a lurking sense of threat. For a time, she is abandoned on her wedding night when her husband has to shut the door blown by the wind and she is left 'Stupid in candlelight'. The image of her face reflected in the twisted candlestick is a macabre touch and conveys something sinister about her sudden loneliness. This confusion of feeling is further felt in her being 'sad/ That any man or beast that night should lack/ The happiness I had'. The poem makes the woman's feelings on her wedding night ambiguous: it conveys her joy but also her vulnerability. One is reminded of some of the remarks in Larkin's letters at this time to James Sutton at the time analysing his own ambiguous feelings about love and the possibility of marriage to Ruth Bowman: 'I am a long way off being capable of any emotion as simple as what is called love'.[5]

Another poem which seems directly related to the Ruth Bowman relationship is 'No Road'. Written in 1950, it deals with the ending of a relationship and evolves, like a number of poems of this period, by elaborating on a single image, in this case a road being allowed to fall into disuse. But 'our neglect/ Has not had much effect' and 'Walking that way tonight would not seem strange'. Nevertheless, the poet avers, before much longer 'no such road will run/ From you to me'. Exploring how he feels about that involves a sudden quickening of ideas and a shift from embellishing an image to a surge of abstract thinking. There is the 'liberty' of awaiting that new world (though it is a 'cold sun') but again the poet is caught in contradictory feelings. He does not want to prevent this new state of affairs but at the same time finds 'Willing it, my ailment', as if he is already disabled by wanting it too much. It is an unsatisfactory poem, with its clotted abstractions at the end, its clumsy negative 'Not to prevent' and its laboured last line. It gives the impression of feelings not quite brought into focus.

A more explicit sense of masculine grievance is given full rein in 'If, My Darling'. 'It was the first poem that made Kingsley [Amis] think that I was some good: he loved it when I sent it to him'[6] and it is easy to understand the poem's appeal to a misogynistic kind of male heartiness. It attempts to shock the girl into realising just how disreputable the male speaker really is. Written in May 1950, it is probably connected with the severance of Larkin's engagement to Ruth Bowman: there is a comical, rather heartless flamboyance in the relish with which the speaker details his true offensiveness. The furniture he imagines the woman expecting to find, all polite Victorian drawing-room décor, is bundled aside by the brute reality of

'A Grecian statue kicked in the privates' and 'A swill-tub of finer feelings'. The real kick comes at the end when the jokey rhyme hammers home the reality he wants the woman to face, that 'the past is past and the future neuter'. This, he thinks, 'Might knock my darling off her unpriceable pivot'. Though interesting for its surrealistic inventiveness (an *Alice-in-Wonderland* fantasy), the poem is really a piece of bluster which makes us feel sorrier for the woman than the man. The language has the muddle of suddenly released exasperation (would it not make more sense to have her knocked off a pedestal rather than pivot?) but it shows a kind of unbuttoned intemperateness which would never have been allowed in *The North Ship*.

'Latest Face' expresses a very different mood from 'If, My Darling', something more tentatively tender but in the end uncommitted. It is reminiscent of Larkin's earlier Audenesque style, with its rapid transitions between images and fleshing out of abstraction ('Lies grow dark around us'). Whilst welcoming the arrival of beauty and toying with the possibility of emotional involvement, the poem in the end seems to suggest that it is preferable to leave the relationship a possibility rather than risk its actuality. The first stanza celebrates the 'effortless' arrival of the woman, as if her most attractive quality is that neither he nor she has had to pursue the other. And this sense of something being held in suspense is present throughout the poem. His look is merely to be recognised; she should not turn again; their embraces 'On a useless level' are more abstract than physical because 'to move/ Into real untidy air/ Brings no lasting attribute –/ Bargains, suffering, and love'. Love, it would seem, belongs to an untidy world of emotional tussle, whereas this relationship can remain one of meaningful gestures, an 'always-planned salute'. The final part of the poem is even more fugitive. It seems to ask what the future of this relationship might be, whether he should actively pursue her until it is too late to turn back, or whether 'Denial of you' can ultimately conclude things.

Written in February 1951, 'Latest Face' expresses a way of dealing with romantic feelings. The language of the poem suggests how erotic desire is preserved not in fulfilment but in deferral. The first encounter is described in a vocabulary of lightness and insubstantiality: 'effortless' 'vagrant' and the neutral 'Admirer and admired'. He 'contains' her 'grace', she his 'judgment', and again romantic attraction is made decorous by the curiously formalised gesture of 'salute'. That he might 'wade' behind her in pursuit is, the verb indicates, an undignified possibility, and whether 'Something' is found or not it will be 'too late for turning back'. Clearly, nothing is to be risked; instead, longing is to remain uncompromised by anything approaching commitment. The object of longing, the poem asserts, is best left remote and unattained, and preserving distance means no-one will be disappointed. One is reminded of the remark Larkin made to James Sutton following the break-up of his engagement: 'Remote things seem desirable. Bring them close, and I start shitting myself'.[7] Desire can remain desire only for as long as its object remains remote.

The poem is notable too for a calculated indefiniteness found elsewhere in Larkin. The theme of beauty's fragility, of the necessary and discomfiting remoteness of the ideal, is one frequently expressed in Larkin's poetry. But here he works by suggestion rather than statement, and the hints and elisions of meaning are appropriate for a poem dealing with deferral as a romantic strategy. Everything about the poem suggests delicacy and indefiniteness, as in the irregular stanzas (do the first two together suggest a sonnet?) and rhyme scheme which approximates to but never quite repeats a pattern.

'Arrivals, Departures' is another poem dealing with the anxieties of love. The simple conjunction of opposites in the title is mirrored in the tripartite structure of the poem, with the first stanza describing the traveller's arrival, the third his departure and the middle stanza acting as a meditative transition between the two. Coming and going, the poem seems to suggest, is the natural condition of things. Boats arriving in the docks awake the lovers in the morning; outward bound at night, the boats' hooting is unsettling for lovers who can never know 'How safely we may disregard their blowing,/ Or if, this night, happiness too is going'. The future is unknowable and security, even in love, illusory. All is transition (the setting of the poem is in a port) and the motif of travellers arriving and departing blends with the poem's anxiety not only about the permanence of love but the illusoriness of all our expectations. The arrivals 'lowing in a doleful distance' awake the lovers once more to 'Horny dilemmas' (with the sexual pun): '*Come and choose wrong*, they cry, *come and choose wrong*', and this is echoed by the horns of the outward bound boats which seem to cry to the traveller, '*O not for long*'. For the traveller, as for the couple in bed, the condition is one of impermanence. Wrong choices await and nothing will last.

Apart from 'Arrivals, Departures', the poems discussed hitherto appeared in *XX Poems* and show, albeit in their different ways, not only a jaundiced romanticism but a more oblique and discontinuous mode of expression than we have become used to in Larkin. Two poems, however, related in circumstance and style, serve to show a more direct use of dramatic situation which Larkin had begun to develop and which marks the major stylistic progression from the lyricism of *The North Ship*. 'Lines on a Young Lady's Photograph Album' (the poem which opens *The Less Deceived* and thus perhaps indicates Larkin's confidence in this style) and 'Maiden Name' are both addressed to Winifred Arnott, a trainee librarian in Belfast University Library. Shortly after Larkin met her, she left Belfast to complete her training in London and there became engaged. The second poem, written in 1955 and some six months after her marriage, expresses Larkin's lurking sense of betrayal. Both poems (the first written in 1953) are written in a style very different from 'Latest Face'. And the feeling is different, too. So far, Larkin in his love poems has adopted a pose of provocative guardedness, either by being brutal (in 'If, My Darling') or saturnine (as in 'Arrivals, Departures'). The very title of 'Lines on a Young Lady's Photograph Album' announces something new: an irreverent mockery which, by seeming to take nothing too seriously, can suddenly modulate, almost despite itself, into seriousness and tenderness.

Mockery, and in particular self-mockery (as here in the picture of the dirty old man leering at the girl's photos), becomes an important and profitable strategy by which Larkin released himself from the poeticising postures of *The North Ship*. The poems in *The Less Deceived* which established Larkin's particular identity as a poet – debunking, unillusioned, wittily rueful and irreverently ironic – represent the expression of the philistine in Larkin which begins to triumph over the aesthete who wrote *The North Ship*. His mockery of all pretentiousness, and particularly of artistic aspiration (as in 'I Remember, I Remember') ridicules and ironises the lyrical ego. As the aesthete gives way to the philistine, so the lyrical mode shifts to dramatic (or, in the terms of the Russian literary theorist Mikhail Bakhtin, the monologic to the dialogic). Instead of speaking from a stable centre of lyrical intensity, 'Lines on a Young Lady's Photograph Album' veers around attitudes, shifts its tones of voice, constructs a process of explanation from which a conclusion emerges with apparent naturalness. This is one aspect of the 'dramatic' effect of these poems, their play of provisionality in following processes of thought and development of attitudes. In this way, too, the personal is made impersonal not by lyrical sublimity, but by the performative construction of a voice, or voices, which are actually detached from a single specifiable poetic identity. A product of Larkin's 'mockery' is the ironic distance which allows him to ventriloquise, to take up attitudes and points of view interrogatively.

The title itself sets up the tone of philistine mockery, poking fun very precisely at a 'poetical' pose. There are further punning ironies: the lines are now lines of age, the creases on the photos and the signs of ageing on the girl herself. The poem seems determined to avoid the 'poetic', either in manner or matter. The mockery becomes self-mockery once the album is opened and the speaker ridicules his swivel-eyed hunger. The implied presence of the woman as the addressee (and spectator of this performance) is part of the 'dramatised' aspect of the poem; other poems similarly imply an addressee, often unspecified but imagined as the 'reader', and this, too, marks a crucial advance on the hermetic aestheticism of *The North Ship*. The exaggerated eagerness creates an instability of tone whereby apparently throwaway remarks (such as the ones about the trilby hat and the sneering dismissal of the 'disquieting chaps') reverberate in all sorts of possibly revealing and/or unrevealing ways. The point about such thoroughgoing irony as Larkin now creates is that personal feelings can get expressed almost unnoticed rather than being laid bare.

The tone shifts into stability when the poem reaches its real subject: not the girl, but via photography, time and nostalgia. Photography now gives Larkin an exemplary anti-romantic aesthetic: like photography, his poetry will aim to be 'as no art is,/ Faithful and disappointing'. After years of failure, his art, all artlessness, will record 'Dull days as dull, and hold-it smiles as frauds'. In recompense, it hopes for the 'grace' of 'candour', a candour which registers the blemishes of empirical reality but, as this poem now does, seeks in compensation the truth about our feelings. For the poet is moved by something more than the representation of 'a real girl in a real place'. His feelings for her intensify when 'you/ Contract my heart by looking out of date', where the enjambement points up the pun on 'Contract'. Her 'looking out of date' is not only a matter of changing fashion, but of her existence in a time now inaccessible. And, with relentless candour, this remoteness is what the speaker finds moving about her photos. Excluded from the woman's past, he is left free to yearn for that past precisely because he is/was uninvolved in it and has no responsibility for it: 'We know *what was*/ Won't call on us to justify/ Our grief'. He can 'mourn (without a chance of consequence)'; his nostalgia is possible only because the past he now observes is isolated from him. A draft version emphasised this separation:

> This is your past that I can never share.
> Developed, fixed and mounted high and dry
> In days I cannot rifle if I try . . . [8]

Her past, 'calm and dry', is 'like a heaven' because it is impenetrable, removed now from decision, choice, guilt, even desire (like the 'padlocked cube of light' in 'Dry-Point'). Larkin can be nostalgic about someone else's past precisely because it is ir-recoverable, safely out of reach, a pure realm of completion and uninvolvement. The poem ends with a compliment, not quite to the woman, but to the image of her, a compliment silently qualified by the pun on 'lie' (a pun Larkin will use at least twice more, in 'Talking in Bed' and 'An Arundel Tomb'). The photograph preserves her as she was for a moment, but preservation is not our condition. She lies 'Unvariably . . . as the years go by'.

   In 'Lines on a Young Lady's Photograph Album' Larkin found a way to express feelings of lyrical plangency without belittling them. He does so by framing them within contrary attitudes, as mockery gives way to something more tender within it. The same movement between antipathies occurs in 'Reasons for Attendance', 'Church Going', 'Toads', 'Poetry of Departures' and many poems in *The Whitsun Weddings*. Larkin's sense of failure and his sense of having been betrayed by his earlier lyrical intensities become the real subjects of his poems as a kind of anti-lyricism which can then persuade itself into a chastened lyricism (or flippancy into seriousness, as in 'Church Going'). Hence the emergence of a performative element in *The Less Deceived*. Poems like 'Lines on a Young Lady's Photograph Album' dramatise attitudes, strike slightly exaggerated poses in front of an imagined audience (either a nominated addressee, or the anonymous 'reader') so as to smuggle in the vulnerable emotions Larkin tried nakedly to expose in *The North Ship*. This involves the construction of a dramatised first-person 'speaker' who undergoes, apparently intuitively, a process of self-interrogation. Critics who have con-demned Larkin for having rigged in advance the internal 'debates' his poems seem to undertake rather miss their performative element: they are 'virtual' rather than 'real' arguments. Larkin 'finds his voice' by finding voices, by incorporating in his writing the forces which threaten it and by exploiting rather than suppressing his satirising philistinism. Bakhtin again: 'The writer is a person who knows how to work language while remaining outside of it; he has the gift of indirect speech'.[9]

'Maiden Name' is an obvious companion-piece to 'Lines on a Young Lady's Photograph Album'. Again addressed to Winifred Arnott, it was written early in 1955, some six months after her marriage. Dealing more explicitly with the notion of identity, it explores the same issues of time and memory and, technically, resembles the earlier poem (and many others) in seeming to create evenness out of oddness. Larkin frequently sets himself a technical challenge by taking stanza units composed of an odd number of lines (seven, in this case) and shaping the poem into an odd number of stanzas (here, three) and then deploying rhyme and rhythm to create a feeling of regularity and completeness. Thus the balanced, even-toned reasonableness of the poem is actually having to work against the grain of disequilibrium in its structure.

Now that the woman has married, the poet teasingly asks what significance her maiden name can have. With mock-philosophical solemnity, he proposes that since she has changed her name, she cannot be identical with what she was before. Discarded, her maiden name belongs to the past, to be found among the other trivia of her girlhood and adolescence. Maintaining a tone of graceful wit, the poet asks what meaning her maiden name can have now, given that it belongs so irrevocably to the past. In what sense can it be true of her now? As the second stanza runs into the third, an answer evolves. The woman's past is embodied in her maiden name and its associations now mean 'what we feel now about you then': her beauty, intimacy and youth remain captured in her former name. The recollection of her maiden name vividly brings to mind all that she once was, so that her old name 'shelters our faithfulness' and now comes to mean all that the poet felt – and still feels – for her. By the end of the poem, the poet has discovered that far from losing its significance, the woman's maiden name has assumed a greater meaning in preserving all his feelings for her – now that she is lost to him.

Under its witty exterior, this is another poem about loss and the threat to identity posed specifically by marriage. The manuscript draft carries a note describing the existential conundrum which lies at the heart of the poem: 'you are not she'.[10] But the loss of the woman brings with it the freedom to feel an unthreatened (and unthreatening) romantic longing. He can now treasure her memory and honour romantic ideals – love and beauty – because they are fixed and preserved in an unchangeable past. 'Disused', her name can now 'shelter' his faithfulness and protect it from change. As in 'Lines on a Young Lady's Photograph Album', the past presents and preserves an ideal which is now remote – and so can remain an ideal. Perfection must remain inaccessible. 'Maiden Name' is also similar to the earlier poem in its construction of a voice which modulates through a variety of tones and feelings performed in the syntax and diction of conversation rather than the compacted obliquities of lyricism. In a poem so concerned with the existential validity of names, marriage is treated ironically as a kind of name-less horror, irrevocably altering identity, 'losing shape and meaning less', a confusion 'By law with someone else'. There is the same direct address in the second-person pronoun, now even more boldly foregrounded as a dramatic strategy: 'Try whispering it slowly./No, it means you'. And there is the same contrivance of reticence and emotion, a reticence which plays out a drama: it is sur-prised by, wary of but ultimately submissive to emotional intensity.

'Maiden Name' has a romantic attachment as its specific occasion but at its heart is a more general question which is present throughout *The Less Deceived*: the question of identity. The poem's opening strategy was to ask what meaning the woman's maiden name could have after her marriage and the implicit suggestion was that in changing her name she had in some fundamental way changed her identity; she could no longer be what she once was. In *The Less Deceived*, Larkin is constantly questioning the assumption that we express our identity by making choices which determine the course of our lives. The same preoccupation is evident in the letters he wrote in the late 1940s. Those failures with his third novel and *In the Grip of Light* together with the romantic complications with Ruth Bowman seem to have forced upon Larkin a bewildered inertia.

> I refuse to believe that there is a thing called life, that one can be in or out of touch with. There is only an endless series of events, of which our birth is one & our death another . . . Life is chiefly an affair of 'life-force': we are all varyingly charged with it and that represents our energy and nothing we do or say will alter our

voltage or wattage . . . great men . . . are those lucky beings in whom a horny sheath of egoism protects their energy, not allowing it to be dissipated or turned against itself.[11]

The Less Deceived can be seen as the result of Larkin's creative energies being turned against themselves, scrutinising motives, probing identity, retreating from all choice in the overwhelming fact of death. 'I search myself for illusions like a monkey looking for fleas. But the process of removing an endless series of false bottoms from one's personality is wearying . . .'[12] *The Less Deceived* represents that process of removing false bottoms. And in the end what *The Less Deceived* most yearns for is an escape from personality, the annihilation of identity. For all their definiteness in terms of empirical observation, these poems are essentially provisional, strategies by which to interrogate the trappings of identity: work, love, childhood, religious faith, everything by which we try to give shape and meaning to our lives. Larkin wants to resist not only romantic involvement but all forms of commitment because any such pledge to a person, article of faith or way of life involves an illusion.

My views are very simple and childish: I think we are born, & grow up, & die . . . Everything we do is done with the motive of pleasure & if we are unhappy it is because we are such silly bastards for thinking we should like whatever it is we find we don't like . . . If we seriously contemplate life it appears an agony too great to be supported, but for the most part our minds gloss such things over & until the ice finally lets us through we skate about merrily enough. Most people, I'm convinced, don't think about life at all. They grab what they think they want and the subsequent consequences keep them busy in an endless chain till they're carried out feet first. As for how one should spend one's time, that's usually decided for you by circumstances & habit.[13]

A little later, Larkin writes:

It has always seemed to me fatally easy to get carried along on the surface of life, & though I agree one would probably do as well that way as any other you do not catch me giving in & being carried. I resist the current, even if it means staying in the same spot all one's life.[14]

The inertia of resistance was to become one of the hallmarks of Larkin's life and work.

One of the currents plainly resisted in *The Less Deceived* is sexual desire. 'Dry-Point' is a poem which proceeds by metaphor but its subject of post-coital *tristesse* is clear enough. Nevertheless, the poem has a revealing history. In *XX Poems*, it appeared under the title 'Etching' with a companion-piece, dropped from *The Less Deceived*, called 'Oils' and the two poems were paired as 'Two Portraits of Sex'. 'Dry-Point is a form of copperplate engraving in which no acid is used and like the original title 'Etching' it indicates the poet's approach to his portrait of his subject'.[15] Written within a few days of each other, the two poems present diametric opposites not only in their view of sex but also in their poetic techniques. The first poem, 'Oils', portrays sexual desire as elemental in its mysterious intensity. Here is the opening stanza:

> Sun. Tree. Beginning. God in a thicket. Crown.
> Never-abdicated constellation. Blood.
> Barn-clutch of life. Trigger of the future.
> Magic weed the doctor shakes in the dance.
> Many rains and many rivers, making one river.
> Password. Installation. Root of tongues.[16]

This is unrecognisable as Larkin and all the more interesting for being so. It represents that symbolist, Lawrentian side of him: an urgent, highly figurative language in which meaning is strained into expression. The title explains the poem's technique: this is a poem about sex as richly coloured and thickly impressionistic as an oil-painting. But the effect is gauche: 'New voice saying new words at a new speed/ From which the future erupts like struck oil . . .'. By contrast, 'Dry-Point' is, as the title implies, a more prosaic, austere, fastidiously hard-edged utterance. As the poem goes on to elaborate, there is also a more saturnine view of sex half-disguised in the title: sex not as eruption but as aridity.

From the outset, sexual desire is perceived as imprisoning. It is a bubble in which we are constantly enclosed and which we repeatedly try to escape from: 'Bestial, intent, real./ The wet spark comes, the bright blown walls collapse . . .'. The image of male orgasm and detumescence leads to further images of shame and disappointment, specifically related to engagement and marriage. But set against failure and remorse, the imprisoning cycle of desire and disappointment, is another image altogether:

> And how remote that bare and sunscrubbed room,
> Intensely far, that padlocked cube of light
> We neither define nor prove,
> Where you, we dream, obtain no right of entry.

The 'you' is the 'time-honoured irritant' of not only sexual desire but all desire. The poem yearns to escape from desire itself as a condition of our lives, to escape into emptiness and solitariness, a 'bare and sunscrubbed room . . . that padlocked cube of light'. Our ordinary desires cannot 'define' or test this remote transcendence, a condition of vacancy rather than longing. 'Dry-Point' suggests that the ultimate desire in Larkin's poems is for desirelessness.

Two other poems in *The Less Deceived* deal explicitly with the illusions bound up with sexual desire. In 'Reasons for Attendance' Larkin again uses a first-person speaker, but this time so as specifically to undermine the drift of the speaker's argument. In this sense, too, many of the poems in *The Less Deceived* are provisional: Larkin uses a speaker to dramatise an internal conflict and then pulls the rug from under the speaker's feet or in some other way reveals the speaker as flawed or partisan. By using these personae, Larkin is able to articulate, juxtapose and take the measure of conflicting attitudes, ones no doubt embodied in himself.

The 'voice' of 'Reasons for Attendance' has all the appearance of reasonableness until the end when the poem's strategy of subversion is revealed. In fact, the central voice of the poem is the trumpet's which on the one hand, 'loud and authoritative', strikes 'the beat of happiness' and on the other is the 'rough-tongued bell/ (Art, if you like) whose individual sound/Insists I too am individual' (the 'bell' being the cone of the trumpet). It is between these two opposing attractions, the one sexual and communal, the other solitary and vocational, that the speaker is poised. (In using the occasion of a jazz-band to prompt these reflections, Larkin is also saying something about his own love of jazz either as an involvement in a shared popular culture or as the pursuit of a solitary aesthetic. Even here, it seems, Larkin is divided between communality and privacy.)

As he passes a dance-hall, the speaker is drawn by the music to peer through the window at the dancers inside. He is the outsider looking in, and for a long moment wonders what it would be like to be inside and enjoying 'The wonderful feel of girls'. What attracts the dancers, he knows, is a sexual desire he feels too ('Why be out here?'). But this is quickly negated by the assertion that happiness is not just to be found in partnership. By contrast, he is drawn another way, towards an individual fulfilment in art rather than the dancers' search for happiness with a mate. His pursuit of 'Art' asserts his unique individuality which it seems the speaker prefers to preserve at the expense of intimacy with another person (one recalls Larkin's wriggling torments during his engagement to Ruth Bowman). Happiness is not to be found by any single means and believing this the speaker can rest content, or so he persuades himself, to remain on the outside, excluded from the dancers who seek happiness in their own, different way. So it seems an even-handed, democratic conclusion is found, until we reach the sting in the tail of the poem: 'both are satisfied,/ If no one has misjudged himself. Or lied'.

The ending of the poem strikes a note of doubt which echoes back through the whole. And on closer inspection, we find that self-doubt constantly threatens to undermine the apparent confidence of the speaking voice. We might begin by noting the exaggeratedly unflattering portrait of the dancers: their faces are 'flushed', they are 'shifting intently' and 'Solemnly' as if stupefied by 'the smoke and sweat' in which they 'maul to and fro'. From the start, the speaker does not want to envisage precisely what would otherwise be the too appealing contrast to his own loneliness. Instead, it is imagined as something furtive and animal (like the frightening urgency of 'Bestial, intent, real' in 'Dry-Point'). Then we listen to another kind of mauling to and fro, in the speaker's internal debate – 'Why be out here?/ But then, why be in there? Sex, yes, but what/ Is sex?' – which in its balance looks reasonable but actually posits a defensively silly question. The speaker knows all too well what sex is, 'sensing the smoke and sweat,/ The wonderful feel of girls'. This defensiveness is clear in the rhetorical 'Surely' and the hectic dash to a blustering assertion: 'sheer// Inaccuracy, as far as I'm concerned'. What look like the shifts and hesitations of reasonableness turn out to be the evasions of a speaker anxious to justify a conclusion on which he has already decided: that in pursuing a bachelor's vocation to Art the speaker is not losing out. And yet even as he announces his individualism, the speaker cannot disguise an uneasy embarrassment: '(Art, if you like)' – bracketed, deferential, not to be taken too seriously for fear of sounding pretentious. The speaker knows all too well that the individuality he thinks is preserved in Art might in fact be nothing more than an imprisoning loneliness. He has not quite managed to lie to himself. Like so many of Larkin's poems, 'Reasons for Attendance' speaks with more than one voice. Its ostensible commitment to 'individuality' is simultaneously challenged by other voices which themselves suggest that the very notion of a stable, coherent, unified 'individuality' is an illusion.

Another poem dealing with our sexual nature is 'Deceptions' (originally 'The Less Deceived'). In using a historical source (Henry Mayhew's *London Labour and the London Poor*), Larkin again dramatises an internal debate about desire and suffering, this time by re-creating the circumstances of a Victorian girl who is drugged and raped. The extent to which Larkin is able to sympathise with both the girl and her rapist has made this poem the subject of some controversy.[17] One critic ends her discussion of the poem thus: 'In sum, I do not think that one can have it both ways: Larkin as detached poetic observer and Larkin as sympathetic to human suffering . . . the callousness which [the poem] exhibits and the sadism which it in part condones ought at the least to be seen as problematic – and as a limitation in Larkin's art'.[18] This states the problem, but fails to consider that the poem knows it is problematical, that Larkin is concerned to show how sympathy can never compensate for suffering and that identifying with suffering is fraught with potential moral dishonesty. For all the poem's participants are victims: the girl, the rapist, Mayhew, the poet and the reader. All are limited in their perspectives by their individual isolation and their contingent historical circumstances.

For these reasons, it is worth pursuing the poem's historical source. Henry Mayhew's documentary study of the London poor was published in 1861. In it, Mayhew gives the story of 'a woman over forty, shabbily dressed, and with a disreputable, unprepossessing appearance'. She was the daughter of a Dorsetshire tenant-farmer who visited London when she was sixteen. She was enticed by a stranger feigning illness into a brothel where, after consuming drugged coffee, she was raped. She was briefly the man's mistress but inevitably fell into prostitution. Mayhew records her as saying, 'You folks as has honour, and character, and feelings, and such can't understand how all that's been beaten out of people like me. I don't feel. I'm used to it'. She went on: 'I don't want to live, and yet I don't care enough about dying to make away with myself. I ain't got that amount of feeling that some has'. Mayhew moralises her story into the discourse of Victorian evangelising philanthropy: 'this woman's tale is a condensation of the philosophy of sinning'. His conclusion is that 'she had become brutal'[19].

Already, the woman's story comes to Larkin through two mediating sources: the woman's recollection of the event and Mayhew's recording of it for his own pedagogic purposes. The poem's specific starting-point is the girl's waking up next morning and discovering herself to have been violated. Then follows her desolation: 'I was inconsolable, and cried like a child to be killed or sent back to my aunt'. The poem immediately seeks to identify with the ruined girl, but it is an identification which has to acknowledge distance: the distance between the original event (when the girl was unconscious), the woman's recollection of it, Mayhew's use of it and the 'Slums' and 'years' which have intervened. That distance is measured in the difference between 'I can taste the grief' and the drug 'he made you gulp', the one volitional and vicarious, the other instantaneous and enforced. Larkin can 'taste', but no more.

Throughout the description of the girl's suffering, Larkin uses a wider frame of reference so as to put her experience into perspective, a perspective that includes the man who raped her. There is the glimpse of sunshine, then the noise of traffic outside widening to include a whole community ('bridal London') which now rejects her. Finally, there is simply 'light, unanswerable and tall and wide'. What 'light' is this? The light of philanthropic Mayhew bringing her story into the open? The light of day, literally and metaphorically? The light of her own understanding which 'Forbids the scar to heal, and drives/ Shame out of hiding'? And is this 'light' connected with 'that padlocked cube of light' to which in 'Dry-Point' desire has 'no right of entry'? The 'Shame' is certainly the girl's, but is it only hers? Does it not also belong to that callously indifferent 'bridal London'? To Mayhew ('She had become brutal')? To the rapist? And to the poet himself? Where in 'Dry-Point' the light is a 'padlocked cube' to which the speaker wishes to escape, here it seems to represent the horrifying truth of (sexual) knowledge and disillusionment. As in 'Dry-Point', the image of light is bound up with the desire to escape identity.[20] But in this case the girl knows only an appalling, self-tormenting exposure: 'All the unhurried day/ Your mind lay open like a drawer of knives'. But in her despair, the girl has at least broken free from the prison of desire. Nevertheless, although Larkin's judgement is more compassionate than Mayhew's, it still – shamefully – falls short of empathy. It is that falling short which is the subject of the second stanza.

Again, we are withdrawn from the situation and reminded of distance: 'Slums, years, have buried you'. It is this perspective that allows the speaker to admit his incapacity: 'I would not dare/ Console you if I could. What can be said . . .'? This is where the poem concedes its perplexed failure. Why would the speaker not 'dare' to console the girl? Because the only consolation he can offer is dispassionate, not empathetic. As the girl herself said, nothing could console. The girl, the rapist and the speaker are fundamentally isolated: the girl in her desolation, the rapist in his delusion, the speaker by history. The proffered consolation is hesitant and deferential: 'you would hardly care/ That you were less deceived'. Less deceived – but at such a cost. As Larkin explained in his letter to George Hartley about the collection's title, 'the agent is always more deceived than the patient . . . On the other hand suffering – well, there is positively no deception about that. No one *imagines* their suffering'. Where the opening description of the girl broadens into a panoramic perspective, the closing description of the man intensifies into identification:

> . . . you were less deceived, out on that bed,
> Than he was, stumbling up the breathless stair
> To burst into fulfilment's desolate attic.

Here, the poet 'is not having to reconstruct the picture: he only just avoids being subsumed in it. He does avoid it because of the contempt which the blustering adjectives suggest. The desire has taken charge of the poet as well; the identification here is grimly complete . . . he is *compelled* to feel the disgusting violence of male desire and the desolation of its fulfilment'.[21]

The poem makes its readers uncomfortable. For we too are victims of the woman's rebuke: 'You folks as has honour, and character, and feelings, and such *can't understand* how all that's been beaten out of people like me' [*my stress*]. The poem refuses to traffic in easy sympathy and instead admits to a more shameful identification with the man violently imprisoned in desire and the delusion that desire can be fulfilled. Where 'Reasons for Attendance' makes its strategy of subversion explicit in the final volte-face it performs, 'Deceptions' gradually discloses its own treachery in extending sympathy from the victim to the perpetrator.

If the speakers of 'Dry-Point', 'Reasons for Attendance' and 'Deceptions' want to escape from sexual desire, other voices in *The Less Deceived* look beyond all forms of desire to death itself. Larkin's poems and letters show him almost preternaturally conscious of death as the final annihilation of all endeavour and identity: even a cursory glance at the early, unpublished poems in the *Collected Poems* shows the young Larkin bemoaning his advancing years. Written in 1954 'Age', another poem which proceeds by discontinuous imagery, worries about what its speaker's life amounts to ('I needs must turn/ To know what prints I leave . . .') and what his past tells him about his identity ('. . . whether of feet,/ Or spoor of pads, or a bird's adept splay'). In 'Wants', the speaker looks through identity to nothingness. Its flat, wearily trudging refrains toll the knell of gloomy nihilism: 'Beyond all this, the wish to be alone. . . Beneath it all, desire of oblivion runs'. Life is starkly reduced to a few tableaux of sex and society – 'the invitation cards', 'the printed directions of sex' – from which the speaker seeks to exclude himself. This sort of escapism represents the oblivion some poems in *The Less Deceived* seek, though as James Booth describes it, '"Wants" is at bottom a disgruntled antisocial satire'.[22]

Disgruntlement is also the keynote of 'Triple Time', the title suggesting the division of time into past, present and future (marked by the three stanzas) as well as a rapid musical tempo (in which time flies). The poem in fact goes on to show this division as false, for the 'present' only exists in relation to other time (its past and future); like 'a reflection', it is itself empty, a moment of transition between present and future, 'unrecommended by event'. And yet this present moment was once eagerly anticipated in childhood which invested the future with potential fulfilment as 'An air lambent with adult enterprise'. But it will also, imminently, turn into the past and be remembered with regret. Moreover, as the object of romantic nostalgia (and here the poem switches from urban to pastoral imagery), it will be remembered as something other than it really was: 'A valley cropped by fat neglected chances/ That we insensately forbore to fleece'. We need this illusion of missed opportunities to constitute 'our last/Threadbare perspectives' so that as we grow old ('seasonal decrease') we can blame the past for our current misfortune. The truth of the matter is that we can only live in a constant alteration of promise and disillusionment as future becomes past and hope turns to disappointment.

This kind of despair is dealt with more wittily in 'Next, Please', the acquisitiveness (or weary boredom) of the title set against the proverbial ship that we wait to 'come in' and which never arrives.[23] The cliché is brought comically to life in the 'sparkling armada of promises' and the 'big approach, leaning with brasswork prinked,/ Each rope distinct,// Flagged, and the figurehead with golden tits/ Arching our way. . .'. But the zest subsides to a sombre ending:

> Only one ship is seeking us, a black-
> Sailed unfamiliar, towing at her back
> A huge and birdless silence. In her wake
> No waters breed or break.

Still, the bravura of the opening is not quite dissipated and there remains a touch of melodrama in the 'huge and birdless silence' (and in the 'black-Sailed' ship broken over the line-ending). The poem's exhilaration is expressed in its mocking language and the stanza structure which casually throws the syntax over the line-endings but reins in everything in the clipped fourth lines, leaving mimetically a sense of falling short. Whilst its conclusion is the same as 'Triple Time' ('it's/ No sooner present than it turns to past'), this time the voice finds more comedy than despair in our delusions.

A poem which similarly makes comedy out of misery is 'I Remember, I Remember'. This is not to say that the comedy alleviates the misery as some sort of 'light relief', but that the cause of our misery, the structure of time, the recurring cycle of expectancy and disappointment, is itself inherently funny. So are the strategies by which we delude ourselves. In mocking Thomas Hood's sentimental version of childhood, Larkin's travelling speaker offers an opposite but equal exaggeration which reduces childhood to oblivion: '"Nothing, like something, happens anywhere"'. Though we enjoy the speaker's mockery of the Wordsworthian and Lawrentian clichés popularly associated with childhood, there is nevertheless something excessive in his mounting irony. The zealous dismantling of childhood takes place, after all, only in his own head and the fellow-passenger's observation ('"You look as if you wished the place in Hell"') makes the speaker's seething resentment look just a little absurd. Again, there is unspoken distance between the 'I' of the poem and the reader so that 'I' should be regarded as another subjective presence, another 'voice', rather than an unproblematic author. After all, the childhood described in 'Coming' as 'A forgotten boredom' is far from forgotten in 'I Remember, I Remember'.

'At Grass' is another poem about oblivion, but this time much more maturely conceived than the lurking self-pity of 'Wants'. As in 'Deceptions', distance between writer and subject (here, retired race-horses) is important. Again, the poem's opening deliberately falls short of identification with the subject. The eye can hardly pick out the horses from their shelter and when one moves about the other only seems to look on. Furthermore, the horses are distanced from their own past, and although the speaker embarks on a loving re-creation of 'faint afternoons/ Of Cups and Stakes and Handicaps,/ Whereby their names were artificed', the anthropomorphic surge subsides: they are not plagued by memories, although the speaker is. These horses have escaped their fables, their past, even their names. Remote now from nearly all human contact ('not a fieldglass sees them home . . .'), they stand for the speaker as icons of anonymity, patiently awaiting their end.

Larkin had seen a cinema documentary about a famous retired race-horse and, like 'Wedding-Wind', the poem attempts to project a particular state of mind. He was drawn to the subject because it allowed him to talk about fame, a fame he had failed to achieve as a novelist, in a way that ultimately discounts it.[24] And yet everything about the poem insists on distance between the speaker and the horses. The poem simply refuses anthropomorphism. The opening is muted; 'Shade' already carries suggestions of death and when the wind 'distresses tail and mane' the curious formality of the word brings the speaker rather than the horses into focus. The stanzas describing their fame busy themselves with the human spectacle and the poem closes with a return to elegy. When these horses gallop 'for what must be joy' it is the speaker who, a touch desperately, confers joy on them. The poem resists the attempted identification with the horses in order to preserve what is most desirable about them: their anonymity. Larkin's draft notes emphasise that 'horses, free at last, become horses'.[25] Simon Petch writes that the horses 'become representations of unconscious identity. Liberated from the past and from the demands of time, they have finally become themselves . . . Their shedding of identity is seen as freedom. . .'.[26] They are, precisely, unknowable (like the raped girl in 'Deceptions') and that is their attraction – if not to the speaker, then to Larkin. The speaker of the poem is only passively dramatised: there is no externalised 'I' in the poem but a kind of anonymous centre of consciousness. 'At Grass', a poem about the loss of identity, succeeds in making itself anonymous.

One of the conditions which in *The Less Deceived* thwarts anonymity is choice, for choice bespeaks desire and what we choose is an aspect of what we are. A number of poems deal with the difficulties of choice – or, perhaps the ultimate unimportance of it. For all too often choice seems another illusion of freedom. And yet 'Places, Loved Ones' seems to be about how we choose to deny ourselves choice so as to avoid real responsibility for our lives. Like 'Reasons for Attendance', it presents a speaker who, embarked on one track of self-justification, switches to another. Choosing a wife and home, says the speaker, 'seems to prove/ You want no choice in where/ To build, or whom to love' so that when disappointment follows 'it's not your fault'. After this pious sanctimoniousness comes a more damaging admission. The rootless bachelor acts in just the same way as the settled husband, pretending that 'what you settled for/ Mashed you, in fact'. Both ways of living were chosen and we settle for what we have precisely so as to close off all the other unsettling options which remind us that had we been braver, stronger, wiser, life could have been better. We pretend to have been trapped by circumstances to avoid the thought that 'you still might trace/ Uncalled-for to this day/ Your person, your place'. The final implication of the poem seems to be that authenticating identity lies somewhere beyond the reach of choice. It is as if, like the women in 'Afternoons' (in *The Whitsun Weddings*), something has pushed us to the side of our own lives and the choices we make are purposeless.

Larkin is frequently accused of indulging in attitudes of willed resignation and easy fatalism. 'Places, Loved Ones' actually seems to rebuke resignation by saying that resignation is just another of our defensive postures. We should note as well the use of the dramatised second-person pronoun which claims for the poem the provisionality and vulnerability of any other speech-act. Perhaps the poem means no more than what Larkin wrote in the letter quoted earlier, about most people living on the surface of life by habit, routine and what circumstances dictate. It is hard to know how seriously to take the speaker of the poem, which seems to be grappling with something unresolved.

Much more finished are poems which Larkin seems, perhaps unfortunately, to have become most closely identified with: 'Poetry of Departures' and 'Toads'. Both are poems of comic disgruntlement which work by deploying clichés and dramatising stereotypes. In

'Poetry of Departures' – the title is a comically literal translation of a phrase used to describe a style of nineteenth-century French poem which imagines romantic escape from the everyday world – Larkin uses two voices to dramatise the conflict between escapist adventurousness and stay-at-home security. The first takes the form of clichés representing stereotypical masculine glamour: '*He walked out on the whole crowd*', '*Then she undid her dress*' and '*Take that you bastard*'. These romantic gestures are stirring but even before the speaker tells us of his own fantasy adventure – only to dismiss it – they have been subverted by irony. For right from the start of the poem, these stereotypes of liberation are treated as mythical fantasies. They are heard 'fifth-hand', you are expected to 'approve/ This audacious, purifying,/ Elemental move' (the exaggerated language already suggesting you will not approve) and the clichés of escapism are almost comically lifeless. It is only when the speaker embarks on his own fantasy that the language of escapism comes to life, but only to appear ridiculous:

> But I'd go today,
>
> Yes, swagger the nut-strewn roads,
> Crouch in the fo'c'sle
> Stubbly with goodness . . .

By this stage in the poem we already know that the speaker, for whatever reasons, cannot accept that chucking up everything and clearing off is a real possibility. The language of his own fantasy ridicules itself, not because it is limited to cliché but because it hilariously goes beyond it. 'Though the phrases here *sound* vaguely familiar . . . and immediately perform their function in conjuring up some Technicolor Gregory Peck or Tony Curtis, they are in fact not familiar verbal clichés. Rather they are a poetic apotheosis of the cliché.'[27] And so we have been softened up for the speaker's self-justifying conclusion: that he will never cut-and-run because to do so would be

> artificial,
> Such a deliberate step backwards
> To create an object:
> Books; china; a life
> Reprehensibly perfect.

To choose between home and flight is no choice at all because each option involves exactly the same illusion: that life can be made happy and fulfilling by choice.

The same sort of technique and conclusion is present in 'Toads' (though in this case the speaker's accidental self-revelations are more damaging), another comic poem of discontented resignation. Both poems have become accepted as representing Larkin's personal credo about life and work but their language and attitudes, whilst they mock the illusion of escape, satirise the speaker as well. Their comedy extends to self-mockery, suggesting lugubrious rue-fulness is itself a pose. Larkin stuck to his career and did not believe in exotic holidays, but was more self-knowing and self-critical than the speakers of 'Toads' and 'Poetry of Departures'.

'Toads' is a poem about desire and necessity, and again its language betrays the fact that the speaker's 'argument' is settled in advance. The poem is light-hearted, but the use of half-rhymes throughout gives it a nervous, fidgety edge of seriousness. Once more, as a defence-mechanism, the alternative to boring security is imagined unflatteringly:

> Their nippers have got bare feet,
>   Their unspeakable wives
> Are skinny as whippets – and yet
>   No one actually *starves*.

True, but it is a calculatedly unenticing alternative to work, however toad-like. In fact, what the speaker really wants to do is only admitted later:

> to blarney
>   My way to getting
> The fame and the girl and the money
>   All at one sitting.

But he is barred from such worldly success, 'For something sufficiently toad-like/ Squats in me, too' and this inner compulsion to settle for the world of work, duty and routine will always win out. The poem ends in a fog of abstraction:

> I don't say, one bodies the other
>   One's spiritual truth;

> But I do say it's hard to lose either,
> When you have both.

This seems to say that 'the toad *work*' which squats 'on my life' should not be assumed to be an externalisation of the inner 'toad' which 'Squats in me', but that when you have both 'toads' (a life of work which answers an inner need) it is hard to give up one of them – all of which sounds like the strained reasoning of bluster. The final stanza fails to answer the poem's opening question: 'Why should I let the toad *work*/ Squat on my life?' Where the question might get answered is in the fleeting description of the 'something sufficiently toad-like' which squats in him:

> Its hunkers are heavy as hard luck,
> And cold as snow . . .

This is not quite a toad (though 'toad-like') and here the imagery intensifies into impressions: heaviness and coldness. The speaker cannot throw over his life, however oppressive it is, because it answers his need to feel hard done by ('heavy as hard luck') and passive, even unfeeling ('cold as snow'). In the poem's conclusion, the speaker tries to argue that his having to settle for the world of work is not his fault: but almost buried within the poem (like 'Reasons for Attendance') is a more personally discrediting admission.

As we have seen, *The Less Deceived* can be read in terms of the 'voices' within individual poems so as to reveal the complex play of linguistic registers by which attitudes are dramatised and often ironised. As one critic has remarked, there is in many of Larkin's poems 'a certain deviousness in the rhetoric'.[28] However, there are other poems in *The Less Deceived* whose strategies appear less devious. One example is 'Church Going'. Much anthologised and widely admired, its rhetoric is in fact all too palpable, complacently modulating from facetiousness to gravity. Those stately final stanzas, with their elevated vocabulary and solemnly end-stopped lines, whilst they satisfyingly express the 'hunger' to be 'more serious', also set about disguising uncomfortable notions. The solace of churches, they assert, is in 'our compulsions' being 'robed as destinies'. The image, compelling as it is, actually suggests that the appeal of church ceremony involves an illusion. The arbitrary, provisional and circumstantial, the 'compulsions' of birth, marriage and death, are euphemised as 'destinies'. The undisturbed rhetoric of the poem represents a kind of wish-fulfilment, a desire to ritualise the randomness of life, to make chance look like order. (These are themes which will come to preoccupy *The Whitsun Weddings*.) If 'Church Going' is less 'devious', it is because it is determined to gloss over its more disturbing questions.

Elsewhere in the volume, the less 'devious' poems ('Coming' and 'Spring', for example, which were written within a few months of each other in 1950) have a lyrical intensity which seems to immerse them in the world rather than observing and making statements about it. 'Coming' looks forward to the spring with an image which might look back to Larkin's own childhood:

> And I, whose childhood
> Is a forgotten boredom,
> Feel like a child
> Who comes on a scene
> Of adult reconciling,
> And can understand nothing
> But the unusual laughter,
> And starts to be happy.

The speaker disowns his own childhood so as to feel its pathos all the more. The same intensification works in 'Spring'. Although its speaker concedes his unhealthy separateness from nature ('Threading my pursed-up way across the park,/ An indigestible sterility'), there is a grateful, even greedy, appreciation:

> And those she has least use for see her best,
> Their paths grown craven and circuitous,
> Their visions mountain-clear, their needs immodest.

In *The Less Deceived* that 'indigestible sterility' tries to find ways of being different from itself. Although some critics find it out of place in *The Less Deceived* the poem which most fully expresses this is 'Absences'.[29] Completed in November 1950, it seems to be rooted in Larkin's move from Leicester to Belfast made a few weeks earlier: 'I am always thrilled by the thought of what places look like when I am not there,' he once wrote.[30] In an undisguised symbolist manner, the poem presents, without context, a scene of a storm at sea. There are no ships, no coasts, only a horizon and a sky 'yet more shoreless' in which clouds are gathered and unravelled. Water, sky, light and wind: these are the only presences, constantly transforming themselves, the sea tilting and sighing, the clouds riddled, shifting and sifting. The poem is entirely absorbed in the scene and in its own protean language. Then, 'the final line shifts vertiginously, and without warning to a completely different image':[31]

> Such attics cleared of me! Such absences!

Larkin wrote of the poem: 'I fancy it sounds like a different, better poet than myself. The last line, for instance, sounds like a slightly-unconvincing translation from a French symbolist. I wish I could write like this more often'.[32] In a volume that rehearses so many 'selves' – the bachelor aesthete, the brazen chauvinist, the disillusioned lover, the lecher, the anti-social recluse, the comic curmudgeon – here is a poem in which Larkin succeeds in negating himself. 'Absences' goes beyond the desire for oblivion in 'Wants'. 'The poet seeks no transcendence himself. Rather he remains passive whilst the seascape transcends him. If there is a metaphysical absolute anywhere in Larkin's verse, it is here, in this negative sublime.'[33] It is an absolute for which Larkin strives throughout the rest of his poetry.

4

Larkin in the Movement

The Less Deceived sold well immediately and, much to Larkin's private annoyance, the Marvell Press struggled to keep copies in print. It was also widely reviewed with, for the most part, generous notices appearing in the major periodicals: *The Times Literary Supplement* referred to Larkin as 'a poet of quite exceptional importance'.[1] Elsewhere, the collection was welcomed as coinciding with a new movement in poetry, one which has since been the subject of some critical debate and hostility. Larkin never deliberately associated himself with, or consciously spoke for, a 'school' of poetry, but the reception of *The Less Deceived* – so very different from the silence which greeted *The North Ship* and *XX Poems* – and Larkin's subsequent reputation are intimately bound up with the emergence of the Movement.

The term came to be applied to a group of poets who rose to prominence in the mid-1950s. Along with Larkin, those most frequently identified as 'The Movement' were Kingsley Amis, Robert Conquest, Donald Davie, D. J. Enright, Thom Gunn, John Holloway, Elizabeth Jennings and John Wain. They began appearing together in journals and anthologies of that time and literary journalists and critics were quick to discern similarities between them. The roots of the Movement (the very title has been seized upon by its critics as indicative of its dullness) disappear in a number of directions, historical, social and cultural. Indeed, the very existence of a 'Movement' has been questioned. There was never a deliberately organised 'school' of poets armed with manifestos and some of its central figures denied any conscious involvement. So in some quarters it has been dismissed as little more than a journalistic invention by which a new generation of poets took control of the literary publicity machine. Nevertheless, it is now generally accepted as a fact of literary history that a distinctive poetic sensibility becomes evident during this period, one whose essential characteristics came to be most closely, and misleadingly, associated with Larkin.

Whatever the ultimate coherence of the Movement, it began as a series of friendships in Oxford (and to a lesser extent, Cambridge), the central one being between Larkin and Kingsley Amis. Something of the nature of this friendship, which remained important to Larkin throughout his life, can be caught from accounts each of them wrote about their undergraduate days in Oxford. Larkin recalled Amis's gift for mimicry: 'not a BBC Variety Hour knack of "imitations". . . . rather, he used it as the quickest way of convincing you that something was horrible or boring or absurd'.[2] They shared a lifelong enthusiasm for jazz and 'devoted to some hundred records that early anatomizing passion normally reserved for the more established arts'.[3] To Amis, Larkin appeared 'an almost aggressively normal undergraduate of the non-highbrow, non-sherry-sipping sort, hard-swearing, hard-belching, etc., treating the college dons as fodder for obscene clerihews'.[4] Clearly, the pose of philistinism, the parade of schoolboy insouciance, represented another facet of Larkin, the obverse of the Lawrence disciple visible in the aspiring novelist's letters to James Sutton. That streak of philistinism is also to be found, in various guises, in many of the Movement's defining principles. Friendship with Amis (and Bruce Montgomery, the pseudonymous novelist Edmund Crispin) meant that pretentiousness was quickly punctured. Larkin has ascribed this worldliness to the prevailing wartime conditions in Oxford. 'Traditional types such as aesthete and hearty were pruned relentlessly back . . . This was not the Oxford of Michael Fane and his fine bindings, or Charles Ryder and his plovers' eggs . . . and I think our perspectives were truer as a result. At an age when self-importance would have been normal, events cut us ruthlessly down to size'.[5] And the passion for jazz, which became the qualification for entry to the Larkin–Amis circle, was part and parcel of their defiant unpretentiousness, their irreverent rejection of the pieties associated with 'highbrow' arts. Lavishing on popular, 'middlebrow' culture the kind of scrutiny usually devoted to the 'classics' in music, their 'anatomizing of jazz' was an iconoclastic gesture which we can find mirrored in other aspects of the Movement's attitudes. In the end, jazz was to become for Larkin 'an epitome of the accessible, unself-conscious art that the modern world seemed to have turned away from'.[6]

One way of accounting for the emergence of the Movement is to see it as part of a general post-war period of reconstruction. As plans were made for the future at a political level, so a post-war generation of poets tried to identify what of their immediate past (the 1930s and 1940s) was worth preserving and what direction poetry might take. A return to traditional forms and regular structures of rhyme and rhythm seems to have been a natural response to a national mood of rebuilding. One of the Movement poets, John Wain, later commented, 'At such a time, when exhaustion and boredom in the foreground are balanced by guilt and fear in the background, it is natural that a poet should feel the impulse to *build*. Writing in regular and disciplined verse-forms is building in a simple and obvious sense'.[7] Donald Davie, who figured as a Movement poet (and subsequently became one of its most severe critics), has written of that period:

> It was a matter of 'picking up the pieces'. What I and my friends of those days took for granted was that the Second World War had invalidated even those radically diminished principles and sentiments that had survived the war of 1914–18. In poetics the assumptions of the 1920s and 1930s had to be questioned . . . We had to go back to basics . . . When every other commodity could be offered only under the acknowledged and overriding necessity of austerity (because of the successful U-boat onslaught on Allied shipping), the commodity called poetry had, simply as a matter of honour, to submit to the same controls.[8]

Seen in this light, the attitudes which characterised the Movement poets express the historical and social circumstances of their time. Davie himself had called, in 1949, for a new approach to the language of poetry, 'a new poetic diction which would testify, as always, to a new movement of spirit in society', a poetic diction capable of secure moral statement and signifying 'a complete change of tone, [not] the nervous jocularity of Auden or that suppressed irritation of Pound . . . The tone will be modest, but firm and dignified'.[9] This sifting of the past and planning for the future were symptomatic: 'The Movement cannot be abstracted from the social and political history of those post-war years'.[10] As Davie reminds us, these were the years of austerity, of rationing, of the beginning of the Cold War, of the establishment of the Welfare State, and along with the work of other Movement poets, Larkin's poems spring from their historical circumstances. Thus, the attitude of sceptical caution so visible in *The Less Deceived*, for example, can be related not only to other contemporary writers but to wider conditions: 'The Cold War tended to freeze public attitudes, and counselled silence about private ones. It recommended a guarded private life, in which only small gestures were possible, gestures chiefly about the difficulty of making a gesture'.[11] We might think of the emergence of the Movement, then, as both symptomatic of and contributing to the values of retrenchment, as expressions of an age of austerity.

The emergence of the Movement as an identifiable group can be traced back to various publications and anthologies of the early 1950s, culminating in what is now regarded as the definitive Movement volume, Robert Conquest's *New Lines* anthology of 1956. To begin with, the Movement was a negative reaction to a 1940s idiom poularised in three anthologies (*The New Apocalypse* of 1940, *The White Horseman* of 1941 and *The Crown and Sickle* of 1944) which were designed by their editors to illustrate 'a new romantic tendency, whose most obvious elements are love, death, an adherence to myth and an awareness of war'.[12] Wild claims were made for some of these poets – the Apocalyptics – but it was a relatively short-lived fashion. Nevertheless, more substantial reputations were established during the 1940s: the works of George Barker, David Gascoyne, Kathleen Raine, Vernon Watkins and, most notably, Dylan Thomas were widely published. With whatever individual differences, they shared certain assumptions about the nature of poetry:

> They were all affected by the doctrines and techniques of surrealism; they all believed that poetry was not primarily concerned with man in society, political aspirations or social commentary, but with the celebration of spiritual truth; all were romantic visionaries, whose view of the world was ritualistic and religious . . . Their employment of myth and symbol, drawn from a wide variety of sources, often esoteric and recondite, was designed to emphasize the sacred character of poetry and to stress the fact that the poet is not a lawgiver, a moralist, a teacher or an entertainer, but a bard and a seer. The tone of their verse was appropriately elevated and incantatory, as they proclaimed the sacred mysteries of vatic poetry.[13]

But the Movement's was not a simple, unambiguous rejection of this 1940s orthodoxy. Certainly, Apocalyptic excesses were ruled out of court, but the examples of some others were more problematical. As we have seen, Vernon Watkins exerted a significant formative influence on Larkin (who even in 1967 was writing warmly to Watkins: 'I wish I had your talent – I shouldn't use it in your way, but I wish I had it'[14]) and Dylan Thomas was admired by the younger Larkin and some other Movement poets as 'the greatest talent of the generation before ours'.[15] Rather, it was the death of Dylan Thomas in 1953 by alcoholic poisoning and the attendant glamorising of his troubled life which, for many of the Movement, became the telling symbol of the prevailing poetic decadence.

Nevertheless, the neo-romanticism of the 1940s was the aberration around which the Movement poets first began to gather, even as Larkin continued to write poems out of romantic mannerisms. In 1949, Kingsley Amis and James Michie co-edited *Oxford Poetry* and in an editorial condemned much of the verse submitted to them: 'The typical furniture of the mass of the poems was not, as we soon came to wish it would be, the telegraph-pole and the rifle, but the amethyst and the syrup . . . the typical rhyme was not of "lackey" and "lucky", but of "bliss" and "kiss"'.[16] This fidelity to contemporary experience ('the telegraph-pole and the rifle') and ordinariness of diction and perception (suggested in the proposed half rhyme of lackey/lucky) came to be central to Movement principles. An alternative tradition to the 1940s neo-romantics was proclaimed in 1950 by John Wain (another contemporary of Larkin's and Amis's at Oxford) who in an influential essay recommended the intellectual sophistication and wit of the 1930s poet William Empson as a model for his contemporaries. (Wain duly led the way in starting a fashion for a neo-Empsonian poetry of densely argued intellectuality.)

But the most complete critical statement of this period comes from Donald Davie, whose book *Purity of Diction in English Verse* was first published in 1952. Born in 1922 in Barnsley, in industrial South Yorkshire, Davie became closely identified with the Movement, sharing a typical Movement background: petit-bourgeois origins, a provincial grammar-school education, English at Cambridge and, after war-service, an academic career as a university teacher. He was one of the most active Movement writers, widely publishing poems and critical essays. His work is of particular importance in describing both the aspirations and, ultimately, the limitations of the Movement, and thus helps to define the distinguishing features of Larkin's work.

In his book, Davie sets out to show how the language, or, more properly, the poetic diction of some late eighteenth-century poets could be 'morally valuable'. He focuses on those poets with whom he feels that a selection has been made from language, 'that words are thrusting at the poem and being fended off from it, that however many poems these poets wrote certain words would never be allowed into the poems'.[17] This 'purity of diction' is also felt in the metaphorical economy of these poets, an economy indicative of intellectual command and bespeaking a set of shared assumptions between poet and reader. This criterion of purity of diction, argues Davie, is 'indispensable to the poetry of Goldsmith's contemporaries, and to that of my own'.[18] As in the age of Goldsmith, what was needed in the 1950s was a period of conservation rather than innovation, of the restoration of dignity and propriety to a language threatened by debauchery. Davie makes quite plain that his subject is not only eighteenth-century poetry but the contemporary situation, and that he is addressing 'the would-be poet of to-day . . . I should like to think that this study might help some practising poet to a poetry of urbane and momentous statement'.[19] Later, in 1966, Davie described his intention in writing *Purity of Diction* as an attempt 'to understand what I had been doing, or trying to do, in the poems I had been writing. Under a thin disguise the book was, as it still is, a manifesto . . . I like to think that if the group of us [i.e. the Movement] had ever cohered enough to subscribe to a common manifesto, it might have been *Purity of Diction in English Verse*'.[20] As a manifesto, what *Purity of Diction* declares is a commitment to a poetry possessing the virtues of good prose: reason, common experience, a sense of shared community, moderation and, above all, poetry conceived of as statement rather than mystery. Since the 1950s, commentary surrounding Larkin has tended to fasten on these characteristics as defining the virtues (or vices) of his poetry, and so has overlooked the more adventurous and disturbing aspects of his work.

The most significant popularisation of Movement poetry came in 1952 and 1953 when John Lehmann and later John Wain broadcast work by new poets on a monthly radio programme. Wain's broadcasts were more partisan than Lehmann's and he actively promoted the Movement's anti-romanticism. (Larkin's reading of 'If, My Darling' was broadcast by Wain on 1 July 1953.) Wain's proselytising soon had the desired effect and the programme was roundly attacked: after six editions, Wain was replaced. But this brief publicity helped establish a group identity: as Larkin later noted, '[we] got attacked in a very convenient way, and consequently we became lumped together'.[21]

At the same time as Davie, Thom Gunn, John Holloway, Elizabeth Jennings, Kingsley Amis, Larkin and other Movement poets were having poems broadcast on the radio, an anthology entitled *Springtime* was published (in 1953) which included amongst its fifty contributors six Movement poets. Five poems which Larkin had selected from his privately printed *XX Poems* appeared there – the first publication of his poetry since two poems ('Plymouth' and 'Portrait') had been printed in *Mandrake* in May 1946, then still an undergraduate periodical started by Wain at Oxford in 1945. Donald Davie has said that it was *Springtime* which first revealed to him that there were others who shared his 'indignant distaste for the Dylan Thomas or George Barker sort of poetry which had been *de rigueur* in London for a decade'.[22] Elsewhere, Oscar Mellor at the Fantasy Press near Oxford and George Hartley at the Marvell Press near Hull were providing other outlets for Movement poets. The Fantasy Press, founded in 1952, published a series of pamphlets including the work of Jennings, Gunn, Davie, Amis and Larkin; it also published the first full-length collections by three Movement poets, Jennings's *Poems* (1953), Gunn's *Fighting Terms* (1954) and Davie's *Brides of Reason* (1955). George Hartley's magazine *Listen*, which began publication in 1954, soon became a regular outlet for Movement writers and Larkin continued to contribute to it until it closed in 1962.[23]

But although some of these writers and other commentators began to perceive and foster a group identity, it was only by a piece of questionable journalism that the Movement sobriquet came to be manufactured. Anthony Hartley, who had known Wain, Amis and Larkin at Oxford, exerted his influence as poetry reviewer for the *Spectator* to help a good deal of Movement poetry appear there. In August 1954, he reviewed four Fantasy Press publications (by Thom Gunn, George MacBeth, Donald Davie and Jonathan Price) under the title 'Poets of the Fifties' and identified in them a similar tone:

> It might roughly be described as 'dissenting' and non-conformist, cool, scientific and analytical . . . this is the poetic equivalent of liberal, dissenting England. A liberalism distrustful of too much richness or too much fanaticism, austere and sceptical. A liberalism profoundly opposed to fashion in the metropolitan

sense of the word . . . Complication of thought, austerity of tone, colloquialism and the avoidance of rhetoric – these provide some common ground and common dangers . . . what is certain is that, for better or worse, we are now in the presence of the only considerable movement in English poetry since the Thirties.[24]

This was followed up by a leading article on 1 October 1954 written by the *Spectator's* literary editor, J. D. Scott (though published anonymously) who subsequently explained that his motives had more to do with increasing the *Spectator's* circulation than with literary analysis:

> The circulation was not behaving as it should, and one day in the autumn the editor, Walter Taplin, gave the staff a pep-talk. What could we do to liven things up, get ourselves talked about, be more influential, more sensational, and so more circulation-building, more money-making? . . . The idea that had occurred to me was to take the movement in poetry and see how far it extended beyond poetry, and specifically into the novel, and to consider the extent to which it represented some historic change in society . . . And so there appeared, on 1 October 1954, an article entitled 'In the Movement' . . . It was designed to grab the attention of any casual reader who . . . might happen on it. It was written in a tone brisk, challenging and dismissive.[25]

Like Hartley, Scott identified the Movement with changes in social attitude, suggesting in particular how idealism now looked to be constrained and limited: 'The Movement, as well as being anti-phoney, is anti-wet; sceptical, robust, ironic, prepared to be as comfortable as possible in a wicked, commercial, threatened world which doesn't look, anyway, as if it's going to be changed much by a couple of handfuls of young English writers'. And according to Scott, the Movement was still incohesive 'and, as a movement, dumb . . . Small as it is, it is nevertheless a part of the movement of that tide which is pulling us through the Fifties and towards the Sixties'.[26] Thus, by a piece of journalistic self-publicity, the movement became the Movement.

A group identity became more firmly established by the appearance in 1955 and 1956 of two anthologies, D. J. Enright's *Poets of the 1950s* and Robert Conquest's *New Lines*. Larkin was well represented in both, with eight poems in *Poets of the 1950s* and nine in *New Lines*. Moreover, each of the editors had quite independently assembled the same set of contributors: Kingsley Amis, Robert Conquest, Donald Davie, D. J. Enright, John Holloway, Elizabeth Jennings, Philip Larkin and John Wain (with Thom Gunn appearing in *New Lines*). Here, if anywhere, we have the corpus of the Movement, and in their editorial essays Enright (whose anthology was published in Japan and hence addressed as an introduction to current English poetry) and Conquest identified the characteristic virtues of their poets. Enright called for a poetry steering a middle course between despairing imitations of T. S. Eliot's *The Waste Land* (published in 1922) and the neo-romanticism of the 1940s: 'What we have to do is resuscitate the idea of the dignity of the human individual . . . this necessitates not only a willingness to recognize the virtues when and where they are met with, but also a fairly tough intelligence and an unwillingness to be deceived.' This sense of 'moderation', of 'chastened common-sense', went hand-in-hand with 'honesty of thought and feeling and clarity of expression'. Like Hartley and Scott, Enright pinpointed the limited horizons of Movement poets in comparison with their antecedents of the 1920s and 1930s: 'And the sense of private responsibility perhaps weighs more heavily on them than the sense of social responsibility on the writers of the 1930s'.[27]

Conquest's introduction to *New Lines* was more outspoken and deliberately provocative. He expressed 'the belief that a general tendency has once again set in, and that a genuine and healthy poetry . . . has established itself'. To its credit, he argued, the poetry of the 1950s submitted 'to no great systems of theoretical constructs or agglomerations of unconscious commands . . . [It is] free from both mystical and logical compulsions . . . empirical in its attitude to all that comes'. Still, a note of reservation is struck when Conquest rather vaguely admits to his poets being dedicated to 'a negative determination to avoid bad principles'[28] rather than a more positive ambition. It is worth setting Larkin in the context of his Movement contemporaries because the poets in *New Lines* did, however briefly and contingently, represent various sorts of coherence. The contributors' resemblances in social backgrounds, poetic attitudes and assumptions about their audience make *New Lines* a particularly revealing document in the development of much modern poetry, including Larkin's.

As Donald Davie later noted, the *New Lines* poets represent the emergence of a new generation of writers (born between 1917 and

1929 and centring on 1922) whose social origins were lower-middle and middle-class and who achieved positions of some influence having first won their way to Oxford and Cambridge through competitive examinations. Amis, Davie and Holloway have described themselves as lower-middle-class and six of the Movement poets (including Larkin) were educated at local grammar schools. Davie, Enright, Larkin and Wain grew up in industrial towns in the North or Midlands and Amis, Davie, Enright and Holloway won scholarships to Oxford and Cambridge. Even more notably, only Elizabeth Jennings has not at some stage worked full-time for an academic institution: all the rest have pursued a part or the whole of their careers within universities.[29]

Its social origins inform many of the Movement's attitudes but the most obviously unifying factor visible in *New Lines* is the academic provenance of these poets. In the small worlds of Oxford and Cambridge, most of these poets knew or knew of each other. More to the point, their poetry is everywhere informed by donnish intelligence and academically cosmopolitan interests. A glance at the Contents page of *New Lines* reveals poems about Florence, the Piazza San Marco, Lerici, Baie des Anges, Nice, and titles such as 'A Head Painted by Daniel O'Neill', 'The Rokeby Venus', 'Epistemology of Poetry' and 'Eighth Type of Ambiguity'. The work of critics such as F. W. Bateson at Oxford and F. R. Leavis at Cambridge was producing, if not a consensus of literary opinion, at least a shared conviction of the centrality of literary study to a liberal education. In short, *New Lines* is the product of an academic community, representing an historical moment when the writing of poetry, the academic criticism of poetry and the teaching of literature were part of a unified cultural activity.[30]

This sense of community is present in the Movement's address to its readers. If the 1930s poets' favoured pronoun was 'you' (the workers, the proletariat, the revolutionaries), the Movement's is 'we': fellow-academics and intellectuals. In one light, the Movement can be seen as marking a moment of post-war political consensus in England; in another, they are a group of poets writing for each other. Whatever the reasons, this imagined intimacy with the reader, the conversational idiom and sociable gestures of 'I suppose' and 'Perhaps', contribute to an impression of community. An assumption of shared intellectual scruple and moderation are part of the very texture of *New Lines* poems, whether in the affable colloquialisms of Larkin or the more elevated 'purity of diction' aimed at by Davie. Blake Morrison has noted how the colloquial asides serve 'to persuade the reader that the poet is modest, friendly, well-mannered and, above all, fair-minded', and cites the following examples from *New Lines*:

> One question, though, it's right to ask,
> Or, at the least, hint tactfully.
>
> (Holloway)

> Yes, true; but in the end, surely, we cry
> Not only at exclusion, but because
> It leaves us free to cry.
>
> (Larkin)

> Better of course, if images were plain,
> Warnings clearly said . . .
>
> (Amis)

> For him, it seems, everything was molten.
>
> (Enright)

> Yes, some attempt undoubtedly was made
> To lift the composition, and to pierce
> The bald tympana – vainly, I'm afraid;
> The effect remains, as ever, gaunt and fierce.
>
> (Davie)[31]

But these impressions of homogeneity can be misleading. For if at one extreme *New Lines* is populated by poems about foreign cities and paintings, at the other are poems expressive of calculated philistinism. This is the 'anti-wet', 'anti-phoney' aspect of the Movement, a mockery of pretentiousness and cultural posing. It is present, for example, in the anti-romantic deflations of Larkin's 'I Remember, I Remember' and it is the Larkin–Amis axis which gives *New Lines* its most robustly undeceived, come-off-it tone. Amis's poem 'Against Romanticism' portrays a landscape symbolic of cool realism, 'Not long, voluble swooning wilderness' but 'a temperate zone / – Woods devoid of beasts, roads that please the foot'. More potent still is his 'Something Nasty in the Bookshop' (later re-titled 'A Bookshop Idyll') which sets out to put poetry (especially love-poetry) firmly in its place:

> Between the GARDENING and the COOKERY
>   Comes the brief POETRY shelf;
> By the Nonesuch Donne, a thin anthology
>   Offers itself.
>
> Critical, and with nothing else to do,
>   I scan the Contents page,
> Relieved to find the names are mostly new;
>   No one my age.

Bored but carping, ready to find fault, interested primarily in fixing competitors, this is a reader glad to find the anthology 'thin'. The Poetry shelf is, after all, sandwiched as another hobby between Gardening and Cookery. At every turn, self-display is sniffed out: titles such as 'Landscape near Parma', 'The Double Vortex' and 'Rilke and Buddha' (and such titles would not be out of place in *New Lines*) signify '"I travel, you see", "I think" and "I can read"'. However, the browser is disconcerted by books of love poems by women and is led to ask a question that could be asked of the Movement generally:

> Should poets bicycle-pump the human heart
>   Or squash it flat?

Although the poem tries to undermine the male speaker's aggressive chauvinism, it cannot escape the conclusion that poetry can be little more than a strangulated emotional outpouring or just something to do between gardening and cookery. Puncturing the pretentiousness of literature in literary ways was part of the armoury of defensive irony with which Larkin and Amis chose to protect themselves. In 'Fiction and the Reading Public', a poem he worked over a number of times before finally publishing in 1954, Larkin debunks his academic title with a cynical account of literature as mutual gratification:

> Give me a thrill, says the reader,
> Give me a kick;
> I don't care how you succeed, or
> What subject you pick . . .
>
> For I call the tune in this racket:
> I pay your screw,

>Write reviews and the bull on the jacket –
>So stop looking blue
>And start serving up your sensations
>Before it's too late;
>Just please me for two generations –
>You'll be 'truly great'.[32]

Later, in 'A Study of Reading Habits', Larkin similarly mocks the self-delusions of reading: 'Get stewed:/Books are a load of crap'.

But even if their irony was more destructive, Amis and Larkin are not alone in *New Lines* in their attack on the romantic self-delusions of writers and readers. In 'Reason for Not Writing Orthodox Nature Poetry', John Wain compares generations of nature-poets to 'a spectacled curator showing/ The wares of his museum to the crowd' who 'yearly waxed more eloquent and knowing/ More slick, more photographic, and more proud'. And in 'The Interpreters (or How to Bury Yourself in a Book)', D. J. Enright attacks the literary academy, 'those critics for whom the outside is a dreadful bore:/ they scrape for the ambiguous, dig for the profound, deep, deep beneath the ground' and thus bury themselves beyond a more urgent and human 'crude vulgarity of meaning'. Too easily characterised as complacently academic, the Movement in fact constantly betrays anxieties about itself.

That anxiety can be felt in ways other than the mocking philistinism of Larkin and Amis. At a profound level, *New Lines* poems are guarded, defensive and emotionally cautious. A reader of *New Lines* comes away from that anthology with an impression of almost obsessive formal correctness. Regularity – of rhyme, metre and form – is the structural principle of these poems, a discipline which can quickly come to feel costive. The issue of formal correctness and its attendant impression of emotional sterility is tackled most directly in *New Lines* by Donald Davie. He is often portrayed as the most drily academic of the Movement poets, but it is actually Davie who is most sensitive to the limitations – his own and others' – of merely technical accomplishment.

A major preoccupation of Davie's poems in *New Lines* is the issue of intellect and emotion. Where Larkin's poems project a dramatised simulacrum of thinking (by using a persona), Davie's poems narrate their anxieties about the propriety of expressing strong emotions. In 'Rejoinder to a Critic', Davie concedes: 'You may be right: "How can I dare to feel?"/May be the only question I can pose' but goes on to justify himself:

> 'Alas, alas, who's injured by my love?'
> And recent history answers: Half Japan!
> Not love, but hate? Well, both are versions of
> The 'feeling' that you dare me to . . . Be dumb!
> Appear concerned only to make it scan!
> How dare we now be anything but numb?

In a post-nuclear age, feelings can be dangerous. On the other hand, Davie also counts the cost of appearing concerned 'only to make it scan'. His 'Limited Achievement' (its ostensible subject the artist Piranesi) is a mordant self-diagnosis:

> Successful in his single narrow track,
> He branches out, but only to collapse,
> Imprisoned in his own unhappy knack,
>
> Which, when unfailing, fails him most, perhaps.

The poem deliberately embodies the failings it talks about and its thesis might be applied to the general debilities of the Movement – technical accomplishments that are imprisoning, conclusions that are glib rather than revealing. That hanging final line which so neatly turns on itself is typical of the Movement's attitudinising and is reminiscent of Larkin's habit of suddenly reversing the drift of a poem, as in 'Reasons for Attendance' and 'No Road'. Moreover, it reminds us how so many of the poems in *New Lines* rely on irony as their chief (often only) rhetorical ploy, an irony that invites the reader to share an attitude of quizzical wariness.

The wariness is not only emotional (and Larkin is in that respect most typical of the Movement) but political. A notable feature of the Movement is its withdrawal from the political activism of the major 1930s poets: Auden, Isherwood, Day Lewis, Spender, MacNeice. This is in part due to the advent of the Welfare State, full employment and a gradual affluence (visible in Larkin's supermarkets in *The Whitsun Weddings*). But a more profound reason lay in the attitude of many 1950s writers to their 1930s forebears. The gulf of the Second World War separated them, a gulf which for those who served in the war could make the 1930s poets look foolish and irresponsible. Davie's 'Remembering the 'Thirties' recalls that

The Anschluss, Guernica – all the names
At which those poets thrilled or were afraid
For me mean schools and schoolmasters and games;
And in the process some-one is betrayed.

In debating who is betrayed – whether 'In time's long glass' poets of political commitment look foolish or heroic – Davie concludes:

A neutral tone is nowadays preferred.
And yet it may be better, if we must,
To praise a stance impressive and absurd
Than not to see the hero for the dust.

That 'neutral tone' has become something of a cliché to describe the Movement but Davie's conclusion is important in conceding to the political engagement of an earlier generation a comparatively heroic stature. As Stephen Regan has noted, 'The pose of neutrality and objectivity could not be sustained indefinitely'[33] and by the 1960s and 1970s Larkin, Amis and Davie were writing poems that were unashamedly polemical.

By the mid-1950s, commentators, critics, journalists and publishers could speak of the Movement, even if some of those supposedly in it continued to doubt its existence. In 1964, Larkin claimed that he had 'No sense at all' of belonging to the Movement: 'Bob Conquest's *New Lines* in 1956 put us all between the same covers. But it certainly never occurred to me that I had anything in common with Thom Gunn, or Donald Davie, for instance, or they with each other and in fact I wasn't mentioned at the beginning'.[34] There might have been reasons why in 1964 Larkin wanted to distance himself from a movement which even by then had a faintly antiquarian air (Conquest put together a *New Lines 2* in 1963 endorsing Davie's suggestion that a more suitable title would be 'Divergent Lines'). But even as the Movement was being announced, Larkin was expressing reservations. To Enright's anthology he contributed a brief statement of poetic principle which has since become notorious. Dismissing literary theory as 'no help to me as a writer', he went on:

I write poems to preserve things I have seen/ thought/ felt (if I may so indicate a composite and complex experience) both for myself and for others, though I feel that my prime responsibility is to the experience itself, which I am trying to keep from oblivion for its own sake. Why I should do this I have no idea, but I think the impulse to preserve lies at the bottom of all art. Generally my poems are related, therefore, to my own personal life . . . As a guiding principle I believe that every poem must be its own sole freshly created universe, and therefore have no belief in 'tradition' or a common myth-kitty or casual allusions in poems to other poems or poets, which last I find unpleasantly like the talk of literary understrappers letting you see they know the right people.[35]

Larkin presents here an appealingly uncomplicated description (he said later he was 'rather dashed' to find his views printed verbatim) of his poetry as preserving an original experience in a way that can transfer that experience as completely as possible to the reader. As for his dismissing a 'common myth-kitty', it could be argued that Larkin's work expresses a private myth-kitty in which elemental presences have an absolute value. What he rejects is the erudite and academic quality of much modern poetry, Eliot's and Pound's in the 1920s, and some of his contemporaries' in the 1950s. As we have seen, Movement poetry did have academic origins and assumed an academic bias in the reader: much of it was written by intellectuals for other intellectuals. By contrast, Larkin's poems in *New Lines* (amongst them 'Maiden Name', 'Latest Face' and 'Born Yesterday') look vulnerably emotional.

In the second edition of George Hartley's *Listen*, Larkin contributed another barely disguised attack entitled (with a tongue-in-cheek reference to Freudian psychology) 'The Pleasure Principle'. Here, Larkin castigates 'a new kind of bad poetry, not the old kind that tries to move the reader and fails, but one that does not even try', suggesting that 'a cunning merger between poet, literary critic and academic critic' is responsible for fostering a new kind of audience. 'Poetry was no longer a pleasure. They have been replaced by a humbler squad, whose aim is not pleasure but self-improvement . . . the modern poetic audience . . . is a *student* audience, pure and simple'. In terms calculated to irritate many of his academic Movement poets, Larkin argued: 'But at bottom poetry, like all art, is inextricably bound up with giving pleasure, and if a poet loses his pleasure-seeking audience he has lost the only audience worth having, for which the dutiful mob that signs on every September is no substitute'. In a final flourish of bluff, no-

nonsense populism, Larkin quotes (without a hint of irony in so doing) Samuel Butler: 'I do not like having to try to make myself like things; I like things that make me like them at once and no trying at all'.[36]

Clearly, Larkin wanted to detach himself from what he saw as the academic sterility of much Movement poetry. After reading Robert Conquest's draft introduction to *New Lines*, Larkin wrote to him privately:

> ... I am not quite so happy when you suggest that 'we' have returned to 'the principle that poetry is written by and for the whole man'; I don't think 'our' poetry stands up for a single second, in this respect, alongside poets who I should say did adopt that principle – Owen, Hopkins, Hardy, Edward Thomas – and I should be chary of suggesting that it does. One reason for this is that much of it seems so 'literary' in inspiration . . . For my part I feel we have got the method right – plain language, absence of posturings, sense of proportion, humour, abandonment of the dithyrambic ideal – and are waiting for the matter: a fuller and more sensitive response to life as it appears from day to day . . .[37]

Larkin can be seen distancing himself not only in the inverted commas around 'we' and 'our', but in his reservations about his contemporaries' (and his own) achievements. His feeling was that their poems were written around literature rather than life, whereas his own were highly personal, even private: 'I always think that the poems I write are very much more naive – very much more emotional – almost embarrassingly so – than a lot of other people's. When I was tagged as unemotional, it used to mystify me; I used to find it quite shaming to read some of the things I'd writen [*sic*]'.[38] Characteristically, Larkin wanted to keep himself at arm's length from any 'school' or 'movement', not only out of distrust for anything that smacked of theorising, but because he wanted to let his own, individual reputation establish itself independently. In 1954 he wrote to a friend: 'People like Anthony Hartley and G. S. Fraser are very stupidly crying us all up these days: take my word for it, people will get very sick of us (or *them*; that is, Wain, Gunn, Davie, Amis) and then, UNLESS they produce some unassailably good work, I think the tide will turn rapidly & they will be rapidly discredited. I'm sure I don't care'.[39] How much of the petulant disdain can be ascribed to ironic bravado it is hard to say, but taken with other evidence this does seem to confirm that Larkin was only ever a half-hearted traveller with the Movement. But whilst it is true that he never actively promoted himself as a Movementeer, he nevertheless profited by exposure with them; and at worst he stands accused (by Donald Davie, as we shall see later) of pusillanimity and just a little disingenuousness in relation to the publicity surrounding the Movement.

Larkin was not alone in wanting to dissociate himself from some aspects of the Movement. Larkin did not like the air of the academy that hung around some of its poetry but even from within the academy there were warning voices. Donald Davie, one of its most self-consciously academic poets, was also alarmed by some of the Movement's limiting attitudes. In a discussion about 'provincialism' current in the literary journals of the time, Davie had tried to detach the notion of 'urbanity' from its modern association with irony and restore to it something of Matthew Arnold's definition of it: 'the tone of the city, of the centre, the tone which always aims at a spiritual and intellectual effect, and not excluding the use of banter, never disjoins banter itself from politeness, from felicity'. For Davie, true 'urbanity' in literature involves an attempt to persuade the reader of one opinion or another, whereas the poetry written by his contemporaries was limited to the practice of irony with opinions and statements neutralised by the refuge of relativity:

> Much art, much great art, is tendentious, at least in the sense that its power not merely vibrates inside it, but thrusts outside, and in one direction rather than another . . . It is this liberalism in critics . . . which explains the high price we are prepared to pay in litera-ture for irony . . . And it is not hard to see why. For no literary tool is so handy for making the thrusts and stresses inside a literary work cancel themselves out, like the two thrusts that meet in a Gothic arch . . . Thus the structure rises, in stress played off against stress, vertical, intricate, and vibrantly at rest, and we like that, but what we really like is that the whole thing is not going anywhere.[40]

Drawing on then fashionable notions of ambiguity (especially William Empson's *Seven Types of Ambiguity*), much Movement poetry is concerned not so much with rendering ordinary experience (Larkin) nor with arguing from conviction and making philosophical statements (Davie) but with taking up attitudes provisionally and thus striking up a particular kind of relationship with the reader. It was in revolt from this position that Davie was later to launch his most vigorous attack on the Movement.

Not that reservations were expressed only from within the Movement. A contemporary poet, Charles Tomlinson, whose work drew freely on foreign writers and artists, famously attacked Movement poetry for its 'general failure to see things anew . . . They seldom for a moment escape beyond the suburban mental ratio they impose on experience'.[41] By 'suburban', Tomlinson meant that Movement poets were deliberately limited and unambitious in subject and technique. He was perhaps remembering Kingsley Amis's 'Statement' in *Poets of the 1950s* saying 'nobody wants any more poems on the grander themes for a few years, but at the same time nobody wants any more poems about philosophers or paintings or novelists or art galleries or mythology or foreign cities or other poems. At least I hope nobody wants them'.[42] But an older generation saw in the young 1950s writers a philistinism they crudely ascribed to the social origins of many of the Movement poets. In their vocabulary, 'suburban' was unambiguously a term of class contempt. Stephen Spender wrote in 1953 that England was experiencing 'a rebellion of the Lower Middle Brows' and Evelyn Waugh spoke of a 'new wave of philistinism with which we are threatened by these grim young people coming off the assembly lines in their hundreds every year and finding employment as critics, even as poets and novelists'.[43] Louis MacNeice, another 1930s poet, had only a slightly less brazen slap at the Movement's social origins: 'As individuals then, we must welcome some of these New Liners, but as a group or a Movement, well, let them go. And behold, they go – with what docile arrogance, with what lowered but polished sights; roped together, alert for falling slates, they scale their suburban peaks – the Ascent of C3'.[44] Just how threatened by the Movement generation an older literary Establishment felt can be seen from this attack on Kingsley Amis's 1954 novel *Lucky Jim* by Somerset Maugham, who saw in Amis's hero a representative type of the new generation:

> They do not go to university to acquire culture, but to get a job, and when they have got one, scamp it. They have no manners, and are woefully unable to deal with any social predicament. Their idea of a celebration is to go to a public house and drink six

beers . . . They are scum. They will in due course leave the university. Some will doubtless sink back, perhaps with relief, into the modest class from which they emerged . . .[45]

Such clamorous snobbery ('the ascent of C3', 'the modest class from which they emerged') from an older generation reveals the most durable aspect of the Movement's success – and another point from which Larkin departs from it. Whatever the limitations of Movement poetry, however shortlived its success as a journalistic takeover, the fact that these particular writers should have achieved prominence at this particular time is of some sociological importance, as Donald Davie noted:

> I'm like Wain and Larkin and others in being a product of the provinces . . . and, like nearly everyone else in the group I'm a product of the lower-middle class . . . Accordingly, my history is the history of my education and duplicates that of all the rest – a winning of the way to one of the ancient universities by competitive examinations, rather than the going there as a matter of course as in the case of products of more privileged classes, such as Spender, Auden . . . [The Movement's] sociological importance is very great, and it consists in this – that for the first time a challenge is thrown down, not by individuals . . . but by a more or less coherent group, to the monopoly of British culture sustained for generations by the London haut-bourgeois.[46]

Given Larkin's own inclination to snobbery (there's more than a hint of it in his 'Pleasure Principle' reference to the dutiful mob signing on at university every September, and much more of it in his letters), he might not have endorsed Davie's gratified tone too quickly. Provincial Larkin might have been, but as the son of Coventry's City Treasurer he stood apart from the lower-middle class origins of some of the Movement poets. In this, too, Larkin was not quite central to the Movement's identity. For all its irreverence, beneath the surface of the Larkin–Amis kind of philistinism lay an inclination to preserve the values of the London haut-bourgeois rather than foster the rise of the petit-bourgeois, as their later political attitudes make clear. In addition, Larkin's suspicion of theory and his distaste for academic erudition in poetry meant that he could never quite be 'in' the Movement, even as in the popular imagination he became its embodiment. Quite simply, he regarded many of its poets as his rivals and did not want his own developing reputation to be too closely associated with any 'school' or 'group'. Perhaps he sensed, too, that the Movement was quickly to fall prey to its own internal contradictions.

For all the journalistic puff surrounding the Movement, its recruits never wholeheartedly presented an image of collective coherence. This is where some damaging accusations have been made: that Movement poets profited from publicity whilst fastidiously appearing not to court or solicit it. Perhaps Donald Davie had Larkin in mind (as well as himself) when in 1959 he published an angry critique of the whole Movement enterprise. As we have seen, Davie was intolerant of the Movement's habitual irony and in a 1957 review of a volume of Enright's poems he criticised what he called Enright's 'common-mannerism' as representing 'a genuine danger that impatience with cultural pretentiousness is turning into impatience with culture; and that humane indignation is dissolving into ready-made sentimentality . . . I cling to the hope that Enright [is] not so out of patience with arti-ness and cultural window-dressing that he's forsworn for good the deeper reaches (and so the deeper humanity) of the art he practises'.[47] By 1959, Davie is much more forthright in condemning Movement 'common-mannerism', that affable philistinism evident in Amis's and Larkin's rejection of foreign cultures and 'common myth-kitty'. This, claims Davie, was what disabled the Movement from the start, the pusillanimity

> of going much further than halfway to meet our readers, forestalling their objections, trying to keep in their good books. Ours was writing which apologized insistently for its own existence, which squirmed in agonies of embarrassment at being there in print on the page at all . . . you can see the same craven defensiveness which led us, when we were challenged or flattered or simply interviewed, to pretend that the Move-ment didn't exist, that it was an invention of journalists, that we had never noticed how Larkin and Gunn and Amis had some-thing in common, or that, if we had noticed, it didn't interest or excite us.

According to Davie, the Movement set out to placate a middlebrow audience by its self-deflating pose of philistinism, and a highbrow one by its xenophobic insularity. Not only that, but the Movement's maidenly timidity in failing to exploit its access to publicity brought about 'the sort of half-hearted falling between two stools which made the Movement abortive'. But the most damaging feature of Movement poetry – and, by implication, Larkin's – is to be found in its attitude to the reader:

> We were deprecating, ingratiating. What we all shared to begin with was a hatred for writing considered as self-expression; but all we put in its place was writing as self-adjustment, a getting on the right terms with our reader (that is, with our society), a hitting on the right tone and attitude towards him.[48]

This is far-reaching criticism and stakes out much of the ground on which Larkin's poetry has subsequently been attacked. The basis of his attack is ultimately aesthetic: in his eyes, the Movement (and Larkin) won over a readership only by selling the art of poetry short. They were unambitious, undemanding and unchallenging. Blake Morrison has identified the Movement's inherent weakness and consequent transitoriness in similar terms:

> On the one hand, the Movement enjoys and exploits the sense of belonging to an academic élite; on the other hand, it disapproves of writing aimed at such an élite. On the one hand, it asserts the importance of university teachers and critics; on the other, it questions and satirizes their function. On the one hand, it declares that to write for a large audience is damaging; on the other, it declares that it is valuable and necessary. On the one hand, its work is dense, allusive, intimate with fellow intellectuals; on the other, its work is simple, 'accessible', intimate with an imagined Common Reader. Previous critics of the Movement have tended to emphasize one side or the other, accusing it of 'academicism' or of 'philistinism'; the truth is that the work of the Movement is characterized by a tension between the two.[49]

By the end of the 1950s, the Movement had dispersed. The poets assembled in *Poets of the 1950s* and *New Lines* were by now establishing individual reputations, with Donald Davie's willingness to experiment and absorb foreign influences taking him furthest away from 'Movement' origins. There is a tendency to see in Larkin the true, unwavering spirit of the Movement, his later poetry faithfully continuing to exemplify Movement attributes. *The*

Less Deceived happened to appear at a propitious moment and Larkin was consistently at pains to detach himself from anything resembling a collective enterprise. His work emerges from impulses much more contradictory than the Movement 'aesthetic' could describe. In fact, the 'Movement' itself could never really take shape. Partly an invention of journalists, partly a bandwagon for a few reputations, it undoubtedly represented the *Zeitgeist* of the mid-1950s. In the novel, Kingsley Amis's *Lucky Jim* and John Wain's *Hurry on Down* portrayed a new type of anti-hero based on an emerging social class:

> Born: Coketown 1925. Parents: lower-middle class. Educated: local council school, grammar school and university . . . Married. One or two children. Occupation: civil servant/ journalist/ lecturer/ minor executive. Politics: neutralist. Ambition: to live well. Interests: people, money, sex. Worries: money, sex. Enthusiasms: Orwell, jazz, Dr. Leavis, old cars. Antipathies: Dylan Thomas, provincial culture, European novels. Future: indefinite.[50]

Later, dramatists such as John Osborne, who were labelled 'Angry Young Men', drew on the same kind of social stereotype. But as a poetic movement, the Movement represents only one aspect of a wider sociological and historical phenomenon: the rise of a petit-bourgeois, provincial intelligentsia, impatient of the Establishment but ultimately committed to neutrality and a slightly rancorous preservation of the political and cultural status quo. The Movement is best thought of as a moment, one in which certain social, political and historical forces crystallised. As for Larkin, he remained, as ever, something of a sceptical spectator, pursuing an identity not by commitment to group programmes and collective activism but to that

> rough-tongued bell
> (Art, if you like) whose individual sound
> Insists I too am individual.

> ('Reasons for Attendance')

5

The Whitsun Weddings

The success of *The Less Deceived* (it was mentioned in *The Times* on 22 December 1955 in its 'books of the year' round-up) and his association, in critics' minds at least, with the Movement were mixed blessings for Larkin. Of course, he welcomed the praise and recognition but his growing reputation imposed burdens too. In *The Less Deceived*, Larkin had learned to deal with deeply personal issues in ways that externalised them. By using slightly differentiated personae, he made his poems 'multivocal' and 'dialogic'[1] and by broadening the range of linguistic registers he could modulate more effectively into lyricism. One of these personal issues was his sense of failure; now, by accepting failure, he had begun to triumph.[2] And now that Larkin knew he had an audience, the strategies by which he protected his essential core of privacy had to become more devious. 'Fame endangered his poems by threatening the delicate balance between a desire for private rumination and a longing for a public hearing. He wondered how he could continue to "be himself" if his self depended on remoteness and disappointment, neither of which he could truly be said to possess any more.'[3] Questions of identity and its relation to love and death remain at the centre of *The Whitsun Weddings*.

In 'Absences', Larkin had pushed perception to the limits of experience by imagining an absence of self. Similarly, in 'Wires', written just a few weeks before 'Absences', he found a simple metaphor to express the limitations of selfhood. As so often in *The Less Deceived*, the subject is desire and the inevitability of disappointment and disillusionment. At the same time, the poem enacts a pattern of encroachment and enclosure which speaks of the fundamental imprisonment of identity. As for the cattle, so for the speaker: there is no going 'beyond' the limits of ourselves:

> The widest prairies have electric fences,
> For though old cattle know they must not stray

Young steers are always scenting purer water
Not here but anywhere. Beyond the wires

Leads them to blunder up against the wires
Whose muscle-shredding violence gives no quarter.
Young steers become old cattle from that day,
Electric limits to their widest senses.

Only in rhapsody have those cattle ever reached the waters, when at the end of 'Wedding-Wind' they were summoned in metaphor to kneel 'by all-generous waters'. There, they were part of a rhetorical question; now, they stand in the real world. The 'purer water' scented by 'young steers' (youthfully and vigorously masculine) is here more urgently sexual in its allure (though water continues to hold a more metaphysically symbolic value in Larkin's work). On one level, these young steers want to explore forbidden territory before they become docile 'old cattle': what they do not yet know is that even 'the widest prairies' have a limit somewhere. This is not just a case of Larkin's willed resignation or chosen fatalism, for ultimately the poem is not simply about how we are always bruised by experience but about how we are trapped in our own identities and personalities. For the object of yearning is always 'Not here but anywhere'; that is, wherever the young steers *are not*. As the syntax indicates, the very fact of wanting to go 'Beyond the wires' is what 'Leads them to blunder up against the wires', for they can never escape the prison of selfhood. Where they are is where they do not want to be and the 'muscle-shredding violence' of the electric fences is their own dissatisfaction with their lot. 'Not here but anywhere' is thus an ultimate existential principle. 'Young steers become old cattle' when they accept their fundamental isolation, that they can only ever be 'here' and that 'anywhere' is always elsewhere.

The schematic allegorising of the poem is even more pronounced in its formal structures. As James Booth points out, the rhyme-scheme (abcd dcba) builds a closed, static structure. To begin with, the young steers are unenclosed in the unrhymed first quatrain, but the 'apparently smooth enjambement into the second quatrain turns out to be brutally ironic, as the line bafflingly wrests us back to the "wires" . . . the words turn out to be a noun phrase: a mere figment in the minds of the cattle, which leads them only to the wires'.[4] The rhymes proceed to turn back on themselves to clinch the irony: the search for 'water' gives 'no quarter' and 'from that day' they will no longer 'stray' because the 'fences' are now part of their 'senses'. Thus the poem enacts its thesis of imprisonment. Booth calls it 'a QED of failed youthful illusions',[5] but its mathematical neatness should not distract us from its brooding import. Here, existence is fenced. Twenty-seven years later, Larkin will still be confronting 'here', but now 'anywhere' else can only be penetrated in the annihilation of death. His appalled recognition in 'Aubade' is expressed in terms strikingly reminiscent of 'Wires': 'Not to be here,/ Not to be anywhere,/ And soon; nothing more terrible, nothing more true'.[6]

Hence, 'The Importance of Elsewhere' for Larkin. Although this particular poem is to be read in its contingent circumstances (Larkin's departure from Belfast to Hull), 'elsewhere' stands for Larkin as an imaginative space, contiguous with experience but never actual, like the 'padlocked cube of light' which in 'Dry-Point' we can never enter. It is a realm of escape, of fulfilment, of fantasy and its presence is everywhere in *The Whitsun Weddings*. It is the 'joyous shot at how things ought to be' which, here, has long fallen wide; it is where the 'unfocused she' does not go dark. In short, 'elsewhere' is the 'unfenced existence' envisioned beyond the end of 'Here': it is the region of the ineffable to which so many poems in *The Whitsun Weddings* aspire.

In March 1955, Larkin left Belfast to take up the post he occupied for the rest of his life as Librarian in the University of Hull. Three months later, he completed 'The Importance of Elsewhere', a poem which explores his feelings about returning to England. 'It was extraordinary how at home I felt [there]', he wrote to his former colleagues on his return, '. . . and how much I disliked leaving . . . Queen's is a perfect little paradise of a library'.[7] Later, he spoke of how his life 'reawoke somehow' in Belfast and recalled that 'The best writing conditions I ever had were in Belfast . . . I can't seem to organise that now'.[8] His personal life, too, had achieved some stability in Belfast, once he had finally severed his engagement to Ruth Bowman and escaped the immediate burden of his widowed mother. Now, a return to England threatened that precarious stability of tensions which had produced most of *The Less Deceived* poems. 'The Importance of Elsewhere' carries a note of nostalgia, but more urgent is its concern with strangeness and separateness.

The first stanza argues that 'Strangeness made sense' in Ireland because 'it was not home'. Loneliness could be accepted as a natural condition and 'difference' ('The salt rebuff of speech') led to 'welcome'. Strangeness 'went/ To prove me separate, not unworkable', suggesting that in the unfamiliar surroundings of Belfast the speaker felt a permissible isolation which in England only makes him feel guiltily 'unworkable'. In England, feeling separate 'has no such excuse' because 'These are my customs and establishments' (Larkin's recorded reading puts the stress on *my*). The separateness he feels in England is more damaging because 'Here no elsewhere underwrites my existence'. In Belfast, he was 'elsewhere' (calling it 'Ireland' emphasises its foreignness) and the sense of strangeness and isolation sharpened his sense of identity. Back in England, his feelings of isolation have no such excuse: he might actually be 'unworkable' rather than liberatingly 'separate'. 'Elsewhere', his existence was authenticated by a legitimised 'strangeness', but being 'Here' (like home, we all hate 'having to be there') obligates him to merge his identity in community.

The relationship between 'self' and 'others', between the individual and society, is a major theme throughout Larkin's work, whether dealt with explicitly as in 'Vers de Société' (*High Windows*) and the earlier 'Best Society'[9], or in the many poems which tussle with the problems of relationships and marriage. It is also bound up with his use of personae as a constant strategy in his poetry. John Goodby notes:

> The ambivalent attitudes towards home, belonging, work and women, are a direct result of Larkin's 'inner émigré' stance and also give rise to his characteristic use of elusive personae in the poetry. These personae are similar to, but not quite, Larkin himself; by employing them he is able to negatively define himself and hence prevent the reader from pinning him down as fatally as he was in *The North Ship* . . . such marginalising, self-deprecatory strategies combine to protect a vulnerable 'self' but can only do so negatively, by dividing the 'self' into non-'selves'.[10]

As we shall see, the collision between the self and society is evident in the very language of Larkin's poems. Essential to his imagination is the need for an 'elsewhere' where such conflicts are resolved; his poems have been well described as 'adventures in feeling and experiencing, journeys into "difference"'.[11]

'Mr Bleaney' was the first poem Larkin appears to have written on his return to England. It takes up very directly the issue of 'difference' and separateness and also presents us with Larkin's strategy of poetic disguise at its most teasing. (By a further irony,

Larkin introduces his recorded reading of the poem with remarks about the representativeness of individual experience: 'I'd imagined that the kind of experience it was based on was the kind of thing that only happened to me: apparently not'.) The poem emerges from the specific situation of Larkin's trying to find satisfactory digs in Hull and it was some months before he was accommodated by the University in the top-floor flat he occupied from 1956 to 1974. Originally, it was entitled 'Mr Gridley'; the change to 'Bleaney' reinforces the bleakness described in the poem. (In fact, Larkin had used the name before: Bleaney is an otherwise anonymous schoolboy contemporary of John Kemp's in Larkin's first novel, *Jill*.[12])

The monologue opens with another voice, the landlady's, who establishes the colloquial idiom the rest of the poem will make use of. In five stanzas, the speaker all too quickly sketches the lineaments of Bleaney's life, its dull routine and meagreness, before the closing two stanzas pass a general reflection both on the frightening emptiness of Mr Bleaney's life and on the speaker's implied similarity to it. Like 'Reasons for Attendance' and other poems in *The Less Deceived*, the poem dramatises, in a way reminiscent of Browning, a process 'from a poise, or a pose, to an exposure or an epiphany', presenting 'a brave deception in the strong and engaging surface, which hid a complex and sensitive disturbance within'.[13] In 'Mr Bleaney', the disturbance is both emotional and syntactical.

At first, the poem seems to be constructed around caricatures. The nagging landlady begins by parading her attachment to her former tenant: '"He stayed/ The whole time he was at the Bodies, till/ They moved him"', the 'Bodies' being slang for a car-assembly works (and here perhaps functioning as a sinister joke: Mr Bleaney's 'hired box' is all too coffin-like). Already, she tries to pressurise the new tenant to take her garden – 'a strip of building land' – 'properly in hand'. Mr Bleaney is soon the hapless bachelor of simple and undemanding tastes. There is no pretence at dignity: the curtains are tatty and shrunken, their flowered pattern serving ironically to emphasise the barrenness inside and outside the room. Mr Bleaney's life was similarly bare, routinised into regularity, punctuated by dulled and futile optimism (he played the football pools without ever winning) and blighted above all by loneliness (summer holidays always taken at the same resort and Christmas spent with his sister). His life seems to amount to the failure that is reflected even in the physical details of the room: it is dull (a 60-watt bulb), confined ('no room for books or bags') and stale (the bed is 'fusty').

But the poem evolves from two contrary assertions: 'I know his habits' and the concluding 'I don't know'. What surfaces in the poem is a growing identification with Mr Bleaney and an accompanying alarm. The final two stanzas come to a recognition that the distinction the speaker wants to make between himself and Mr Bleaney (the speaker is, after all, an intellectual, worried about where to store his books) is illusory. In occupying Mr Bleaney's room, he may be stepping into Mr Bleaney's shoes – indeed, he might already be in them. For his decision to take the room, in spite of its tawdriness, seems unpremeditated: '"I'll take it"' is blurted out almost impulsively. The speaker finds himself wrestling with this emerging identification with Mr Bleaney. But Larkin's later comment on the poem suggests, conversely, that Mr Bleaney is closer to the speaker than the speaker yet supposes:

> The first two-thirds of the poem, down to 'But if', are concerned with my uneasy feeling that I'm becoming Mr Bleaney, yes. The last third is reassuring myself that I'm not, because he was clearly quite content with his sauce instead of gravy, and digging the garden and so on, and yet there's doubt lingering too, perhaps he hated it as much as I did.[14]

This shifts the balance of identification somewhat: it is not a case of the speaker settling for Mr Bleaney's undemanding complacency, but of recognising that, like him, Mr Bleaney might have loathed his 'yearly frame'. The compassion is for imagined suffering, the unhappiness Mr Bleaney might have silently endured. 'I know his habits', the outward garments of his life. What the speaker cannot know, or does not want to know, is how Mr Bleaney felt about his life. The speaker's feelings about Bleaney shift uneasily from fearful disdain to fearful compassion: perhaps he hated his life as much as I do and neither of us adds up to much. As with 'At Grass' and 'Deceptions', identification stops short of complete empathy.

This is the burden of the last two stanzas, marked off from the rest of the poem by their complex syntax and shift to more metaphorical language. H. G. Widdowson has analysed them in terms of their grammatical construction: 'The clause is both adverbial and nominal, and so neither, a newly crafted syntactic metaphor devised to express precisely a confusion of thought and attitude which could not otherwise be expressed. The meaning depends on the ambiguity remaining unresolved ... The normally distinct categories of third and first person conflate so that the identity of Mr Bleaney is superimposed on that of the present lodger'.[15] At the same time, the convolution expresses resistance to identification in a kind of syntactical squirm which both ventures and disclaims the judgement that, if 'how we live measures our own nature', Mr Bleaney warranted no better than his hired box. Amongst the competing presences in the poem – the landlady's, the 'jabbering set' (radio) which perpetuates Mr Bleaney's presence – the speaker's remains inviolable. Beneath the surface of the poem are troubling stirrings of compassion for a comical stereotype. By the end of the poem, there are disturbing cross-currents of feeling. For Mr Bleaney, 'this was home' and there is no 'elsewhere' to underwrite his alienation from it, the 'hired box' of his life. The speaker shivers with him. The world is indifferent to them both: the 'frigid' wind tousles the clouds purposelessly. But in the end, the speaker contrives to resist a painful identification with Mr Bleaney. The final, isolated, exhausted 'I don't know' is both an admission of failure and a triumph of self-preservation.

The degree of compassion felt for the gallery of characters in *The Whitsun Weddings* is fundamental to the sense of identity which lies behind all Larkin's work. The 'cut-price crowd' of 'Here', the young mothers in 'Afternoons', the married couples of 'The Whitsun Weddings', the crowds acting 'their solemn-sinister/ Wreath-rubbish' in 'Naturally the Foundation will Bear Your Expenses', Arnold in 'Self's the Man': all are treated with subtle variations of irony and approval. Moreover, amongst these 'characters' are the speakers of the poems, dramatised versions of the 'selves' in Larkin, carefully masked self-revelations. What, for example, are we to make of the women in 'Faith Healing'? 'Moustached in flowered frocks', they are already vaguely rebarbative. But they are made even uglier in their emotional intensity, 'stiff, twitching and loud/ With deep hoarse tears'. When joy arrives, 'Their thick tongues blort, their eyes squeeze grief'. They seem to be foolish participants in a calculated illusion ('Stewards tirelessly/Persuade them onwards'), the final illusion being of love itself. They are victims not only of delusion, but of a narrator who seems determined to mock them. But even at their most foolish and ugly, there is compassion for them, not explicitly stated but suggested in the poem's narrative technique which situates us in the women's collective consciousness. Only this degree of sympathy could coin 'blort', a variation, Larkin thought, of the dialect word 'blore' (meaning to bellow like an animal) and which, like 'yowl' in 'Lines on a Young Lady's Photograph Album', releases overwhelming feelings of pain and longing.[16] A draft manuscript version of the final stanza began:

> What's wrong! Moustached in flowered frocks they heave,
>   Grunting, then quieten down.[17]

The subsequent alterations show a modification towards compassion with the softening of the bestial imagery. The ending of the poem returns us to the onlooking speaker, detached enough to see (cruelly) that time has 'disproved' all their yearning for love. But again, the poem has drawn towards compassion. Even if it does not itself do so, it knows what it is to 'blort'.

This tension between isolation and community is only completely resolved in poems which cleanse themselves of attachment to people and narrative, and immerse themselves in contemplation of natural phenomena. This is the residue of the romantic lyricism of *The North Ship*, but now denuded of personality. The agnostic of 'Church Going' satisfies the 'hunger in himself to be more serious' by yielding up to sensations of absolute repose, 'unprotected by any sleight of tone or persona'.[18] In 'Water', Larkin offers benediction to the elemental presences of water and light. The poem combines a kind of 'man of the world nonchalance'[19] (raising a glass being akin to 'Cheers!') with unembarrassed homage:

> And I should raise in the east
> A glass of water
> Where any-angled light
> Would congregate endlessly.

The poem makes use of the traditionally religious associations of water (as in baptism) and secularises them. Water in this poem is associated with the capacity to change ('a fording/ To dry, different clothes'), perhaps even to make oneself different from oneself. In congregating endlessly, the light in the final image represents coherence, difference become unity.

It is tempting to see 'Water' as an almost 'voiceless' poem in which attention is so absorbed in the object that identity is neutralised into a kind of impersonality. Andrew Motion isolates the poem as being only a rare exception in *The Whitsun Weddings* to a collection which otherwise 'conforms almost exactly to the attitudes and styles associated with the Movement'.[20] He describes the glass of water as being treated symbolically, 'transformed into an imaginative apprehension of endlessness, in which all knowledge of time and its constraints, and of self and its shortcomings, is set aside'.[21] This describes very well the impulse of the poem, but as Heaney suggests, such impersonality is not quite achieved: there's the slightly embarrassed 'nonchalance' of the conditional 'If I were called in'. Nevertheless, what Motion describes is more generally true of *The Whitsun Weddings* than he allows. Escaping 'knowledge of self' is one of the most powerful longings in *The Whitsun Weddings*.

One way in which such 'escape' is attempted in the poems is by a kind of ventriloquism approaching self-parody, but which is never quite so stable as parody. This can lead to all sorts of interpretative conundrums. Thus, Jonathan Raban describes 'Annus Mirabilis' (in *High Windows*) as 'so promiscuous in its ironies that it turns into a maze, a stylistic labyrinth in which no directions are certain'. In turn, Neil Powell, who himself regards 'Water' as 'a kind of pastiche', takes Raban to task: 'the poet seems to have set out to write not a parody of a Larkin poem but a poem which might be mistaken for a parody of a Larkin poem. I suppose it is therefore ... a parody of a parody'.[22] Thus does Larkin gloriously sidestep his readers not by withholding himself but by giving them distortedly loud versions of himself.

As this example suggests, the strategy is more fully developed in *High Windows*. But there are poems in *The Whitsun Weddings* which seem to wear their masks very conspicuously. Rather like 'Annus Mirabilis', 'Naturally the Foundation will Bear Your Expenses' caused its first readers some confusion. Its speaker is a free-loading academic milking the system and now about to fly south ('Auster') to do some more name-dropping. His lecture, constantly recycled, is now due to be given in Bombay before being delivered as a radio talk and finally published. His taxi is delayed by the crowds gathering for an Armistice day memorial service: petulantly, the speaker wonders 'when will England grow up?' before selfishly immersing himself in his own careerist plans. The poem first appeared in a 'Humour' section of the magazine *Twentieth Century*, though Larkin described it as being 'as serious as anything I have written ... I've never written a poem that has been less understood; one editor refused it on the grounds, and I quote, that it was "rather hard on the Queen'".[23] Reviewers of *The Whitsun Weddings* discussed the poem as an unsuccessful piece of social satire in the manner of Betjeman. The confusion comes about because the reader's sympathies are ostensibly enlisted by the poem on behalf of the speaker and against the crowds of whom he is so contemptuous. But the tonal structure of the poem suggests, by irony, that our sympathies should be directed away from the speaker and that he, not the crowds, should be the object of our contempt. But even this straightforward alternative is jeopardised by Larkin's disclaimer in the interview already quoted: 'Why he should be blamed for not sympathising with the crowds on Armistice Day, I don't quite know'. This now seems to shift sympathy back to the poem's speaker. In fact, the root impulse of the poem lies not so much in sympathy or antipathy, but in something more complicated: envy. Whilst decrying the speaker's attitudes, Larkin treats him as he treated many of his university lecturer colleagues, with a mixture of contempt and jealousy (they are amongst the work-dodgers in 'Toads'): 'I hope it annoys all the continent-hopping craps',[24] he wrote privately on the poem's first appearance. What the problem illustrates is the instability of these dramatic monologues; seemingly so unproblematic, they are better seen as part and parcel of Larkin's devious rhetoric.

Another of what John Bayley in a different context calls 'a fine performance on the Larkin'[25] is 'A Study of Reading Habits'. Like 'Send No Money', is is a portrait of human inadequacy and failure. Where other poems in *The Whitsun Weddings* approach despair and disillusionment with varying degrees of compassion and pathos, in these two poems Larkin's mask is of the brutal dogmatist. This is not to say that they are insincere (Larkin quoted 'Send No Money' to himself more often than any of his other poems[26]) but rather that they are calculated verbal performances which disguise as much as they disclose. They are personal revelations which aspire to the impersonality of epigram.

During 1960, a romantic relationship began to develop between Larkin and Maeve Brennan, one of his library assistants. 'A Study of Reading Habits' was finished in August of that year. In it, the professional librarian jokes absurdly that 'Books are a load of crap'. What he means, of course, is that the romantic illusions fostered by youthful reading are a load of crap: 'The women I clubbed with sex!/ I broke them up like meringues'. The imagery mocks its basis in voyeuristic fantasy which owes something to popular Gothic fiction and, in the light of Andrew Motion's biographical disclosures, to Larkin's pornographic interests. Now, his reading presents him only with disquieting reflections of his own failure:

> ... the dude
> Who lets the girl down before
> The hero arrives, the chap
> Who's yellow and keeps the store,
> Seem far too familiar.

So, 'Books are a load of crap' because they present either unrealisable fantasies of sexual success or grim reminders of discreditable reality. (After all, with Ruth Bowman, Larkin knew all too well what it felt like to let the girl down. Moreover, the angry rejection of literature is also fuelled by his failed ambitions as a novelist.) The poem seems to make a universal assertion about the absolute disjunction between fantasy and reality. But if we restore the poem to its contingent circumstances, it is charged with other meanings. For at the time, Larkin was helping Maeve Brennan prepare for her Library Association exams. What more appropriate lesson could the tutor offer than the earnestly bibliographical-sounding 'A Study of Reading Habits' – which turns out to be a joke? And within that joke is an admission of sexual fantasy, rejected but none the less thrillingly present. Motion writes, 'Maeve aroused all his most romantic feelings. Small, with a good figure, short brown wavy hair, an eager face and unusually hairy forearms and legs (which Larkin found "very exciting"), Maeve was unsophisticated, conservative, cautious and capable of behaving coquettishly ... and ... he thought – someone he could easily control and pamper'.[27] Motion is in no doubt that Maeve is the imagined addressee of the poem. 'All experience, no matter what its nature, became charged and alluring because of his feelings about her ... the fact of her existence helped bring [these poems] into being. She was his secret sharer'.[28] So this most 'public' of poems, sententious and epigrammatic, is softened and made oblique by its biographical context. Behind its voice of certainty is another teasing and privately coquettish voice.

Similarly, 'Send No Money' presents the familiarly rueful, resigned Larkin. But like 'A Study of Reading Habits', its performative elements are very strong. The exaggerated relish of women succumbing to sex 'like meringues' is echoed in 'Send No Money' by the comically alliterated conclusion, 'Tracing the trite untransferable/ Truss-advertisement, truth'. The poem's fatalism ('the blows of what happened to happen') can be read as self-parodying: as these final lines indicate, there is something strenuously *willed* about this kind of resignation. To some extent it is an exaggerated pose, for although it seems to speak in an undisguisedly 'authentic' voice there is an element of ventriloquism about it. It makes a caricature (Time as a 'fobbed/ Impendent belly', a loud avuncular or headmasterly figure, 'booming' worldly wisdom) out of deep feeling, pantomime out of philosophy: *'watch the hail/ Of occurrence clobber life out/ To a shape no one sees'*.

These three poems – 'Naturally the Foundation will Bear Your Expenses', 'A Study of Reading Habits' and 'Send No Money' – illustrate how by using dramatic monologue Larkin's poems might actually distort the portrait of his own identity and so escape, in Motion's phrase, 'knowledge of self'. Another way of escaping is, as we have seen in 'Water', to retreat, or launch, into a kind of rapt inarticulacy. 'Here', one of the central achievements of *The Whitsun Weddings*, takes up these themes of identity, isolation and community, and resolves them into images of light and silence and the ineffable disappearance of self. 'Here' manages to speak for all of us because 'here' is where we all are.

In 'Wires', young steers ran up against 'electric fences' even on the widest prairies. 'Here' similarly explores the limits of our freedom, but this time looks beyond the fences. It begins in isolation – the poet on a train – and ends in an even more profound solitariness as the poem arrives at land's end beyond Hull, on the Holderness peninsula, facing the North Sea. The poem itself offers no precise geographical clues and this is one of the ways by which it makes itself significantly disembodied. Like the other journeys in *The Whitsun Weddings* ('The Whitsun Weddings' and 'Dockery and Son'), it is both literal and a metaphor of imaginative flight. In a remarkable feat of syntactical control, Larkin makes the first sentence last twenty-four lines. Its suspended present participle, 'Swerving', which anticipates a subject, actually turns out itself to be the subject of the main verb 'Gathers'. As the sentence journeys through a rapid succession of realistic details, the essential theme of the poem emerges only as we approach journey's end and complete the sentence with an inversion: 'removed lives/ Loneliness clarifies'. It is an almost unnoticeable virtuoso performance, which for three stanzas keeps the reader syntactically suspended and, more to the point, refuses to supply a personal-pronoun subject. In this way, the presence of the speaker is withdrawn and the reader experiences the journey without, it seems, a mediating voice. In a poem about emptiness, the grammar contrives its own sort of deprivation.

Having turned from 'traffic all night north' (again a curiously verbless phrase), we are taken through landscapes of increasing solitude before encountering the sudden surprise of urban Hull. Here, with its crowded commercialism, is contemporary life at its most familiar. The transferred epithet in 'cut-price crowd', the apparently indiscriminate list of its desires which puts 'sharp shoes' next to 'iced lollies' to suggest not only confusion but the transitoriness of desire, might suggest an attitude of disdain, though it is hard to pin down in a poem which so resolutely avoids a 'voice'. Lying beyond the town are isolated villages, and in contrast to the mechanised, impersonal town of 'flat-faced trolleys', the silent solitariness of the countryside 'clarifies' the sense of existence beyond the immediate. The contrasting brevity of 'Here silence stands/ Like heat' mimes the sensation of a journey concluded, of arrival, stillness; and the simile gives us a thickened synaesthesia after the three-stanza catalogue of rapid empirical observation. After the onward rush of the first uncoiling sentence, the end of the poem achieves stillness by rhythmical repetition and an adjustment in the rhyme-scheme which now gives a full rhyme to the couplet 'thicken/quicken' (the equivalent couplet of stanza two is a half rhyme, 'cluster/water'). Finally, we end in dissolving vagueness: the land ends in the 'bluish' distance, beyond a beach of 'shapes'. And in that bluish distance of sea and sky is 'unfenced existence:/ Facing the sun, untalkative, out of reach'.

But the syntax once again leaves a teasing ambiguity. The poet is poised on the threshold of ineffable transcendence, but 'unfenced existence' isn't 'Here'. It lies beyond, out 'there', 'out of reach'. 'Here' is where the poet stands, facing the sky and sun, himself 'untalkative' and 'out of reach'. As he stands, secluded from the urban crowds and community, so he is excluded from 'unfenced existence'. Nevertheless, the poem clearly endorses a freedom which is found only in an isolation so intense as to suggest the disappearance of self. In 'Mr Bleaney', the poet wanted to refuse complete identification with another person; 'Here' embraces identification of the self not with people but with elemental presences. Disdain felt for the urban community does not constitute the rejection of all communion, although it is only in isolation that the poet responds most intensely to the presence of a natural life which is almost hidden from us, 'unnoticed' and 'neglected'. His elation is emphasised by an image portraying the very opposite of vacancy, for '*Luminously-peopled* air ascends' [*my italics*]. This suggests that it is in states of solitariness that we become most vividly aware of other, almost ghostly presences of non-human life and even of life itself. Moreover, that 'unfenced existence', whilst it is contemplated with thrilling, self-forgetting absorption, nevertheless conveys in its infinite nothingness a darker prefiguring of death. 'Here', for all its eagerness to get away from community, actually carries movements of integration in its accumulative syntax and its immersion in 'otherness'.

'Mr Bleaney' and 'Here' debate the attractions of solitariness: 'The Whitsun Weddings' debates the attractions of marriage. It is one of the many poems in the collection which implicitly and explicitly take up the problems of relationships, particularly of love and marriage, which so dominated Larkin's personal life. In 'Wedding-Wind', he had tried a vignette of a woman on her wedding night; in 'The Whitsun Weddings' he gives a narrative of newly-married couples. The poem was begun in the summer of 1957 and completed in October 1958; chronologically, it belongs to the same period as those other poems about love and marriage, 'Love Songs in Age', 'Self's the Man' and 'Home is so Sad'. The train journey, this time away from Hull towards London, allows the poet to survey the landscapes of contemporary England and externalise the insider/outsider dualism which the poem tacitly explores. It also gives rise to a familiar effort in Larkin's poetry to find coherence in randomness and purpose in contingency. The train journey – the speaker isolated behind his window, travelling but actually trammelled, unifying a rapid succession of disparate and fleeting impressions – offers Larkin a ready metaphor by which to explore issues of identity and choice.

Critical comment on the poem has tended to focus on two issues: the portrait of the wedding-parties and the concluding imagery. Like the 'cut-price crowd' in 'Here', the wedding-parties seem to be treated with sneering superiority:

> The fathers with broad belts under their suits
> And seamy foreheads; mothers loud and fat;

> An uncle shouting smut; and then the perms,
> The nylon gloves and jewellery-substitutes,
> The lemons, mauves, and olive-ochres . . .

This, critics argue, expresses contempt for a society 'where mass tastes and values prevail, and the charming yokels of an earlier pastoral have turned into menacingly actual travelling companions, claiming equal rights with the egregious and refined spectator of their shoddy ordinariness'.[29] As we have seen, one of the arguments in Larkin is undoubtedly between communion with 'ordinary people' and disdain for them; but this kind of criticism unquestioningly accepts the voice speaking these lines as one it is intended we approve. At this point in the poem, the speaker has been distracted from his reading by 'whoops and skirls' and is only now beginning to take an interest: 'Struck, I leant/ More promptly out next time, more curiously,/ And saw it all again in different terms'. The poem, in fact, continues to see these weddings 'in different terms' and its speaking voice, by its conclusion, has corrected itself into an attitude altogether more democratic and humble than those isolated lines can suggest. The speaker's aloofness affords him the privileged position of onlooker but also, as the end of the poem concedes, isolates him so that it is he who is 'Marked off . . . unreally from the rest'.

Like 'Here', 'The Whitsun Weddings' seeks integration, a vision which will unify everything in the poem that is disparate: the Odeon, the cooling tower and 'someone running up to bowl' with the dozen marriages at which 'each face seemed to define/ Just what it saw departing'. Only the detached onlooker can memorialise what the participants are unaware of: 'none/ Thought of the others they would never meet/ Or how their lives would all contain this hour'. Hence, the image of London which immediately follows, 'spread out in the sun,/ Its postal districts packed like squares of wheat', combines separateness ('squares of wheat') within unity ('spread out') like these couples on the train. So, 'this frail/ Travelling coincidence' is both precious and transitory, like the 'hothouse' which flashed 'uniquely'. For each of the participants – the couples and the wedding-guests they left behind – the experience is unique, but universalised by the presence of the perceiving onlooker. For the speaker, what stands 'ready to be loosed' as the train slows is 'all the power/ That being changed can give'. There is no irony here: the metaphorical association between these newly-married couples and the 'sense of falling' as the train slows confers real power on them. They have perhaps become different from themselves. From mockery, the voice has modulated to reverence, and as the couples launch themselves into their new lives, the poet transposes the literal 'sense of falling' into a mysterious simile: 'like an arrow-shower/ Sent out of sight, somewhere becoming rain'. As with these newly-weds, the simile celebrates the power of change, from 'arrow-shower' to 'rain'.

But it is an image that causes difficulties. Though Larkin told an interviewer that he meant to give an unqualified assent to hopefulness at the end of the poem,[30] the image suggests the dissolution of what the poem has integrated. The drafts of the poem reveal that Larkin had speculated on some of these subsequent married lives, deciding on success for some and unaccountable misfortune for others. Buried within the image is Larkin's memory of the English bowmen in Laurence Olivier's film of *Henry V*. 'Dipped in the blood of patriotic fervour, Larkin's arrows serve Cupid's purpose, not Mars' . . . As he prepares to watch them disappear, he reminds himself that the arrow-shower of love wounds as well as inspires'.[31] So the poem cannot quite endorse an unqualified optimism for these couples. The speaker has shared in an experience of which the other participants remain ignorant (and in that sense is characteristically voyeuristic) and the poem carries an undertow of scepticism which resists a fairy-tale ending. The couple's lives carry the momentum of 'change', but change is in itself neutral and transitory. The speaker, by contrast, though he is elated by the experience, enjoys it only by virtue of his isolation from its central participants. That is his privilege, and the price he must pay.

Poems written about the same time as 'The Whitsun Weddings' similarly argue about emotional involvement. Written a few weeks after 'The Whitsun Weddings', 'Self's the Man' is another dramatic monologue which again sets about subverting the apparent security of the speaker. His exaggerated sense of inferiority to the married 'Arnold' is no inferiority at all, but actually expresses grateful relief at having escaped Arnold's domestic torment. So it comes as no surprise when the speaker argues that in fact Arnold is no more self-less than the speaker: 'He still did it for his own sake,/ Playing his own game./ So he and I are the same'. This leaves the way open for smug complacency before the sting-in-the-tail reversal, the sudden recognition that chosen bachelorhood might not be tolerable after all. The poem functions in much the same way as Ogden Nash's comic verse as described by Larkin:

> Nash's let-down rhymes and wait-for-it metrics are perfect stylistic equivalents for the missing chairs and slow burns of which civilized masculine living is compounded: waiting for women, putting up with children, social boredom and humiliation, having to work . . . He is, in fact, in line with those humorists who make you laugh at things not because they are funny but because laughing at them makes it easier to stand them . . .[32]

In fact, 'Self's the Man' wipes the smirk off its own face.

'Love Songs in Age' and 'Home is so Sad' are much more melancholy reflections on the failure of love. Where some poems use a tone of bitter disillusionment, 'Love Songs in Age' is much more tender in its treatment of the widow's disappointment (Motion identifies the widow as Larkin's mother). As the widow looks through her old song-books, she is reminded of her youth and the promises of romantic love offered by the songs. They purvey a sentimental illusion: love is a 'glare' which sails above us out of reach, 'Still promising to solve, and satisfy,/ And set unchangeably in order'. But though the widow weeps, the poem avoids cynicism. Love is 'Still promising' and the woman is not condemned for having been deluded. The whole poem aims for a kind of Hardyesque plangency ('That certainty of time laid up in store/ As when she played them first') and mourns the passing of time and the regrets of old age as much as the disappointments of love. 'Home is so Sad', though it owes less to Hardy, also looks back regretfully, this time without a narrative frame and leaving its feelings more exposed, particularly in its oddly vulnerable conclusion:

> You can see how it was:
> Look at the pictures and the cutlery.
> The music in the piano stool. That vase.

Motion concludes: 'His [that is, Larkin's] mother's house preserves all the odds and ends . . . which represent the original good intentions of a couple making a home together. But all that remains of their "joyous shot at how things ought to be" is faded hope. What will survive of us, the poem says, is not love but the wish to love – and indelible signs of how the wish has been frustrated'.[33]

The dominant attitude to love in *The Whitsun Weddings* is of baffled and resigned disappointment, often turning to rancour. 'Talking in Bed' looks to put it at its bleakest. It is a poem of declarative statement within which there is working a more lyrical mode of feeling and expression. We begin with the couple 'Lying together' (the pun on 'lying' is all too obvious), 'An emblem of two people being honest'. But contrary to the poem's title, there is no talking in bed. The poem hurries to its gloomy conclusion: 'At this unique distance from isolation/ /'It becomes still more difficult to find/ Words at once true and kind,/ Or not untrue and not unkind', where the characteristic double negatives of the final line serve to twist the knife a little more. But contrasting with these prosaic statements is the more elaborately metaphorical centre of the poem which takes us outside the silent couple's bedroom and challenges the logic of the poem's surface. As 'more and more time passes silently', what is heard is the wind's 'incomplete unrest'. As we have seen, from his earliest work the wind is contemplated in Larkin's poems as a disruptive and distracting force ('Wedding-Wind', 'Absences', 'Mr Bleaney'). Here, it is as if the lovers' ears are attuned 'Outside', listening to the wind which mirrors their own condition of unsettled incompleteness. The wind is ceaselessly roaming, changing, sifting, reflecting the unfinished ebb and flow of the lovers' feelings for one another. The strangely insubstantial 'dark towns heap up on the horizon' suggests random purposelessness, as if the world is governed by accidental and capricious forces, forces which brought these lovers together quite arbitrarily. And this world outside is indifferent and impersonal. The motion of the wind and clouds, the sprawling mass of the towns, all seem incalculable and inexplicable: 'None of this cares for us'. But this central moment in the poem is oddly consoling. That 'Nothing shows why' the couple cannot be both 'true and kind' is not quite true: the wind expresses a universal condition of purposeless change in which relationships are inevitably fragile. But by introducing the wind, the poem withdraws from the couple and insists on a presence (as so often in Larkin, an elemental force) which, though it is indifferent to them, nevertheless couples them. The wind functions rather as the onlooker in 'The Whitsun Weddings' who draws into unity otherwise separate experience, and as the glass of water in 'Water' where 'any-angled light/ Would congregate endlessly'. It is by talking that the couple hurt one another; in silence there is a shared isolation. Contrary to first impressions, 'Talking in Bed' is another poem which wants to integrate what lies separated.

The sacrifices involved in romantic entanglements are enumerated many times in Larkin's poems. As we have seen, commitment to another person represented for Larkin a threat to personal identity and, especially, his creativity as a writer. The poem 'Love' (which Larkin chose to exclude from *The Whitsun Weddings*) takes up familiar arguments frequently rehearsed in much earlier poems. 'To My Wife' and 'Marriages' (both dated 1951 in the *Collected Poems*), for example, represent marriage as a choice which denies all other choice ('Choice of you shuts up that peacock-fan/ The future was': 'To My Wife'[34]), an agreement 'That words such as liberty,/ Impulse, or beauty/ Shall be unmentionable' ('Marriages'[35]). 'Love' repeats the same argument as 'Self's the Man', that love is never selfless.

> The difficult part of love
> Is being selfish enough,
> Is having the blind persistence
> To upset an existence
> Just for your own sake.
> What cheek it must take.
>
> And then the unselfish side –
> How can you be satisfied,
> Putting someone else first
> So that you come off worst?
> My life is for me.
> As well ignore gravity.[36]

Although the subsequent final stanza slightly changes the tack of this logic, and although the comically querulous voice asks us not to take it too seriously, 'My life is for me' is a sentiment running through all Larkin's love poetry. It is given more problematical expression, for example, in 'Broadcast', which Larkin said on his recording of *The Whitsun Weddings* 'seems to be about as near as I can get in this collection to a love-poem: not, I'm afraid, very near'.

The poem's occasion is the broadcast on radio of a concert attended by the poet's loved one and listened to by him at home. The tenuousness of this connection sets up the muted tenderness of the speaker's attempts to imagine the woman at the concert. Everything in the poem conspires to all but efface her. The music prompts a mocking distaste the speaker cannot keep in check: the violins 'snivel' and are followed by 'Cascades of monumental slithering' and 'rabid storms of chording'. When he tries to imagine her, it is her venialities he sees: the dropped glove on the floor and (more cruelly) the new but 'slightly outmoded' shoes. As in 'Talking in Bed', the focus of attention turns outwards when in the gathering darkness he loses 'All but the outline of the still and withering/ / Leaves on half-emptied trees'. The putative object of his devotion has rapidly receded behind his involvement in the outside scene, and then in the noisy climax of the music. He is 'shamelessly' overpowered and now 'desperate to pick out/ Your hands, tiny in all that air, applauding', guiltily trying to compensate for his forgetfulness of her during the concert. Throughout the poem, his hold on her is precarious. The object of his love remains distant, removed, unspecified. The imagery of the gathering darkness itself suggests something fragile and vulnerable in their love. Just as he loses sight of the trees outside, so the woman at the concert recedes from him, herself surrounded by impersonal space, an impersonal audience and brought to him by the impersonality of the radio. Try as he might (and he does not try very hard), the poet cannot resist absorption in himself: his witty sarcasm about the music, his concentration on the trees outside. By contrast, the woman is presented merely in terms of conventional attitudes: 'Beautiful and devout'. 'Broadcast' fails as a love poem to just the extent it succeeds as a portrait of self-centredness.

'On me your voice falls as they say love should,/ Like an enormous yes' ('For Sidney Bechet'). In poem after poem in *The Whitsun Weddings*, Larkin wonders why the voice of love has failed to fall on him. He tries various voices of his own, from the plangent melancholy of 'Love Songs in Age' to the self-taunting ironies of 'Wild Oats'. Although Larkin chose 'The Whitsun Weddings' as the title-poem to foreground its note of celebration, the collection's emotional centre is 'Dockery and Son', an extended self-scrutiny which weighs bachelorhood and marriage, isolation and community. Again cast as a dramatic monologue, the speaker's return to his Oxford college and the news that his junior contemporary, Dockery, now has a son there prompt a series of reflections in which the speaker tries self-justifyingly to deny the differences between Dockery's life and his own.

What should be an occasion for self-indulgent nostalgia turns out to be much more threatening. The first stanza develops the speaker's uncomfortable isolation: he is 'Death-suited' (not a gratuitous morbidity: Andrew Motion records that Larkin was returning from a funeral) and when he tries the door of where he used to live it is significantly locked. Once familiar lawns are now 'dazzlingly wide'. He catches his train 'ignored' and glumly watches his past disappear. Already feeling a disconcerting sense of exclusion, the speaker broods on how young Dockery must have been when he became a father. He drifts into sleep, but wakes still tormented by the thought that as a young man Dockery made a definite choice about marriage and children. But such a thought threatens the speaker's complacency and he retreats from it: 'No, that's not the difference . . .'. Self-defensively, he decides that in having children Dockery acted on the false premise that 'adding meant increase' whereas, in a blusteringly evasive semantic scruple, to the speaker it means 'dilution'. The speaker wants to argue that such assumptions are not 'Innate' but 'more a style/ Our lives bring with them'. Significantly, his reasoning begins to get foggier here: the question 'Where do these/ Innate assumptions come from?' unwittingly confirms what it wants to deny, and the proposed alternative, that our assumptions are 'more a style/ Our lives bring with them', sounds suspiciously tautological. Once we get into the 'sand-clouds', we really are in a fog of self-justifying bluster by which the speaker wants to assert ('Self's the Man' again) that between Dockery and his son, and the lonely bachelor-speaker, there is no essential difference. Both cases represent the triumph of circumstances rather than of personal will: what we 'most want to do' warps 'tight-shut, like doors' (in a telling contrast, the moon is 'strong/ / Unhindered'). This questionable reasoning is the context for the poem's epigrammatic conclusion:

> Life is first boredom, then fear.
> Whether or not we use it, it goes,
> And leaves what something hidden from us chose,
> And age, and then the only end of age.

Undoubtedly, the biographical Larkin speaks in this conclusion. Andrew Motion calls the poem 'a compressed autobiography. It encapsulates Larkin's views about the effect of his parents on his personality, it reports spiritedly on his undergraduate career, it grimly sketches the attitudes which dominated his adult life'.[37] Nevertheless, the conclusion is one the poem takes care to portray, even parade, as just a little one-sided. The dramatic monologue essentially allows Larkin to attitudinise. The conclusion asks for our assent, but does not necessarily expect it. Its rhetoric is persuasive but palpable. As Stephen Regan notes, '"Something", like "nothing", is one of those words that allows Larkin's poems to remain uncommitted about what determines the nature of "being", while retaining a sense of urgency and distress in response to common suffering'.[38] In its idiomatic language and conversational address, the poem keeps faith with Wordsworth's real language of real men. We might choose to resist the embrace of the conclusion's 'we', but for all its bleakness the poem does believe in community, above all in its community of readers.

In 'Dockery and Son' (the title suggests the established continuity of a family firm), 'To have no son, no wife,/ No house or land still seemed quite natural'. The poem placed at the end of *The Whitsun Weddings*, although written amongst its earliest, is not so securely self-reliant. Supporting the prominence given to the volume's title-poem, 'An Arundel Tomb' wants to end the collection on a note of positive optimism by celebrating the triumph of love over time. In fact, the poem cannot offer such comfort, and it is that thwarted desire which gives the poem its own 'sharp tender shock'.

Larkin visited the tomb of the Earl of Arundel and his wife in Chichester Cathedral at the end of 1955. The poem begins with neutral description, though the opening detail notes their 'blurred' faces and 'vaguely shown' vestments. The style of the carving is plain and unadorned and there seems little to interest us until we notice 'with a sharp tender shock' the earl's left-hand gauntlet held empty in his right hand, thus leaving his left hand free to hold his wife's hand. The speaker's tone modulates into scepticism, refusing to be deluded by this apparent memorialisation of love. It was 'just a detail friends would see', incidental to 'The Latin names around the base', soon eroded by 'soundless damage'. With the passage of time, the couple can only signify now 'an attitude' and 'Time has transfigured them into/ Untruth'. Their held hands have come accidentally to be 'Their final blazon'. But the significance we attach to that romantic gesture is only one we will upon it. We impute to it the meaning we want it to have but which was in truth never intended. Their joined hands do not represent the triumph of love over time, but our delusory wish that it might be so. Thus they 'prove/ Our almost-instinct almost true:/ What will survive of us is love'. Isolated, that final line has an aphoristic romantic appeal; in its context, it stands in apposition to our 'almost- instinct': it is what we want to believe. 'Love isn't stronger than death just because statues hold hands for 600 years',[39] wrote Larkin on the manuscript draft. But in the tension between what the line wants to say and what it actually says is the poem's emotional ambivalence, its 'immense slackening ache' ('Faith Healing').

Rather than love, 'An Arundel Tomb' memorialises time. The couple undergo a 'supine stationary voyage' and the paradox expresses time's passage as a permanent state of change. 'Rigidly they// Persisted', and the fact of that persistence charges the poet's imagination. Their images are eroded literally and metaphorically by the tide of 'endless altered people' who wash at their identity. Now they are 'helpless', a 'scrap of history' extant in an age which is itself an insubstantial 'trough/ Of smoke in slow suspended skeins'. Even the poem's grammar (in stanza four) works to enact the discontinuity between their world and ours by losing 'their grammar of conditional futurity' in 'a modern indicative present'.[40] But for all the unillusioned emphasis it puts on time's triumph, the poem is imaginatively drawn to images of recurrence and anonymous presence:

> Snow fell, undated. Light
> Each summer thronged the glass. A bright
> Litter of birdcalls strewed the same
> Bone-riddled ground.

In an emotional shift we have seen before, consolation is found not in romantic love but in elemental processes which endure remotely and unconscious of human presence. These are the values constantly endorsed in Larkin's work, and it is the sense of life as *otherness*, over-mastering our own brief lives, which his poetry seeks to express.

Like 'Dockery and Son', other poems in *The Whitsun Weddings* ask where our 'innate assumptions' come from, especially about women and sexual desire. *The Whitsun Weddings* is full of the pressure of contemporary commercialism, reflecting the increasing affluence of society as the 1950s turned into the 1960s. Advertising functions in these poems as a means of pointing the contrast between our longings and reality. But at a deeper level, it participates, in some poems, in a more complex fantasy-life.

In 'Essential Beauty', Plato's ideal forms have been ironically diminished to images on advertising hoardings. But the irony is only partial. On the one hand, they represent 'a crudely exploitative economy ... the coercive ideology of modern consumerism'[41] from which the poem will dissent in a general way. But there exists simultaneously with this resistance a deeper attraction because, however exploitative, such images do speak of 'essential beauty'. (Billboards, Larkin once told Anthony Thwaite, 'seem to me beautiful and in an odd way sad, like infinitely platonic essences'.[42]) They externalise our 'innate assumptions' about beauty, fulfilment, perfection and 'how life should be'. Advertising, like clichés, offers Larkin a lexicon of a community's deepest wishes.

The opening of the poem emphasises how these gigantic advertising hoardings, 'In frames as large as rooms', obscure the grim realities of ordinary life: they 'block' streets, 'Screen' graves and 'cover' slums. Their images both camouflage and contrast with the dreariness of urban existence: amongst the streets, graveyards and slums they 'shine/ Perpetually' as well-ordered and flourishing 'groves'. The opening, exaggerated but enthralled, renders both the exploitativeness and attractiveness of these images, and the rest of the poem works similarly to express both their sadness and their beauty. These images promise everything: contentment, prosperity, even perpetual youth are available in 'that small cube' or the 'cups at bedtime'. They are windows on the world of our dreams, reflecting 'none of the rained-on streets and squares// They dominate outdoors'. Taunting us with our ideals of flawlessness, these advertising images are indeed 'cold', remote from our 'live imperfect eyes' which seek 'the home/ All such inhabit'. Reality is what these advertisements cynically overlook (in both senses of the word). Pursuing their promise of success leads only to disillusionment, the boy 'puking his heart out in the Gents' and the pensioner paying more for his brand of tea only 'To taste old age'.

The poem's final image intensifies these painful feelings of desire and exclusion. Advertising's association of smoking with sexual success, crudely trading on masculine fears and desires, yokes together for Larkin two powerful forces: sex and death. The 'dying smokers' momentarily sense the object of their desires 'Walking ... As if on water', miraculous and other-worldly, an 'unfocused she/ No match lit up, nor drag ever brought near', a vision of female attractiveness which floats out of reach. That 'unfocused she', combining the vagueness of 'unfocused' and the urgent, sharp simplicity of 'she', stands as a ubiquitous icon of feminine seductiveness. Literally 'unfocused' she might be, but 'she' stands as the intensely focused object of male sexual desire, a desire that exists beyond the possibility of fulfilment. There's no irony by the poem's end, only the pathos of unsatisfiable desire. She stands 'newly clear' at the same time as 'going dark', a glamorised fantasy-object who complicitly recognises her adorers but fades beyond their grasp, 'a decadent, beautiful harbinger of death'.[43]

'Essential Beauty' belongs to a group of poems which, with varying degrees of rancour, imagine stereotypically glamorised women as participating in a frustrating sexual fantasy. Andrew Motion has explicitly linked Larkin's pornographic interest to the presence in his poems of photographed women (as in 'Lines on a Young Lady's Photograph Album' and 'Wild Oats' as well as more glamorised icons in adverts): 'In all these, working unseen, Larkin transforms a masturbatory impulse and an addiction to solitude into poems of great beauty and sociable truthfulness'.[44] 'The Large Cool Store' confesses to a kind of male bafflement in the face of femininity. Trying to equate the daytime world of those 'Who leave at dawn low terraced houses/ Timed for factory, yard and site' with the night-time erotic promise of 'Modes for Night' ('Bri-Nylon Baby-Dolls and Shorties/ Flounce in clusters') only shows

> How separate and unearthly love is,
> Or women are, or what they do,
> Or in our young unreal wishes
> Seem to be: synthetic, new,
> And natureless in ecstasies.

The conclusion concedes a natural self-delusion in men's 'young unreal wishes' about women, but it is a delusion of which the speaker of the poem cannot rid himself. In 'Wild Oats' he continues to keep in his wallet, like the contraband of fantasy smuggled into the real world, 'two snaps/ Of bosomy rose with fur gloves on./ Unlucky charms, perhaps'. Talismanic and taunting, they thrill the speaker with unsatisfiable erotic yearning. For the object of male desire remains 'separate' and 'unearthly', 'synthetic' and 'natureless', thrillingly 'out of reach'.

In 'Sunny Prestatyn', this longing for what must remain unattainable is most evident as a communally male erotic dissatisfaction. The girl pictured on the poster is the sex object of male fantasy, exploited (she is selling herself to suggest the holiday pleasures of Prestatyn) and exploitative. The opening of the poem knows that we are being manipulated, but beneath its tone of mocking, come-off-it exaggeration (as in rhyming 'poster' with 'coast, a') is an altogether more complicit excitement. She is 'Kneeling up' in an attitude of willing submission and her 'tautened white satin' – pure, virginal, exotic – suggests a specifically male arousal. The 'hunk of coast' sounds threateningly masculine and the hotel 'palms' are not only visually but grammatically connected (as part of the subject of 'Spread') with her 'breast-lifting arms', so that punningly her breasts are lifted by caressing hands. The tone shifts abruptly to worldly-wise bathos – 'She was slapped up one day in March' – and the rest of the poem documents the graffiti which then defaces the poster. 'She was too good for this life' seems both to honour and to dismiss her, as the poem measures dream-image against bleak reality.

But the language of defacement and the manipulation of our attitude to 'Titch Thomas' are highly problematic. The poem does not simply lament the remoteness of fantasy; 'this isn't degraded reality replacing unavailable ideal . . . but the translation of one image of desire into another'.[45] The very fact of translating the 'unfocused she' into a public image is itself a kind of violation, expressed in the casual brutality of her being 'slapped up' one day. She is too good for this life and should not be embodied in it. Hence, there is an 'undertow of approval'[46] not only for Titch Thomas's 'enraged insistence that the image on the poster accords with no reality whatever',[47] but for the savagery of his treatment of it. The autographed name 'Titch Thomas' suggests, however jokily, a male anxiety about sexual deficiency and the defacement of the poster might express 'every man in every penetration, a hatred, an assertion of ownership, a desecration of a false ideal'.[48] The brutality of the nouns – 'Huge tits and a fissured crotch . . . A tuberous cock and balls' – is only less brutal than the triumphant verbs: 'scored well in' and 'set her fairly astride'. The manuscript drafts show an intensification of this brutality: for example, the first drafts had a vaguer 'floating cock and balls'. The ending, too, was less lacerating:

> Another week, and a giant tear
> Ripped everything off but some blue.
> Next week there were farm sales there.[49]

The process of composition is towards ferocity: 'the glimpse of beauty, paradise, escape, is also pretentious mockery of "this life", our life, and therefore deserving of assault'.[50] The pristine girl as one image of desire is translated by her violation into another: an expression of vengeance on everything that is tantalisingly unattainable. It is not that the image is 'unreal', but that its representation of sexual longing is all too urgently real. The poem's satirisation of the female fantasy figure gives way to the gleeful destruction of an erotic icon; behind that destruction there lies an attitude of sexual self-disgust. The poem's conclusion pastes over the desecration with what at first appears a chastening reminder of mortality: 'Now *Fight Cancer* is there'. But this poster holds out a promise as fraudulent as the first, for we can satisfy neither our desires for erotic bliss nor for immortality. 'The cancer advert is the last twist of Larkin's ironic knife. Our girl then takes a sordid journey into oblivion and the male participants in the drama queue up to follow her: Titch Thomas, the knifer, the ripper, the poet – and you and me, hypocrites lecteurs'.[51]

If 'Sunny Prestatyn' and other poems which make use of fantasy female figures betray complex feelings of longing and loathing, 'MCMXIV' searches for a pristine innocence. Like 'Here', it does so by imagining silence and solitariness, and by preserving a moment in a timeless suspension. Larkin achieves this (accidentally, he claims on the recording of *The Whitsun Weddings*), as in poems of similar feeling, by a syntactical manoeuvre. The poem has no main verb ('As changed itself' rather than 'Has changed itself') and this helps create the poem's lingering tranquillity.

The Roman numerals of the title immediately suggest how remote the pre-1914 era now seems, separated from us by the carnage of the First World War that was yet to be unleashed on the world of the poem. As well as historical distance, the numerals suggest a kind of respectful reticence: 'the emotional impact of nineteen-fourteen in Arabic numerals was too great for anything I could possibly write myself'.[52] What follows is a decorous sequence of the conventional typologies of the Edwardian–Georgian era seen through the sentimental haze of late twentieth-century nostalgia. But the poem is not a simple piece of patriotic nostalgia. It knows that it is dealing in cultural myths as potent as those purveyed in the advertising images of other poems. The lines of men queueing up to enlist, 'Grinning as if it were all/ An August Bank Holiday lark', are viewed with pathos but also a subdued irony which surfaces again at the end of the poem: 'the men/ Leaving the gardens tidy,/ The thousands of marriages/

Lasting a little while longer'. After all, we are all 'innocent' of the future, and the present, which has always 'changed itself to past/ Without a word', is treated elsewhere much less sentimentally by Larkin. So the end of the poem, 'Never such innocence,/ Never before or since . . . Never such innocence again', with its liturgical rhythms, asserts, like the end of 'An Arundel Tomb', an emotional attitude rather than accepted fact. It is self-consciously rhetorical and knows it is dealing in myths. That they are not treated satirically is the measure of how far Larkin can go in honouring 'the fragile human idealism which these myths embody'.[53] Myths of beauty, innocence, permanence enlist his sympathy for the human longings they embody. But they are still treated as myths, not truths.

The awareness of time passing, treated with such urgency in *The Less Deceived*, is a more muted theme in *The Whitsun Weddings*. When it is dealt with explicitly, as in 'Reference Back', there is the familiar sense of helplessness. Bored and resentful on a visit home, the poet plays a favourite jazz record only to suffer his mother's banal comment. The moment is charged with disappointment both for the speaker (for whom this is 'A time unrecommended by event' as 'Triple Time' put it) and his mother, who had earlier fallen into the perennial trap of expecting too much of the future (her son's visit home). Henceforth, that record will always recall to the poet this moment of rift between mother and son, just as it has stored up 'The flock of notes those antique negroes blew' since it was made thirty years before. Now, past, present and future are brought by this record into an unhappy alignment as the moment when her 'unsatisfactory age' and his 'unsatisfactory prime' collide. The future offers only disappointment and, worse, the opportunity for painful and still self-deluding retrospection:

> Truly, though our element is time,
> We are not suited to the long perspectives
> Open at each instant of our lives.
> They link us to our losses: worse,
> They show us what we have as it once was,
> Blindingly undiminished, just as though
> By acting differently we could have kept it so.

Some seven years later, on the eve of his fortieth birthday, Larkin expressed the same bleak determinism in a letter:

Looking back on my first 40 years, I think what strikes me most is that hardly any of the things that are supposed to happen or be so do in fact happen or are so. What little happens or is so isn't at all expected or agreeable. And I don't feel that everything could have been different if only I'd acted differently – to have acted differently I shd have needed to have *felt* differently, to have *been* different, wch means going back years and years, out of my lifetime.[54]

Although in one poem 'it leaves/ Nothing to be said', the consciousness of death pervades *The Whitsun Weddings* as the nullity which threatens to render everything purposeless. It is prefigured at the conclusion of 'Here'; elsewhere it makes a mockery of love and as 'the only end of age' ('Dockery and Son') makes speculation about choice futile. 'Life is slow dying', and only humdrum routine offers any kind of consolation: 'Give me your arm, old toad;/ Help me down Cemetery Road' ('Toads Revisited'). 'Ambulances', however, whilst it insists on final things, succeeds in rising above a sense of futility and manages a tender regard for individual life.

The first stanza presents ambulances as impersonal, frightening reminders of unpredictable fate. Onlookers find themselves randomly caught up in someone else's tragedy, accidental spectators of 'A wild white face' which interrupts their mundane routine. For a moment, normal life stands still and the onlookers apprehend with a shock the tenuousness of their own lives. For a second, they are vividly conscious of their own mortality. As the ambulance drives off in 'deadened air', its shut doors signify the close of a unique, individual life. The constituent elements of that life, all its accidental, unforeseen, haphazard events, its self-made continuity, 'the unique random blend/ Of families and fashions' finally begin to come apart. 'Far/ From the exchange of love', a life suddenly unravels. Watching the ambulance, we are brought closer to the nothingness of our own deaths. It 'dulls to distance all we are' in both removing us from and clarifying the shape of our lives.

Characteristically, the poem moves to a moment of intense perception of nothingness. In doing so, it assembles particularities and gathers them into coherence. The narrative perspective silently shifts from third to first person plural as individuality merges in the shared isolation of 'we'. That humdrum line about 'women coming from the shops/ Past smells of different dinners' is powerfully arresting and represents in miniature the pattern of the whole poem. It renders the sudden preciousness of the ordinary; it is a 'unique random blend' which stubbornly insists on the uniqueness of the ordinary and the ordinariness of uniqueness. The 'solving emptiness/ That lies just under all we do' is universal, and frighteningly particular. It solves, resolves and dissolves. As the patient's particular identity dissolves, the poem accumulates noun phrases ('the sudden shut of loss', 'something nearly at an end', 'the unique random blend') in a studied contemplation of substance becoming insubstantial. What cohered and now begins to unravel – 'At last begin to loosen' – is already treated as plural by the verb. Finally, in 'one of the most hauntingly intricate constructions in Larkin's work',[55] the syntax of the last sentence itself looks to unravel. For the subject of 'Brings closer' (and the parallel 'dulls to distance') is the whole, complex infinitive noun-phrase: 'To lie far from the exchange of love unreachable inside a room [which] the traffic parts to let go by'. The poem's conclusion embodies a coherence which the poem itself has integrated in the face of 'dissolving' death. It dissolves and resolves. The final, convoluted sentence, even in confronting extinction, ends affirmatively with the exposed present indicative: 'we are'.

It is in the complexities – and simplicities – of Larkin's language that his sensitivity to life and death, isolation and communion, desire and despair, is most precisely registered. The strained, self-conscious lyricism of his earlier work is in *The Whitsun Weddings* traceable as nothing more fulsome than a perceptible refinement of ordinary language. His use of stereotypes, of clichés, of the recognisable idioms and registers of particular voices, creates the representativeness of so many poems in *The Whitsun Weddings*. By trading on the familiar, Larkin can seem to speak for the common man. But it is always at one remove and Larkin is always the voyeur, observing from behind the window of his railway carriage. He 'dulls to distance all we are' to 'for a second get it whole,/ So permanent and blank and true'. But dulling experience is not what these poems do. On the private edge of elsewhere/ somewhere/ nowhere, they suddenly pitch themselves higher. Abstract nouns and inactive verbs have a special force in Larkin because they speak of a kind of negative sublimity, of what is just 'out of reach'. The syntactical upheavals which occur at the most intense moments of perception in his poems are a step towards the ineffable, the 'untalkative'. Larkin's 'fundamentally passive attitude to poetry (and life too, I suppose)'[56] continues to find expression in *The Whitsun Weddings* within the very structure of his language. At the same time, that 'passive attitude' seeks active identification with something other than itself. After the self-absorption of *The Less Deceived*, *The Whitsun Weddings* expresses a yearning for the self's absorption in otherness.

6
High Windows

Of *High Windows*, Andrew Motion has written: 'The book changed Larkin's life more decisively than any of his previous collections. *The Less Deceived* made his name; *The Whitsun Weddings* made him famous; *High Windows* turned him into a national monument'.[1] But in order to construct that monument, Larkin's eager public had to overlook or explain away the most disturbing aspects of *High Windows*. Where *The Less Deceived* was tormented by questions of love and *The Whitsun Weddings* by loneliness and death, *High Windows* is charged with anger. Forces which in *The Whitsun Weddings* were held delicately in tension can be seen disintegrating in *High Windows*. Poems celebrating continuity and communal ritual remain, and there is a tender regard for futile human gestures of compassion (the 'wasteful, weak, propitiatory flowers' of 'The Building'). But the collection also lays bare feelings of fury and rancour which show Larkin's lyrical impulse being threatened by its twin: a mocking philistinism. This is most obviously apparent in the taunting coarseness of Larkin's language in many poems. It seems that at times *High Windows* wants to say again, with the fury of disappointment, that 'books' and all they represent really are 'a load of crap'.

In *The Whitsun Weddings*, a poetry-reading public found its representative voice. The first 4000 copies were sold in two months[2] and Larkin found himself, only a little unwillingly, something of a celebrity. 'You wouldn't see the frenzy of activity on Northern broadcasting services, I expect: today I had a Guardian feature writer for nearly 4 hours. I long to be anonymous again', he wrote to Barbara Pym.[3] Critical attention was not universally flattering, but even less enthusiastic reviewers such as Al Alvarez recognised Larkin's importance as representing a particular culture. 'Perhaps his special achievement is to have created a special voice for that special, localised moment: post-war provincial England in all its dreariness, with the boredom of shortages no longer justified, the cheap, plastic surface of things which nobody wants and everybody buys.'[4] Emerging a decade after *The Whitsun Weddings*, *High Windows* was awaited and consumed by an expectant public: the first 6000 copies were sold in three months and 13,500 copies reprinted in the following few months.[5] Reviewers argued about Larkin's 'development' ('Only mediocrities develop', Larkin had already tartly observed, quoting Oscar Wilde[6]) but could not then know the bleakest significance of *High Windows*: that by its publication in 1974 Larkin had largely written himself into silence. Only half-jokingly, Larkin wrote to Barbara Pym in 1975: 'the notion of expressing sentiments in short lines having similar sounds at their ends seems as remote as mangoes on the moon'.[7] Larkin had always been anxious about the meagreness of his output but the remark he made in a radio broadcast in 1972 expresses this anxiety in a different way:

> There is great pressure on a writer to 'develop' these days: I think the idea began with Yeats, and personally I'm rather sceptical of it. What I should like to do is write different kinds of poems that might be by different people. Someone said once that the great thing is not to be different from other people, but to be different from yourself.[8]

This replaces the notion of 'development' with an altogether more radical aspiration and reflects the pressure of imminent poetic silence Larkin felt. Although these sentences have been applied to the more adventurous poems in *High Windows* (by Simon Petch, for example), their importance is central to the whole of Larkin's work. *High Windows* can be read as the sometimes despairing conclusion to Larkin's lifelong quarrel with himself about his own identity and the value of art.

In 'Toads Revisited', Larkin once again settled for the world of work, duty and responsibility, but not without first taking the measure of himself against 'the men/ You meet of an afternoon . . . All dodging the toad work/ By being stupid or weak./ Think of being them!' Beneath its gruff surface, the poem does indeed 'Think of being them',

> Turning over their failures
> By some bed of lobelias,
> Nowhere to go but indoors,
> No friends but empty chairs – . . .

Indeed, *The Whitsun Weddings* repeatedly thinks of 'being them': Mr Bleaney, the widow, the women in 'Faith Healing', all of them in some way damaged, or failures, or casualties. The willingness to feel compassion in the poems expresses a shared sense of fear and deprivation. The poems' integration is not only of a social kind, but of meaning, whereby the contingencies of circumstances are assembled into a more enduring significance. David Trotter has pointed out how meaning emerges differently in *The Less Deceived* and *The Whitsun Weddings* poems. Citing 'Church Going' and 'I Remember, I Remember', he writes:

> Both poems complete their description of a particular event before paying attention to the feelings it has aroused . . . Only then, in the ebbing of event, does the significance of either occasion become apparent. Meaning occurs after the event . . . Larkin relates individual experience to shared significance by organising them into temporal succession: first event, then meaning.[9]

But later poems such as 'Here' and 'The Whitsun Weddings' work differently: '. . . meaning does not occur in the aftermath of event. It is produced by the final act of the journey, the moment when the tightened brakes take hold . . . Event and meaning, so distinct in "Church Going" and "I Remember, I Remember", have begun to merge'.[10] This marks another stage in the process of 'self-forgetting' and asserts a faith in implicit meaning, in a shared understanding between writer and reader.

But it is possible to read in *High Windows* a loss of faith in this consensus.[11] The rancorous tone, the general sense of desperation, whilst they can obviously be linked to the increasingly horrified contemplations of old age and death, suggest also a deepening anxiety about the relationship between self and community. There are still poems in which Larkin thinks of 'being them' and they remain amongst his most moving achievements. But other poems wilfully resist integration. The voice of 'The Old Fools', for example, is patently egocentric, with the focus on *me* being them. Other poems in *High Windows* are more daringly lyrical because they can no longer lose themselves in the lyrical moment, but jeopardise it by making their moralising more explicit. Trotter concludes that

> The glancing agnosticism of poems like 'Here' and 'The Whitsun Weddings' was no longer sufficient . . . And Larkin responded . . . by shifting to a far more militant and assertive stance than he had

ever adopted before . . . between *The Whitsun Weddings* and *High Windows* Larkin began to affirm a connection between individual experience and shared meaning which he might once have left to chance. The shaming pragmatism of the sixties drove him to speak his mind, to give his poems the authority of conscious and unequivocal dissent.[12]

Stan Smith has argued in much the same way, suggesting that in *The Whitsun Weddings* Larkin's attitude to 'welfare-state social democracy, where mass values prevail' was usually 'to maintain an equivocal balance in his responses to such a world, poised between annoyance and deference. In more recent work, such as the poems in *High Windows* (1974), this balance has gone, and the mood is a more tight-lipped one, of disdain sharpening to odium'.[13]

So in *High Windows* the attempt 'to be different from yourself' is more strenuous, and sometimes more strenuously defeated. The impulse to celebrate is now more defensive and cornered. Where in *The Less Deceived* and *The Whitsun Weddings* the poetic personality modulated and mediated itself by way of slightly shifting ventriloquisms, in *High Windows* it is more declarative and dogmatic, or else absents itself within the manifestly fictitious creations of 'Livings'. It is as if in *High Windows* the need 'to be different from yourself' is both more desperate and more difficult to fulfil. The lyricism is more risk-taking because it emerges side by side with its opposite: the philistine.

As Janice Rossen has observed, 'Larkin's habitual melancholy is so clearly driven by intense fury.'[14] During the period when the *High Windows* poems were written, there was much to fuel Larkin's fury. His personal life grew increasingly complicated, unsatisfactory and guilt-inducing. To Monica Jones he wrote in 1966: 'it's my own unwillingness to give myself to anyone else that's at fault – like promising to stand on one leg for the rest of one's life. And yet I never think I am doing anything but ruin your life & mine'.[15] A little later, he expanded:

I feel rather scared these days, of time passing & us getting older. Our lives are so different from other people's, or have been, – I feel I am landed on my 45th year as if washed up on a rock, not knowing how I got here or ever having had a chance of being anywhere else . . . Of course my external surroundings have changed, but inside I've been the same, trying to hold everything off in order to 'write'. Anyone wd think I was Tolstoy, the value I put on it. It hasn't amounted to much. I mean, I know I've been successful in that I've made a name & got a medal & so on, but it's a very small achievement to set against all the rest. This is *Dockery & Son* again – I shall spend the rest of my life trying to get away from that poem.[16]

As he sank further into unhappiness and apathy, so his sense of general worthlessness intensified. Writing to his old college friend Norman Iles in 1972, Larkin confessed:

For the last 16 years I've lived in the same small flat, washing in the sink, & not having central heating or double glazing or fitted carpets or the other things everyone has, & of course I haven't any biblical things such as wife, children, house, land, cattle, sheep etc. To me I seem very much an outsider, yet I suppose 99% of people wd say I'm very establishment & conventional. Funny, isn't it? Of course I can't say I'm satisfied with it. Terrible waste of time.[17]

The continuing stream of honours towards the end of his life only served to increase Larkin's sense of fraudulence as a national poet who had all but stopped writing. Responding to a request for a poem in 1983, Larkin wrote: 'poetry gave me up about six years ago, and I have no expectation of being revisited'.[18] Indeed, Larkin wrote very little between the appearance of *High Windows* in 1974 and his death in 1985. Thus, one central significance of *High Windows* is that it represents the period when Larkin wrote himself into silence. We can now read these poems in the full recognition that on their margins, and sometimes at their centre, is the battle to get them written.

Amongst the competing forces in that battle are contradictions seen before in Larkin's work, fundamentally between the aesthete and the philistine. The aesthete earlier revered Lawrence, preserved in lyrics moments of heightened perception, combined Yeatsian vision with Hardyesque pathos. The philistine was iconoclastic, recognised itself as a failed writer who never won 'the fame and the girl and the money/ All at one sitting', and satirically mocked romantic illusions. Larkin found a way of expressing this argument with himself as one between 'Beauty' and 'Truth': 'When I say beautiful, I mean the original idea seemed beautiful. When I say true, I mean something was grinding its knuckles in my neck and I thought: God, I've got to say this somehow, I have to find words and I'll make them as beautiful as possible'.[19] The experience of beauty is in Larkin's poetry always in peril and his most lyrically thrilling moments contemplate negation: 'One longs for infinity and absence, the beauty of somewhere you're not'.[20] In *High Windows* it is possible to see the lyrical, beauty-creating Larkin now much more obviously threatened by the mocking philistine. Trotter and others read the poems as belligerent reactions to the changing social and political circumstances of the 1960s and early 1970s and they are right to emphasise the tension in the poems between consensus and conflict. Nevertheless, the fury in these poems is the fury of disillusionment not only in life but in art. Yet that philistinism, that refusal to take 'Art' as a theology, is what guarantees Larkin's poetic integrity. 'The whole poetic career', writes Barbara Everett, 'in so many ways so prudently managed, is also a drive to extinguish the false artistic ego.'[21]

In *The Less Deceived* and *The Whitsun Weddings*, it was possible to distinguish between the various speakers of the poems who were subject to varying degrees of irony. In that way, the poems could be read as complex projections of attitudes which were actually self-scrutinising. But in a significant number of the *High Windows* poems, the degree of critical distance between author and speaker is much harder to determine. This might simply be a way of saying that in *High Windows* Larkin speaks much more unambiguously *in propria persona*, sacrificing the earlier masks (often ironically self-revealing) for a bluntly declarative directness. This instability of tone can be read in 'The Old Fools'. Is this a poem in which Larkin expresses his fear and disgust with unmediated frankness? Or are we to see it as the projection of an attitude which is subverted by its own language and then corrected into compassion? This latter view is taken by R. P. Draper, for whom the poem's progress 'is one of deepening attention, moving from a seemingly detached, jeering stance . . . to an increasingly sympathetic identification with the subject of senile decay'.[22]

Certainly, 'fury' drives the language at the opening:

What do they think has happened, the old fools,
To make them like this? Do they somehow suppose
It's more grown-up when your mouth hangs open and drools,
And you keep on pissing yourself, and can't remember
Who called this morning?

Clearly, there is a mock ingenuousness about the rhetorical questions and the venom they direct at senility. This loud aggression is self-defensive: it loathes old people because they remind the speaker of his own old age and death. Booth calls these lines an 'embarrassingly obvious' displaced terror of death.[23] But that is their point. There are no strategies of refinement in the language, no rhetorical deviousness which places this voice within a structure of ironies. The terror, like the language, is naked and has gone beyond embarrassment. Just as other poems in *High Windows* flaunt their certainty, this flaunts its outrage: 'Why aren't they screaming?'

The poem shifts ground to consider death and to imagine what it feels like to be old before curving back in horror to 'The whole hideous inverted childhood'. But although there is fascination, there is no compassion. The language refuses throughout to modulate into pathos. Despite the amplitude of the stanzas, there is no real development of attitude or disguised self-scrutiny. The effect of the abrupt half-lines is to bring up short both the stanza and any possible sympathy. Terry Whalen wants to rescue a 'tough compassion and bewildered reverence', arguing that ' "the million-petalled flower/ Of being here", coming as it does from Larkin's more open and romantic impulse as a poet, highly qualifies the terror of the uglier images and feelings which the poem seeks to transcend'.[24] But the image Whalen isolates cannot stand up to the brute force of description surrounding it: 'Ash hair, toad hands, prune face dried into lines . . .'. Larkin's 'million-petalled flower' is rawly sentimental. Against the forces of age and death, it desperately wants to assert the preciousness of life. But its sweetness, its own 'bloom', its rhythmical lilt, look fragile compared with the simple, terrifying, anatomising plainness of

> At death, you break up: the bits that were you
> Start speeding away from each other for ever
> With no one to see.

This is truth rather than beauty. Even when in the third stanza the poem imagines what it feels like to be old, the picture of solitariness 'describes something so purely "over" it seems asphyxiated'.[25] The language remains inert, a trudging sequence of clauses in a tiring sentence. So when towards the end of the poem the phrase 'the old fools' recurs, its tone has not been altered. The ending of the poem, 'Well,/ We shall find out', is brutally laconic. In earlier poems, 'well' was a conversational gesture or a shrug of the shoulders; 'now it is properly vicious, full of menace'.[26] Of course the poem is cruel and implicates us in its cruelty. It does not expect fair-mindedness and its bad-mannered language signals the rejection of rhetorical niceties. It desperately fends off old age and silence. 'The Old Fools' illustrates one of the 'developments' in *High Windows*. Rather than integration and reconciliation, it represents a disturbing intensity and urgent directness.

'The Building' approaches the subject of death more indirectly, but the stealth knows that it is evasive. The tone is more subtle and glancing than 'The Old Fools' and the poem manages to affirm human value in the face of death, though it is hardly consolatory. The strategy is different: rather than head-on confrontation, the poem adopts a *faux-naif* periphrasis, pretending not to know that it is describing a hospital (the draft title was 'The Meeting House'[27]). This allows Larkin eventually to unveil the truth as if it were a new discovery. Like 'The Old Fools', the poem wants to convey renewed shock in the face of familiar horror. But where 'The Old Fools' was essentially personal (despite its 'you' and 'we'), 'The Building' assumes consensus. The hospital is portrayed as the place where we discover our essential sameness; at a rhetorical level, the poem relies on the reader's complicity in the pretence of not knowing that a hospital is being described. This also gives the hospital the force of a gradually emerging symbol.

As a symbol, the building allows Larkin to develop the familiar insider/outsider antithesis, this time to intensify the contrast between routine life, and life when it faces death. Inside the building is a dislocating familiarity. We recognise scruffy 'porters', vehicles which 'are not taxis', a room 'Like an airport lounge', though its inhabitants suggest it is 'More like a local bus': the building assembles fragments of the familiar which will not cohere. This is 'ground curiously neutral' which erodes difference and individual identity in a situation representing 'The end of choice'. Awareness dawns of 'more rooms yet, each one further off' in increasing isolation, before attention turns outside. Suddenly, the ordinariness outside takes on a new preciousness, and freedom is walking out of the car-park. As the affectionately demotic language indicates, the humdrum world of 'kids' and 'girls with hair-dos' fetching 'Their separates from the cleaners' represents a miracle from which those imprisoned inside the building and its final realities are excluded. Larkin clarified this for himself in a manuscript note:

'Once removed from the outside world we see it as a touching dream to wch [*Larkin's abbreviation*] everyone is lulled, but from wch we awake when we get into hospital. In there is the only reality. There you see how transient and pointless everything in the world is. Out there conceits and wishful thinking'.[28]

Where in 'The Old Fools' Larkin tried to convey a 'miracle' by a lift in the language ('the million-petalled flower/ Of being here'), in this poem the commonplace is suddenly numinous because of the way Larkin has situated the speaker. There, he looked at death from life; now, he looks at life from death. The ordinary can no longer be taken for granted:

> O world,
> Your loves, your chances, are beyond the stretch
> Of any hand from here!

The 'conceits/ And self-protecting ignorance' which constitute life outside the building have collapsed: what 'Ambulances' called 'the unique random blend of families and fashions' is reduced to undiscriminating categories: 'women, men;/ Old, young'. Again, the approach of death is conceived in terms of a levelling anonymity in a language drained of rhetoric: 'All know they are going to die./ Not yet, perhaps not here, but in the end,/ And somewhere like this'.

But where 'The Old Fools' was unremittingly harsh, 'The Building', although it rejects religious consolation, offers an affirmation of social routine. Outside the new hospital 'close-ribbed streets rise and fall/ Like a great sigh out of the last century', representing an enduring community where in 'short terraced streets' kids and young girls will compose from 'loves' and 'chances' their universally unique lives. They are amongst the 'crowds' who 'each evening' try to disperse 'The coming dark . . . With wasteful, weak, propitiatory flowers'. As so often before, Larkin asserts the value of human life in terms which recognise its ultimate futility. That final hanging line, superfluous to the syntax and metrically stumbling, nevertheless welcomes life, however attenuated. Thus, 'The Building' recalls the integrating movements of *The Whitsun Weddings*. This time, though, its voice speaks as an insider looking jealously outside, rather than as the outsider looking suspiciously in.

The building isolates those suddenly 'picked out' of the 'working day' from their ordinary lives and confers new value on the humdrum routines that are now imperilled. 'I don't want to transcend the commonplace, I love the commonplace, I lead a very commonplace life. Everyday things are lovely to me', Larkin told an interviewer.[29] His remark illustrates that resistance in Larkin to the transcendent and helps explain the impetus behind a group of poems in *High Windows* which, severed from any defining context, render in miniature the very stuff of ordinary life. 'Friday Night in the Royal Station Hotel' and the sequence called 'Livings' represent what we might call, following Barbara Everett, a 'philistine' aesthetic in Larkin. This is to be distinguished from the 'philistinism' hitherto identified in Larkin: the hatred of 'abroad' and foreign poetry (though even these should not be taken at face value), the dogmatic attitudes and political bigotry. But the aesthetic which loves the commonplace and which risks expressing itself with an air of artlessness, and which most of all escapes 'personality', is a 'philistine' one in a more positive sense. Everett has suggested how 'the factuality' of these poems (there in 'The Building' as the welcome perception of 'Red brick, lagged pipes') 'is something other than *just* a sense of place: it is, rather, a sense of life . . . The "philistine" conditions, sufficiently loved, offer up an unused, fresh symbol of life in its workaday transience and in its moments, like the poem itself, of fugitive, wasted, inexplicable glory . . .'.[30] This 'philistine' Larkin puts at the centre of these poems a kind of modesty. He manages to be different from himself by finding fictional identities which absorb his own, and preserves in these poems fragments of ordinariness. The escape from personality means that, in Everett's words, 'The artist as such has no standing, but sets his goods among the "lambing-sticks, rugs,/ Needlework, knitted caps, baskets, all worthy, all well done,/ But less than the honeycombs": a bee could do better'.[31] The silence surrounding these poems is the silence of modesty, convinced of its own unimportance, become mute.

These poems run counter to the declamatory tendency in *High Windows*. They signally fail to disclose their contexts. In this way, they resemble the most absorbing of *The Whitsun Weddings* poems such as 'Here' and 'The Whitsun Weddings' ('Friday Night in the Royal Station Hotel ' was written in 1966) by merging, in Trotter's terms, 'event' and 'meaning'. In fact, by dispensing with 'event' altogether, they go one stage further. 'Friday Night in the Royal Station Hotel' describes the emptiness of a hotel and the three poems in 'Livings' are monologues spoken by three anonymous individuals imagined in entirely different circumstances. These are quite 'causeless' poems, quite without narrative structure or moralising purpose. Larkin's 'symbolist' tendency here finds its most extreme expression in these most 'philistine' of poems. Their beauty lies in the simple truth of the things they name.

'Friday Night in the Royal Station Hotel' is absorbed in emptiness, silence, and self-protective isolation. But it thrills to residual presences: the 'full ashtrays' of the salesmen now returned to Leeds, the dining-room of 'knives and glass', the lights still on in 'shoeless corridors'. This 'fort' protects dormancy, lull, a between-times; this hotel represents a strange 'exile' from 'home', event, purpose. From here, in the suspension of activity, 'letters of exile' might be written, letters which communicate solitariness and a rapt attentiveness to elemental presences: '*Now/ Night comes on. Waves fold behind villages*', where the metaphor transforms the actual into an image of calming comfort. But of course this letter is not written. The ending of the poem retreats into abeyance, the might-have-been-written which finds itself written. It is like the poem itself. 'Friday Night in the Royal Station Hotel' is a love poem, a sonnet addressed to the merely contemplative imagination which broods on empty chairs and passing hours simply because they are there. It is a poem in which nothing comes into being except the experience of imagining. 'Philistine' in Barbara Everett's sense, its wilful modesty means that the poem offers nothing except its own contrivance. In that way, the poem refuses to be 'symbolist' in the conventional sense:

> . . . his poetic objects – the empty chairs, the corridors, the ashtrays – which could hardly be perceived with more intensity if they *were* symbols, have a complex burden to bear: that of not even being capable of symbolizing the absence which they happen to remind one of. For Symbolism necessitates and is arrogant . . .[32]

This 'philistinism' is an art which refuses to be Art and, in conjuring it, Larkin is purely anonymous. In this way, he manages to be different from himself.

The triptych of poems entitled 'Livings', written separately over three successive months at the end of 1971, can be read as further attempts to escape from personality, what Everett describes as 'the concentration of personal feeling . . . accompanied by an extreme circumscription of any merely personal expression of the self'.[33] Larkin himself described them as 'miniature derivatives of Browning's dramatic lyrics' which were not intended to have a unified meaning.[34] '. . . I thought I was going to write a sequence of lives, or livings, little vignettes, but it petered out after three.'[35] Although Larkin cites for 'Livings' the example of Browning's dramatic monologues, they merely extend that strategy of projecting different 'voices' which has been central to all Larkin's work; this time, the voices are fictionalised as monologues (recalling 'Wedding-Wind' written twenty five years earlier). In that very obvious sense, then, they are 'impersonal'. The first is spoken by a grain merchant. He has inherited his father's business and is passing the time in a rural hotel he uses every three months to conduct business. The year is 1929. The second is spoken by a lighthouse-keeper and the third by a seventeenth-century Cambridge scholar. The poems are dense evocations not so much of people or places as circumstances, of the particularities of three different sensibilities. They are interested in minutiae, in the currency of ordinary living. Like 'Friday Night in the Royal Station Hotel', they are 'philistine' in their modesty, wanting only to render the everyday, the glory and pathos of the usual.

For the speaker of 'Livings I', the usual is this three-monthly hotel stay, the single beer, the soup and stewed pears, the Smoke Room chatter. The poem is stocked with lists, the apotheosis of routine: 'Births, deaths. For sale. Police court. Motor spares', and 'Who makes ends meet, who's taking the knock,/ Government tariffs, wages, price of stock'. These routines fill a life, however grudgingly accepted: 'I drowse . . . wondering why/ I think it's worth while coming . . . It's time for change, in nineteen twenty-nine'. Suddenly, the historical perspective opened up by the poem fills it with melancholy. The factuality of its details, the comic pictures on the walls – 'hunting, the trenches, stuff/ Nobody minds or notices' – take on, from this remote distance, the pathos of the 'Red brick, lagged pipes' seen from inside 'The Building'. Somebody has noticed, and minded. ' "Things like dips and feed": the phrase itself half-ironically half-salutes that densely actual commonplace existence that all Larkin's poems "invent" as their subject.'[36]

'Livings III' is even more historically remote and as a result a little more mannered, an effect pointed up by the strict iambic tetrameters and self-conscious diction. But the poem follows the same movement as the first, from 'inside' to 'outside' and with it comes an intensification of emotional pressure. The 'big sky' (of 'Livings I') and 'Chaldean constellations' which 'Sparkle over crowded roofs' situate these poems simultaneously in their imagined historical time and our own. Thus, as in many of Larkin's most affirmative poems, they merge difference and unity, individuality and timelessness, contingency and continuity.

In the two side-panels of the triptych, two speakers betray some anxiety about their isolation and constricting routines. In the central poem, however, isolation and routine are embraced joyously. 'Keep it all off!' it shouts. Cut off in a storm, the solitary lighthouse-keeper listens to the radio 'Telling me of elsewhere' and exults in his self-sufficiency. In terms of 'The Importance of Elsewhere', the 'elsewhere' of everywhere else underwrites his existence here in a lighthouse which is thrillingly exposed but 'Guarded by brilliance'. The adventurous imagery, taut lines and exclamatory tone convey the intense excitement of living so far beyond the social. As before, it is the simple presence of elemental forces which charges the affirmative gesture, when human presence is dwarfed and chastened by vastness. Taken together, 'Livings' express the contrarieties in Larkin: the yearning for difference, self-sufficiency and remoteness; and the grateful acceptance of sameness, community and mutual reliance.

It is worth stressing how *High Windows* represents a more risk-taking Larkin, not just in the didactic and hectoring tones of its most disenchanted poems, but in their obverse: the purer, symbolist, freely imaginative poems. 'Money' is an instructive case. It starts in typically curmudgeonly fashion. Then, after three stanzas of sour resentfulness, the poem suddenly lifts:

> I listen to money singing. It's like looking down
>   From long french windows at a provincial town,
> The slums, the canal, the churches ornate and mad
>   In the evening sun. It is intensely sad.

Whilst this does not alter the saturnine mood of the poem, the vertiginous shift from aggressive colloquialism to this mysterious simile transfers us from the worldly to the imaginative, from a kind of truth to a kind of beauty. The poem risks incongruity, sentimentality, affectation: all the 'artiness' that the 'philistine' Larkin avoided. 'Money' persuades because, for all its sudden extravagance, it remains exact to feelings of anger, self-reproach and finally an impersonal dismay. It shows in miniature how in his later poems Larkin is more willing to juxtapose contrary modes of expression rather than integrate them and, sometimes, to leave meaning tantalisingly implicit. It is in such self-reflexive poems as 'Friday Night in the Royal Station Hotel', 'Livings' and 'Money' that we find the adventurously post-modernist Larkin.

The title-poem, 'High Windows', is risk-taking in these and other ways. The most obvious is its frank language, designed partly to shock ('. . . these words are part of the palette. You use them when you want to shock. I don't think I've ever shocked for the sake of shocking'[37]). The candid vernacular, so visible in a number of *High Windows* poems, is part of the idiom of bluff, plain-speaking to which many of these poems are drawn. Even more startlingly than 'Money', 'High Windows' juxtaposes contrasting idioms and states of feeling. 'As with much of the later verse, this starts out looking like a poem about sex, and becomes a poem about religion.'[38] The feelings of contempt and jealousy expressed in the speaker's attitude to sex are, without warning, suddenly overtaken by the awed sublimity of the end of the poem. This kind of development is reminiscent of 'Here', but the lyricism of 'High Windows' is more daring in its vulnerability, in its having to overturn language and attitudes so vehemently anti-lyrical.

The 'bad language' of 'High Windows' works to define its speaker. The brutality of 'couple of kids . . . he's fucking her and she's/ Taking pills or wearing a diaphragm', the 'paradise' with its teasing run-on which modifies ironically its meaning, serve as attempts to mask feelings much more ambiguous and troubling. For this is the paradise 'Everyone old has dreamed of all their lives'. Of course, it need not be 'paradise' for the 'couple of kids', but it seems so in the eyes of an older man jealous of youth's sexual freedom. The unfolding first sentence which surges across stanza breaks and grabs at slightly off-key images (the 'outdated combine harvester' and 'the long slide') suggests feelings that are only just kept under control. The superficial disgust for sex made mechanical expresses something else. This is envy, and not a little rage. So the speaker's conjecture about an older generation having envied his own ('*No God any more, or sweating in the dark/ / About hell and that*') is a way of distancing his own feelings of unfulfilled desire. In each case, it is a version of freedom – 'the long slide' – that is envied, but a freedom the logic of the poem suggests is illusory. For the speaker plainly feels that '*He and his lot*' never in truth went down the long slide to happiness, and by extension the 'couple of kids' he now envies are not in 'paradise'. Part of the poem's anger lies in the implicit recognition that freedom is only ever relative, a recognition felt in the absurd simile of going *'down the long slide/ Like free bloody birds'*. Hence, the poem's sudden lift represents an imagined escape into pure freedom, a freedom from all desire and language, an escape from identity and expression. This is 'that padlocked cube of light' of 'Dry-Point':

> Rather than words comes the thought of high windows:
> The sun-comprehending glass,
> And beyond it, the deep blue air, that shows
> Nothing, and is nowhere, and is endless.

This is an authentic paradise (and the 'high windows' have religious associations). But as the effortful repetitiousness of the last line indicates, it is a vision which must remain even beyond words. Unlike 'Here', the poem confesses its own inadequacy: it is the glass which is 'sun-comprehending', not the speaker who can 'know' only the illusory 'paradise' of mortal longings. The poem is often seen as the expression of a transcendent Larkin, with its 'sublime emotional elevation out of negatives'.[39] But the poem knows it is thwarted. The ultimate freedom it posits is a wordless 'thought': the 'air' shows 'nothing' which is imagined as boundlessly 'nowhere'. Characteristically, these negatives function as teasing positives, but ultimately they are not reassuring. The sky shows 'nothing'. It is an endless 'nowhere'. Whilst it is true that 'Once again it is the contemplation of his own absence which most thrills him'[40], the poet of 'High Windows' finally admits that in poetry the ultimate freedom of absence can only ever be a rhetorical contrivance. Outside the poem true absence beckons: silence.

So there are complex cross-currents of affirmation and denial in the poem: that the freedom others seem to enjoy is denied us; that such freedom is actually an illusion; that true freedom, an escape from the self and all desire, is inaccessible to language. This helps to explain why there is an undertow of anger in the poem, an anger and movement towards silence which characterise *High Windows* as a whole. Andrew Motion's biography describes Larkin's first drafts of the poem, where the conclusion was:

Rather than words comes the thought of high windows
The sun pouring through plain glass
And beyond them deep blue air that shows
Nothing, and nowhere, and is endless

and fucking piss.

Motion comments: 'The poem grows out of rage: the rage of unsatisfied desire, the rage of "shame", the rage of having to persuade everyone that "the thought of high windows" guarantees happiness. The poem's beautifully achieved shift from the empirical to the symbolic cannot disguise or subdue Larkin's appetite for what he has never had'.[41] Nor, it seems, for what he will never have: not just sexual fulfilment, but the fulfilment of desirelessness and the poetic expression of the inexpressible. Written in 1967, the poem is the natural successor to 'Here' but also suggests why, to use Larkin's formula, poetry was beginning to leave him.

The poem also reflects the philistine iconoclast in Larkin which constantly threatens the aesthete. The 'fucking piss' of the draft is a comment on the poem's transcendental yearnings, 'and yet the way it sabotages the high hopes of the preceding lines forms an important part of the poem's meaning'.[42] 'Sabotage' is a useful way of describing a significant number of poems in *High Windows*, poems which relish their rancour, their saturnine irony, their intolerant political dogmatism. The most obvious example is 'This Be The Verse'. It returns to familiar preoccupations with parenthood and childlessness. But where 'Dockery and Son', for example, gave the appearance of arguing its way to its bleak conclusion and framed its 'philosophy' within narrative devices, 'This Be The Verse' bullies us into assent. It is a deliberately 'bad mannered' poem in its direct language and monosyllabic bluntness. As so often in Larkin, the problem is to know how seriously to take the speaker, how to judge the critical distance between author and persona. Much depends, in Larkin's poems, on pronouns which assume the reader's involvement and consent so as to speak on behalf of the reader, and on strategies which ironise the 'I' of the poem. But in these more outspoken poems, Larkin seems less concerned to develop rhetorical strategies and so they are more defiantly dogmatic. Constructing personae in Larkin's poems can lead to debatable conclusions. Simon Petch, for example, wants to argue that the speaker of 'This Be The Verse' 'uses sardonic humour to mask the bitterness of his attitude to experience . . . and the poem uses its speaker to take a swipe at the very fatalism of which Larkin has been accused'.[43] But this depends on emphasising the 'humour' at the expense of the 'bitterness'. It is true that the nursery-rhyme lilt is comical, but the comedy does not necessarily make the sentiments ironic. The comic jingle seems rather to reinforce the dogmatic conclusiveness of the poem: 'the truth is as simple as this', is what the epigrammatic terseness suggests.

Certainly, the poem is ironic, but not about its fatalistic attitude. As Thomas Hood's 'I Remember' stands behind Larkin's 'I Remember, I Remember', so Robert Louis Stevenson's 'Requiem' stands behind 'This Be The Verse':[44]

> Under the wide and starry sky,
> Dig the grave and let me lie.
> Glad did I live and gladly die,
>   And I laid me down with a will.
>
> This be the verse you grave for me:
> *Here he lies where he longed to be;*
> *Home is the sailor, home from sea,*
>   *And the hunter home from the hill.*

Stevenson's epitaph gives Larkin the epigrammatic model and the object of his irony: that stoical acceptance of life and death. Larkin's equivalent epitaph is anti-death by being anti-life:

> Man hands on misery to man.
>   It deepens like a coastal shelf.
> Get out as early as you can,
>   And don't have any kids yourself.

'It's perfectly serious as well', said Larkin when commenting on the poem's humour (its opening, for example, which punningly suggests the literal conception of children as well as how parents 'bugger you up once you are born'). The poem teases us by not quite telling us how seriously to take it. In that way, it gets away with being viciously cynical and uncompassionate. As Larkin said of the *High Windows* collection: 'There are some quite nasty ones in it'.[45]

Shortly after completing 'This Be The Verse', Larkin wrote 'Vers de Société' (an ironically pretentious title), another satirically saturnine poem. It again argues about society and solitude and its dramatised structure means that, unlike in 'This Be The Verse', a conclusion appears to evolve and its satire works more explicitly. Even so, its opening, to use Motion's word again, is another example of 'sabotage'. Warlock-Williams (a sinisterly comical name) does not actually write '*My wife and I have asked a crowd of craps/ To come and waste their time and ours*'; the speaker's voice has already sabotaged the language of decorum with its own brute cynicism. (Janice Rossen takes the opening literally, 'an attempt to appear sophisticated by being off-hand and at ease',[46] but if War-lock-Williams is himself being ironical, it rather ruins the irony of the rest of the poem.) The invitation triggers a familiar debate between the claims of community and solitariness. Being sociable requires an effort of politeness 'to catch the drivel of some bitch/ Who's read nothing but *Which*', and is a waste of 'spare time that has flown// Straight into nothingness by being filled/ With forks and faces'. The tone modulates to something more reasonable – being sociable is idealistic, 'It shows us what should be' – before quickly collapsing into rancour: 'Too subtle, that. Too decent, too. Oh hell,// Only the young can be alone freely'. On the other hand, solitariness is associated with lyrical attentiveness: 'Day comes to an end./ The gas fire breathes, the trees are darkly swayed . . .' and 'spare time' is

> repaid
> Under a lamp, hearing the noise of wind,
> And looking out to see the moon thinned
> To an air-sharpened blade.

'*Virtue is social*', but the poem's rhetoric wants to argue that solitari-ness is fulfilling. As so often in Larkin, the poem asserts that it is in states of isolation that receptive communion is found with intensely perceived external presences: the light, the wind, the moon. But what 'High Windows', and *High Windows*, recognises is that this kind of raptness entails silence. And in the end, 'Vers de Société' settles for sociability because

> sitting by a lamp more often brings
> Not peace, but other things.
> Beyond the light stand failure and remorse
> Whispering *Dear Warlock-Williams: Why, of course* –

The poem rehearses familiar tensions in Larkin: between the compassion of community ('we should be careful// Of each other, we should be kind/ While there is still time': 'The Mower'[47]) and society's erosion of individual freedom; between the lyrical pleasures of solitariness and the fear of loneliness. Each stanza has a short three-stress line (the third in the opening and closing stanzas, the penultimate elsewhere); the first and last stanzas are written in rhyming couplets whilst the other stanzas variously deploy three rhymes. Technically, the poem represents a kind of loose symmetry equivalent to its process of reasoning. Its conclusion represents not the reconciliation of contraries but a grudging acceptance of the lesser evil, for in the end 'how hard it is to be alone'.

Though 'Vers de Société' partly counterbalances the nihilism of 'This Be The Verse', poems such as 'Homage to a Government' and 'Going, Going' confirm the impression of dogmatism in *High Windows*, an intemperate philistinism which is the obverse of Barbara Everett's 'sense of life' in the mundane. It is in such poems of social comment that Larkin seems to abandon the rhetorical finessing of his best poems in favour of coercion. Where there was a perhaps confusing level of irony in 'Naturally the Foundation will Bear Your Expenses', the irony of these poems is plainly directed at their objects of scorn rather than emerging from a more sophisticated rhetoric. 'Homage to a Government' – heavy-handed irony – is the most explicit response in *High Windows* to the growing political, industrial and economic difficulties of Britain in the late 1960s, and its socio-political context explains much of the rancorous tone and some of the characteristic imagery of *High Windows*.[48] It laments the closure of a British colonial base in Aden (now in the Republic of Yemen) for economic reasons and condemns the decision as an index of Britain's imperial decline and moral corruption. The lame irony of the repeated 'it is alright' betokens the general naivety of a poem which expresses only a single attitude of political dissent. The conclusion – 'Our children will not know it's a different country./ All we can hope to leave them now is money' – attempts an unearned plangency. Whereas the best of Larkin's poems work towards emotional honesty, this is a mess of inchoate feelings which wants to blame the masses for the shameful loss of colonial power: 'We want the money for ourselves at home/ Instead of working'. Clearly, 'ourselves' does not include the speaker. Whilst the poem tentatively opposes the values of 'money', it fails to construct a genuine dialectic or to engage with real feelings. Instead, it relies on appeasing the reader's predisposition.

These social satires reveal the most damaging aspects of Larkin's philistinism. In them, Larkin's political prejudices are all too vulnerably exposed. Quizzed about the poem, Larkin said:

> Well, that's really history rather than politics. That poem has been quoted in several books as a kind of symbol of the British withdrawal from a world role. I don't mind troops being brought home if we'd decided this was the best thing all round, but to bring them home simply because we couldn't afford to keep them there seemed a dreadful humiliation. I've always been right-wing. It's difficult to say why, but not being a political thinker I suppose I identify the Right with certain virtues and the Left with certain vices. All very unfair, no doubt.[49]

Written in 1969, 'Homage to a Government' is in truth no more substantial than the reactionary political squibs which begin to appear in Larkin's private correspondence at this time. Together, they represent an increasing belligerence which in *High Windows* is allowed to threaten the poetry.

Larkin should have resisted more strongly the temptation to versify his political prejudices. When in 1972 he was asked by an acquaintance sitting on a government working party to produce a poem about the environment, he wrote 'Going, Going'. The poem represents the predicament in which Larkin's fame had now trapped him: the poet whose earlier work had been 'nothing if not personal' now had a public persona to project, one designed to protect his privacy. And the public poet was all too ready to offer his readership hand-me-down opinions and prejudices designed to flatter expectations about himself. In 'Going, Going', stereotyped attitudes and sentimental cliché are deployed unquestioningly. 'I have actually finished *a* poem, and thin ranting conventional gruel it is', he confessed in a letter.[50]

At first, the elegiac tone holds back the polemic, but then impatience breaks through. The lament for a pastoral England threatened by commercial greed turns into an intolerant attack on caricatures: 'The crowd/ Is young in the M1 café;/ Their kids are screaming for more', and 'On the Business Page, a score// Of spectacled grins approve/ Some takeover bid'. As in 'Homage to a Government', rancour hardens into attitudes of disdain which seek easy targets, in this case the 'cast of crooks and tarts'. Against this dystopia, the poem tries to measure an ideal England: 'The shadows, the meadows, the lanes,/ The guildhalls, the carved choirs'. Significantly, all it can manage is this tourist-brochure list of clichés. It is worth comparing this with the England of 'MCMXIV':

> And the countryside not caring:
> The place-names all hazed over
> With flowering grasses, and fields
> Shadowing Domesday lines
> Under wheat's restless silence . . .

The difference lies not just in the more intense visualisation of the latter, but in its apprehension of a real relationship between the speaker and the landscape. In 'Going, Going', the list is expected to trigger a predictable response; in 'MCMXIV' the language 'cares' in despite of 'the countryside not caring'. 'MCMXIV' constructs a particular historical moment as its context, but 'Going, Going' only manages to suggest 'the landscape of a nebulous golden age'. The poem is 'a little smaller than life where it means to grow larger',[51] a failure generally true of the weakest poems in *High Windows*.

In poems like 'Homage to a Government' and 'Going, Going', Larkin signally fails to be different from himself. They are philistine in the sense that they are content to mock, that their 'opinions' are not mediated by self-interrogative rhetoric, that they offer no antithesis to their resignation. The aesthetic impulse of 'Friday Night in the Royal Station Hotel' and 'Livings', Barbara Everett's positive 'philistinism', honours the commonplace and the empirical, and preserves fragments of ordinary human experience without wanting to transcend them. But elsewhere, that impulse capitulates to a philistinism which wants to mock all artistic enterprise and which develops into the reactionary boorishness apparent in some aspects of Larkin's later life.

These tensions between the aesthete and the philistine which underlie so much of Larkin's work are dramatised in 'The Card-Players'. Posing as 'a verbal *tableau vivant* from a former century, an enactment of an interior scene painted by a Dutch Old Master',[52] the poem (a sonnet) subverts its artistic frame by revelling in the base, the primitive, the disgusting. Whilst the extravagant language might suggest an element of parody, it is not clear what is being mocked, and long before its end any satire has been overwhelmed by excited complicity. The scatalogical language ('Jan van Hogspeuw . . . pisses at the dark . . . Jan turns back and farts') and the grossly vulgarised names are part of the poem's wild uninhibitedness. It is a picture of animal comfort – the pissing, belching, farting and gobbing, the smoking, drinking and singing. 'This is a world without families, an exclusively and gloatingly male world where mothers, wives and mistresses are not admitted.'[53] More than that, it is a world without pretentiousness or artiness. Someone 'croaks scraps of songs . . . about love', but only as an accompaniment to the ale, the mussels and 'the ham-hung rafters'. 'This lamplit cave' is a vision not of Platonic essence, but of its opposite: ripe, self-sufficient earthiness. The dislocated last line, reminiscent of the ecstatic conclusion of 'Absences' and the urgent 'Bestial, intent, real' of 'Dry-Point', welcomes retreat into gross, elemental sensuousness. Although at first sight the poem suggests a way of Larkin being different from himself (the manuscript draft bears the note '*Unlived lives*'[54]), it in fact releases that deeply-felt vulgarian in Larkin . Buried under 'Wet century-wide trees', this is a low life which is the natural antithesis of the aspiring, wordless transcendence of 'High Windows'. In effect, it picks up where 'High Windows' left off – 'and fucking piss' – before that poem found its edited equilibrium. *High Windows* makes more explicit than any earlier collection the collision in Larkin between the aesthete and the philistine and the relative silence following its publication in 1974 tells its own story.

As Andrew Motion has shown, that story involves amongst other things the death of Larkin's mother and increasingly complicated and guilt-inducing relationships with women. Larkin's love poems are more usually poems about lovelessness, but in *High Windows* there is a deafening silence about love (though the subject returns vividly in a few poems written after 1974). In fact, a long, unfinished love poem called 'The Dance' was in progress as *The Whitsun Weddings* was published. Although it combines incident and reflection in the self-interrogative manner of 'Dockery and Son' and 'Reasons for Attendance' (which it resembles in other ways too), 'The Dance' is more startlingly intimate and 'confessional' than either. It describes the emotional turmoil of attending a dance with a woman to whom the poet is disturbingly attracted. Its feelings are a familiar mixture of scorn and self-loathing, of desire and fear. The dance is '*Alien territory*'; when in front of the woman, the speaker yearns 'desperately for qualities// Moments like these demand, and which I lack'. When he senses sexual responsiveness, desire merges with panic at 'something acutely transitory/ The slightest impulse could deflect to how/ We act eternally'. Shame confirms 'How useless to invite/ The sickened breathlessness of being young// Into my life again!' But when he dances with the woman again

> I feel once more
> That silent beckoning from you verify
> All I remember – weaker, but
> Something in me starts toppling. I can sense
> By staring at your eyes (hazel, half-shut)
> Endless receding Saturdays, their dense
> And spot-light-fingered glut
> Of never-resting hair-dos . . .[55]

'Its five printed pages in the *Collected Poems* are a fascinating ruin, their fragmentariness powerfully reinforcing the poem's theme of incompletion.'[56] A poem so nakedly exposed to the moment-by-moment intensities of recollected feelings looks therapeutic, and it is no surprise that Larkin could not finish it.

Written some ten years later, 'The Life with a Hole in it' (a bitter allusion to a famous advert) returns to the illusions and disillusionments of choice, the 'something acutely transitory' which deflects 'To how/ We act eternally'. The contrast with 'The Dance' is instructive. There, choice is fully acknowledged and recognised as frightening and perilous. Now, an attitude of self-pitying belligerence opts for the comforts of resignation and fatalism. The life he might have had ('the shit in the shuttered château') and the life he is glad to have avoided ('that spectacled schoolteaching sod') are 'far off as ever'. Life is not a matter of free choice, but of being imprisoned:

> Life is an immobile, locked,
> Three-handed struggle between
> Your wants, the world's for you, and (worse)
> The unbeatable slow machine
> That brings what you'll get. Blocked,
> They strain round a hollow stasis
> Of havings-to, fear, faces.
> Days sift down it constantly. Years.[57]

This is another fine 'performance on the Larkin'. But where the similar 'Send No Money' dramatised its resentments so as to leave room for self-parody, 'The Life with a Hole in it' offers no such critical distance. Only the final line shifts the poem to a more impersonal register, an echo of the faith in lyricism which in Larkin's earlier work transformed rawly personal feeling into a larger awareness. 'This is brilliantly effective "bad" writing. The poet presents himself as flailing about, unhappily aware that his exasperation is out of proportion to its apparent occasion.'[58] But it also confirms the impression that in his later poems Larkin is boxed in by apathy, resignation and a sense of futility. Where earlier the clash of contrary impulses reverberated in complex ironies, now 'bad language' carries the force of simple odium.

Nevertheless, a significant number of poems in *High Windows* do affirm their faith in the lyrical moment, although even here are undercurrents of darker feeling. 'The Trees', for example, with its simple rhymes and soothingly end-stopped lines, wants to welcome renewal: 'Begin afresh, afresh, afresh'. Still, 'Their greenness is a kind of grief' because they mark the passing of the old, just as 'Their yearly trick of looking new' is a reminder of our own mortality. So it comes as no real surprise to learn that in the privacy of his manuscript notebook Larkin wrote beneath the poem, 'Bloody awful tripe'.[59] Larkin's lyricism knows it is wishful thinking. As Donald Davie reminds us, 'The pristine and definitive form of lyric is the song; and the singer is not on oath. The sentiment and the opinion expressed . . . are to be understood as true only for as long as the singing lasts. They are true only to that occasion and that mood . . . '.[60]

Larkin's deflating comment is a kind of retaliation, a self-protective acknowledgement that lyricism can only ever be transitory and thereby delusory. A different sort of acknowledgement is made in 'Cut Grass', which focuses on an image of transitoriness. The simultaneity of life (the 'young-leafed June . . . With hedges snowlike strewn') and death ('Brief is the breath/ Mown stalks exhale./ Long, long the death/ / It dies . . .') is captured in the poem's final image of weightlessness and slowness: 'that high builded cloud/ Moving at summer's pace'. In effect, the poem works by an accumulation of images, all intensifying a lyrical moment but incapable of adding to it. Instead, they emphasise the fragility not only of the cut grass, but of the lyrical moment it comes to symbolise. As Larkin wrote more intemperately of the poem: 'Its trouble is that it's "music", i.e. pointless crap'.[61]

Written in 1964, 'Solar' was the first poem completed after *The Whitsun Weddings* and is amongst the most purely symbolic of

Larkin's poems. It represents one of his most extravagantly romantic and Lawrentian gestures, a prayer to the sun more unembarrassedly devotional than 'Water'. Seamus Heaney has commented: 'The poem is most unexpected and daring, close to the pulse of primitive poetry . . . The poet is bold to stand uncovered in the main of light, far from the hatless one who took off his cycle-clips in awkward reverence.'[62] It reverently addresses a personified sun as an idealised image of self-sufficiency which yet pours 'unrecompensed' and gives 'for ever'. It rises above the emotional entanglements of its predecessor, 'The Dance', to escape into a sublime impersonality, an overwhelming 'You'. There is nothing else quite like it in Larkin's work and it is hard to resist the conclusion that Larkin was making an ironic comment on the poem by printing next to it 'Sad Steps' in *High Windows*. Together, they represent once again the conflicting impulses of celebration and mockery, 'the two halves of his poetic personality in dialogue'.[63]

As before, the literary allusion in Larkin's title functions ironically. The thirty-first of the Elizabethan poet Philip Sidney's sequence of love poems, *Astrophel and Stella*, begins 'With how sad steps, O moon, thou climb'st the skies,/ How silently, and with how wan a face', wherein the moon is made to stand in the poem as a symbol of dis-appointed love. Larkin's poem wants to assert, on the contrary, that the moon is just the moon, although in fact the moon ends the poem as an anti-romantic symbol. Nevertheless, although 'Sad Steps' challenges 'Solar' by debunking the stereotypes of literary symbolism, its witty inventiveness and play of linguistic registers develop strategies whereby Larkin is able to rise above mere mockery.

The poem begins with defiantly idiomatic language. Sidney's moon climbed with sad steps; the poem's speaker gropes his way back to bed 'after a piss'. Parting the curtains, he is 'startled' by the moon's brightness and unsure of his response. 'There's something laughable about this', and the off-key imagery catches the confusion of emotions: the clouds 'blow/ Loosely as cannon-smoke' and the moon is tamely apostrophised as 'High and preposterous and separate'. Then the poem tries comically for an elevated rhetoric, before collapsing gratefully into conversation and literalness:

> Lozenge of love! Medallion of art!
> O wolves of memory! Immensements! No,
>
> One shivers slightly, looking up there.

But it is from the reductive, earth-bound 'shivering' that the poem curves towards its real emotional centre. It does so by deploying a language that looks unembarrassingly empirical but catches the fullness of impressions and experience, and which in its plainness honours the moon's plainness:

> The hardness and the brightness and the plain
> Far-reaching singleness of that wide stare
>
> Is a reminder of the strength and pain
> Of being young; that it can't come again,
> But is for others undiminished somewhere.

The poem makes it appropriate that the painfully affirmative symbolic resonance of the moon should be expressed in a negative prefix: 'undiminished' (like the 'strong// Unhindered moon' of 'Dockery and Son'). The rhetorical control of the poem resists, predictably, the urge to grandeur and, more importantly, the plunge into the self-pitying brashness seen elsewhere in *High Windows*. Indeed, it achieves a more impersonal elegy by arguing its way (unlike, for example, 'Cut Grass') to an emotional centre. Like the moon, the language has a 'hardness' and 'brightness' which fend off easy sentiments either of exaltedness or of mockery. The envy of youth expressed in the conclusion carries with it 'a sense of shared endeavour'. [64] 'Sad Steps' shows ('Dublinesque' is another example) that there remain moments of integration in *High Windows*.

It is in the three central set-piece poems – 'To the Sea', 'Show Saturday' and 'The Explosion' – that these moments of integration are most fully realised. Each of them is set within a community: a seaside crowd; a country fête and a mining village. The first of them to be written, 'To the Sea', is a tribute to habit and duty. There are no metaphysical yearnings here, just a contented contemplation of ritual. The opening infinitive noun-phrase ('To step over . . . Brings . . .') establishes a sense of suspension in time which the poem celebrates in its enumeration of repeated ritual. So, the waves' 'repeated fresh collapse' and the 'white steamer stuck in the afternoon' are instances of sustained continuity, of change become stasis, just as for the poet this visit 'Brings sharply back something known long before'. Stepping over the dividing 'low wall' is to step into a realm where time seems to stand still: 'Still going on, all of it, still going on!' Even when the day begins to fade, it does so with almost unnoticeable gentleness: 'The white steamer has gone. Like breathed-on glass/ The sunlight has turned milky'. The continuity the poet feels with his own past and with his parents' past (who 'first became known' here) is extended in the observation of other families who are 'teaching their children' and 'helping the old'. So, 'through habit these do best'. The continuity of these annual visits to the seaside, of the mutuality of the generations, of the shared recognition of duty as a way of countering 'our falling short': these constitute the affirmative values of the poem. At the heart of this affirmation lies an acceptance of time's passage perceived not as division but as continuity.

'Show Saturday' expresses the same solace in communal ritual. It is a symphony of details, a gradual orchestration of difference into a wonderful harmony. Starting with the country show, it spreads outwards to absorb the rhythms of numberless individual lives. In this, the poet resembles the observer of 'The Whitsun Weddings' who memorialised what 'none/ Thought'; but now, rather than placing himself at the centre of the web, the poet is just another point of interconnection in this 'recession of skills'. For five long, elaborately constructed stanzas the poem simply *lists*: it is a cornucopia of makings and showings, even if they are all 'less than the honeycombs'. Then, as the crowd disperses, the poem tracks its participants

> to their local lives:
> To names on vans, and business calendars
> Hung up in kitchens; back to loud occasions
> In the Corn Exchange, to market days in bars,
>
> To winter coming, as the dismantled Show
> Itself dies back into the area of work.

As in the most celebratory of Larkin's poems, there is a recognition of the miraculousness of the ordinary. The integration of the individual and the universal is achieved in the poem's return

> to private addresses, gates and lamps
> In high stone one-street villages, empty at dusk,
> And side roads of small towns (sports finals stuck
> In front doors, allotments reaching down to the railway) . . .

The list insists on the singular become plural, and the parenthesis, far from mocking welfare-state sameness as some of Larkin's poems do, modestly honours shared uniqueness. So the annual Show becomes, like everything else in the poem, part of an organic rhythm, 'something people do' to disperse 'time's rolling smithy-smoke'. The poem's conclusion swells into a prayer and a command:

> something they share
> That breaks ancestrally each year into
> Regenerate union. Let it always be there.

This time, the poet is not figured as an excluded observer or unwilling participant, but as an intermediary who negotiates with the reader for 'them'. Still, the ending 'is as much a plea as an assertion' [65] and the poem's vision of a shared, common culture is willed into being by its eager accumulation of separateness. In that sense, like all Larkin's lyrics, it refuses to delude itself. Nevertheless, the poem expresses its faith in the power of lyrical perception to hold in significant order experiences that are otherwise random and arbitrary. It is as much a contrivance as the other objects on show. As Barbara Everett writes:

> The virtue of the poem is its impassive, interested, packed inventiveness . . . Within a world void of any reassuring concept, the world of sense takes on the semblance of innocence, an extraordinary steady gravity, a weighty floating-free in time and space: as the 'folk' endlessly poise on their random straw dice, and the wrestling match shines for ever against the empty sky . . . The very *un*reality of this poetic world, its beautiful hollowness and the severe limits to the kind of reassurance it can give, are really the solid terms which give poet and readers a meeting-place, like the 'great straw dice' on which 'folk sit'.[66]

When Larkin said in a radio broadcast that he wanted to write 'different kinds of poem that might be by different people', he went on by way of illustration to read 'The Explosion'. Various features of the poem are notably untypical, but its central affirmations are absolutely characteristic of the lyrical Larkin. As Peter Hollindale has shown, the poem is uncharacteristic in its 'two contrasting lines of ancestry',[67] the use of Longfellow's *Hiawatha* rhythm, and the working-class ballad of industrial disaster (and, more vaguely, the influence of Lawrence for the description of mining villages).

The trigger for the poem was a television documentary about the mining industry that Larkin watched during Christmas 1969, though the poem's values are enduring ones in Larkin's work.[68] The importance of the *Hiawatha* metre in a poem which merges death with a vision of after-life is that it is 'a verbal and experiential rhythm of continuity . . . The power of the *Hiawatha* metre is that it causes nothing to stop: condition merges with condition, like season with season, by almost imperceptible gradations'.[69] Reinforcing the effect of the metre is the alteration between verbs in the past tense and present participles. Moreover, Larkin's unrhymed triplets, though they modify Longfellow's metrics, propel the poem forward even as they frame the poem's ballad-like narrative stages. And in necessitating 'an isolated and resolving final line', Larkin's structure 'provides imaginative space for the poem's two great images of affirmation to be completed'.[70]

The narrative structure is designed to suggest circularity: we know at the opening of the explosion to follow in the middle, and the nest of lark's eggs will become the final affirmative symbol. The image of the sun recurs to mark the poem's three stages. In the morning sun 'the slagheap slept' as the men, 'Shouldering off the freshened silence', walk to work. At noon, 'there came a tremor' and as the masculine endings of the lines take hold, the 'dimmed' sun marks a pause. Then the narrative seems to cut forward, with the pastor's italicised words, to the funeral service. But the manipulation of tenses (from the continuous present of the pastor's quoted words, to the past 'It was said' and 'Wives saw men', and forward to the present participles of the momentary vision) creates the syntactical logic by which men walk 'Somehow from the sun' at the very moment it has 'dimmed' for the underground explosion. The effect of this, quite miraculously, is to annihilate the moment of death, not by meekly editing it out of the poem, but by silently building it in to what survives that moment of death. The men are unbroken, like the eggs. They have simply passed 'Through the tall gates standing open'.

In 'The Explosion', Larkin manages to modify his fear of death by making the moment of death continuous with life, so that like the closing of the day in 'To the Sea' there is an imperceptible change of state. Equally, the poem is careful not to be seduced by the wives' understandable need to see an after-life. They see only 'for a second', and it is their vision, not the poem's. The emphatic 'Somehow', typical of Larkin's indefiniteness at his most intensely lyrical moments, preserves 'the protective uncertainty which keeps a margin of reservation between the poet's needs and the risk of deceptive fulfilments'.[71] The ending is not a religious consolation. Its beauty resides in an ordering of human experience which asserts the fragile preciousness of compassion. A single line silently conjures up a network of human relationships: 'Fathers, brothers, nicknames, laughter'. These miners, 'Coughing oath-edged talk and pipe-smoke', shoulder their way into the poem's opening silence. Anonymously,

> One chased after rabbits; lost them;
> Came back with a nest of lark's eggs;
> Showed them; lodged them in the grasses.

As the man took care of these eggs, so the poem with the men. It shows them, and lodges them in their community, amongst their nameless wives and families. The poem makes them 'Larger than in life they managed'.

In choosing to conclude *High Windows* with 'The Explosion', Larkin continued the pattern of *The Less Deceived* and *The Whitsun Weddings*. He ends with poems of qualified affirmation: the enviable anonymity of the horses in 'At Grass'; the 'almost true' proof of our 'almost-instinct' about love in 'Arundel Tomb', and now the visionary intensity of 'The Explosion'. Though Larkin cited this last as a 'different kind of poem', its central concerns are ubiquitous in Larkin's work, so much of which is taken up with being 'different from yourself'. The poems he wrote after the publication of *High Windows* continue to show his obsession with questions of love, identity and death. For all their emotional power, 'The Explosion', 'To the Sea' and 'Show Saturday' represent only moments of relative serenity. For the rest, perhaps the most significant feature of the poems written in the final fifteen years or so of Larkin's life is their infrequency. The lifelong quarrel with himself about the value of art, about the circumstances of his own life, about the rival claims of the aesthete and the philistine, seem to have yielded to a silence occasionally punctuated by a few poems of 'required writing' (amongst them birthday tributes and some 'official' verses) and a few agonised meditations on death and love.

In 'Aubade', which Larkin published in 1977, the traditional dawn which separates the lovers is now a horrifying reminder of mortality. It is a poem which brings 'the solving emptiness/ That lies just under all we do' to the surface and stares at it, 'blank and true' ('Ambulances'). The confrontation is sustained in language 'resolutely declarative, unwavering in its intent, with none of the hesitation of discovery imitated in "Dockery and Son" – none of the self-doubt of the earlier poetry'.[72] As the poem broods on 'nothing more terrible, nothing more true', it can only find ways of saying the same thing in negatives drained of sublimity: 'Not to be here,/ Not to be anywhere,/ And soon'. Religion is dismissed as a pretence and 'Courage is no good:/ It means not scaring others'. Only in the final stanza, added some time after the others had been written,[73] does the poem shift its gaze.

> Meanwhile telephones crouch, getting ready to ring
> In locked-up offices, and all the uncaring
> Intricate rented world begins to rouse.
> The sky is white as clay, with no sun.
> Work has to be done.
> Postmen like doctors go from house to house.[74]

The ordinary, workaday world is 'uncaring' and 'rented'. But as always in Larkin, that world also secures his deepest affections. Tucked between the two dismissive adjectives but prominent at the beginning of the line, 'Intricate' pays tribute to whatever resists, however temporarily, the encroachments of death. It is the 'Intricacy' of 'smells of different dinners' ('Ambulances'), of 'sports finals stuck/ In front doors' ('Show Saturday'), of 'Fathers, brothers, nicknames, laughter' ('The Explosion'). A draft ending of 'Aubade' made a sense of survival more explicit:

> Postmen go
> From house to house like doctors to persuade
> Life to resume. [75]

The final 'Postmen like doctors' are emblems of that workaday world which sustains itself by individuals' mutual reliance. They contribute to that 'Intricacy', representing every tender pre-servation in Larkin's poems of an empirical, stubbornly material reality.

Honour that world as Larkin's poems do, it is a world from which he feels himself ultimately excluded. 'Love Again' rehearses with shocking intensity all the resentments and despair which finally overwhelmed Larkin as a poet. It remained unpublished in his lifetime.

> Love again: wanking at ten past three
> (Surely he's taken her home by now?),
> The bedroom hot as a bakery,
> The drink gone dead, without showing how
> To meet tomorrow, and afterwards,
> And the usual pain, like dysentery.
>
> Someone else feeling her breasts and cunt,
> Someone else drowned in that lash-wide stare,
> And me supposed to be ignorant,
> Or find it funny, or not to care,
> Even . . . but why put it into words?
> Isolate rather this element
>
> That spreads through other lives like a tree
> And sways them on in a sort of sense
> And say why it never worked for me.
> Something to do with violence
> A long way back, and wrong rewards,
> And arrogant eternity. [76]

Andrew Motion shows how the poem 'summarizes the conflicts between "life" and "art" that had shaped Larkin's whole existence'.[77] The need to 'say why it never worked for me' is why even the most triumphant of Larkin's poems are about failure, and why the poems ultimately prefer silence to words:

> Then there will be nothing I know.
> My mind will fold into itself, like fields, like snow.
>
> ('The Winter Palace'[78])

7
Larkin's Identities

In 'Posterity', Larkin pretends to construct his own epitaph. Its ostensible joke is that the poem's speaker will be posthumously saddled with an uncomprehending American biographer, just as the American will have to tolerate this boring Englishman. Otherwise so different, they are the same in feeling thwarted and forced to settle for second-best. Within this irony, Larkin plays with self-revelation, just as the opening plays with self-referentialism ('Jake Balokowsky, my biographer,/ Has this page microfilmed'). Balokowsky is in the same tradition as the self-seeking academic in 'Naturally the Foundation will Bear Your Expenses' and seems paraded mockingly before us as the biographer who will fail to pluck out the heart of the poet's mystery, getting only as far as the uncomprehending intemperateness of 'Oh, you know the thing ... One of those old-type *natural* fouled-up guys'.

But the question remains: how far do we imagine that the poet agrees with this conclusion about himself? Again, the ostensible joke is that he does not at all. The point of the poem seems to rest in the feeling that the American has got it all callously wrong. But this in turn makes the poem too sentimental, smug and vain, and the poem simply does not leave its speaker with that kind of triumph. For Balokowsky's uninhibited idiom dominates the poem, and in the characteristically cautious English irony is expressed admiring envy that 'he's no call to hide/ Some slight impatience with his destiny'. At the end, the speaker does suffer a defeat. Not only are he and Balokowsky more alike than they seem, but Balokowsky's complacent cliché might well describe the poem's speaker perfectly. The poem cuts both ways. As a poem bent on non-disclosure, it wants to say that its speaker reckons to rise above the sweeping, simple-minded psychoanalysing of an unsympathetic biographer. But the non-disclosure is suddenly the poem's most revealing aspect: Balokowsky's diagnosis is grotesquely right.

The same sort of reversal is evident in another biographical sketch, 'Self's the Man'. It seems to be an attack on the idiocy of

154

marriage by a relieved bachelor who suddenly confesses to uncertainty. But the real confession in the poem is its rebarbative smugness in arguing that 'self's the man' for everybody. Other poems disintegrate more calculatedly into self-subversive doubt: am I better than those I accuse? They do so by exploiting a multiplicity of tonal registers which undermine authorial stability. In a simple sense Larkin's poems, together and separately, are multivocal. Explicitly or implicitly, an 'I' addresses a 'you' and they thus take on the condition of speech-acts. They are 'performative' in being constructed with an explicit consciousness of the impression they are creating; their 'voices' express attitudes sometimes ecstatic (as in 'Solar' and 'Water'), often mocking, and frequently epigrammatic in pursuing a philosophical 'truth'. Even at their most declarative (as in their use of coarse language), the poems carry a highly self-conscious rhetorical persuasiveness.

The English philosopher J. L. Austin thought of all language as 'performative', that is, not so much involved in making statements as in making gestures of intention and producing calculated effects. Terry Eagleton paraphrases: 'Literature may appear to be describing the world, and sometimes actually does so, but its real function is per-formative: it uses language within certain conventions in order to bring about certain effects in a reader. It achieves something *in* the saying: it is language as a kind of material practice in itself, discourse as social action'.[1] Or, in Larkin's case, discourse as social interaction. The personae or 'masks' by which Larkin ventriloquises attitudes evolve from his command of idiom, often of caricature: the landlady's chatter in 'Mr Bleaney', the *'Then she undid her dress'* of popular fiction, the newly-wed's excited *'I nearly died'*, the academic's complacent hypocrisies in 'Naturally the Foundation will Bear Your Expenses', Balokowsky's Americanisms and finally the whole argot of advertis-ing imagery. Populated by social types and embodiments of stereo-typical attitudes, Larkin's poems foreground the metonymic aspect of language, the capacity to suggest the whole by the representative part. They are the dramatised speech-acts of a speaker who, seeming to participate in, actually manipulates the drama of his poems. George Watson has defined in terms applicable to Larkin what he calls the 'eccentric stance' in poetry:

It arises out of a highly insular tradition of conversation: amusingly semi-learned talk, richly allusive, vivified by a speaker into social performance – the British, as foreigners often remark, tending to be actors, or at least mimics – and by a speaker conscious of himself as a character and eager to impart that consciousness to others, whether as entertainment, self-defensive deceit, or both . . .[2]

Larkin once ended an interview by saying of his poems, 'Don't judge me by them. Some are better than me, but I add up to more than they do'.[3]

Fundamentally, the construction of 'selves' is a function of the way language operates in Larkin's poetry and his work represents a striking instance of Mikhail Bakhtin's descriptions of dialogic discourse. Bakhtin wanted to evolve a poetics of the novel which would account for its historical rise to pre-eminence as a genre, but the terms he used offer a helpful approach to Larkin, particularly when we remember that Larkin began to write the poems by which he came to be known at just the point he was abandoning his novels.

David Lodge has explained that for Bakhtin literary discourse is performative, that a word is not so much a two-sided sign as, in Bakhtin's words, a 'two-sided *act* . . . It is determined equally by whose word it is and for whom it is meant . . . A word is territory *shared* by both addresser and addressee, by the speaker and his interlocutor'.[4] For Bakhtin, this multi-vocal polyphony is the medium of the novel:

> Herein lies the profound distinction between prose style and poetic style . . . for the prose artist the world is full of other people's words, among which he must orient himself and whose speech characteristics he must be able to perceive with a very keen ear. He must introduce them into the plane of his own discourse, but in such a way that this plane is not destroyed. He works with a very rich verbal palette.[5]

The peculiar triumph of Larkin's lyricism is precisely to incorporate 'other people's words' in just the way described by Bakhtin. Moreover, the use of direct speech in the poems works in the way described by Lodge:

> Characters, and the persona of the authorial narrator . . . are constituted not simply by their own linguistic registers or idiolects, but by the discourses they quote and allude to.

A corollary of Bakhtin's insight is that language which in itself is flat, banal, clichéd and generally automatized can become vividly expressive when mimicked, heightened, stylized, parodied and played off against other kinds of language in the polyphonic discourse of the novel.[6]

'*My wife and I have asked a crowd of craps/ To come and waste their time and ours: perhaps/ You'd care to join us?/* In a pig's arse, friend.' This is polyphonic enough, the framing automatised formality of the social invitation synchronised with its opposite idiom, the recipient's far from automatised feelings (attributed by him to the host or actually belonging to the host?) and merging in the anti-social mutuality of 'friend' (addressed to Warlock-Williams, or to the reader, or to both?). Lodge shows how Bakhtin came to doubt that any literary text could be purely monologic, and to conclude that all literary discourse is to some extent inherently dialogic. He quotes this passage from Bakhtin:

> Doesn't the author always find himself *outside* of language in its capacity as the material of the literary work? Isn't every writer (even the purest lyric poet) always a 'playwright' insofar as he distributes all the discourses among alien voices, including that of the 'image of the author' (as well as the author's other *personae*)? It may be that every single-voiced and nonobjectal discourse is naive and inappropriate to authentic creation. The authentically creative voice can only be a *second* voice in the discourse. Only the second voice – *pure relation*, can remain nonobjectal to the end and cast no substantial and phenomenal shadow. The writer is a person who knows how to work language while remaining outside of it; he has the gift of indirect speech.[7]

The development of Larkin's poetry can be seen as the progress towards manipulating language 'while remaining outside of it', when the embarrassed aestheticism of the early lyrics gives way to the dramatisation of unaesthetic experience; when the novelist's ear for other people's words is used to construct idiolects not in plots, but in the suddenly intense moments of poems.

Bakhtin's remarks are useful because they distinguish between the writer and what he writes by reminding us of the materiality of the writer's medium. Moreover, they offer an approach to Larkin's poems which begins to get us away from the familiar Larkin criticism which describes his 'themes' (the more 'unchanging' – love, time, death, and so on – the better) or analyses his poetic style in terms of its faithfully mimetic representation of an unmediated 'reality'. This study has focused on Larkin's rhetoric, on the ways in which his poems construct themselves as speech-acts in order to persuade the reader into one point of view or another. Its primary 'theme' of identity has arisen naturally from Larkin's situation as a writer 'outside' his language. His poems are not 'confessional', because they know the fictiveness of 'self-revelation'. But they represent the effort to achieve self-definition. Balokowsky is right: the speaker's fouled-upness is *natural*. Larkin's poetry is constantly striving for what is always 'out of reach': the ultimate expression of an absolute selfhood.

The critical arguments surrounding Larkin have not changed very much since the battle-lines were drawn by Charles Tomlinson in 1957 and Al Alvarez in 1962. Tomlinson, as we have seen, interpreted the poetry of the Movement as a philistine rejection of Modernist experiment and a xenophobic ignorance of American and European examples. His review of *New Lines*, in a piece provocatively entitled 'The Middlebrow Muse', was an angry polemic which attacked the Movement, including Larkin, on a number of fronts. The first, particularly interesting in view of Bakhtin's remarks quoted above, was its brazen soliciting of the reader's approval: 'For a movement in writing which purports anti-romanticism there is at work an unconscionable amount of self-regard, of acting up to one's mirror image of oneself'. The second became a more enduring criticism: 'My own difficulty with [Larkin's] poetry is that, while I can see Mr. Larkin's achievement is, within its limits, a creditable one, I cannot escape the feeling of its intense parochialism. Moreover, the tenderly nursed sense of defeat, the self-skitting go hand in hand with an inability to place his malaise and an evident willingness to persist in it'.[8]

'Parochialism' and its variants – provincialism, xenophobia, insularity – became the charge most frequently laid against Larkin. It is hard to know just what Tomlinson meant by it, for its shades of meaning are never exactly defined. On one level, it represents a kind of metaphysical incuriousness: 'They show a singular want of vital awareness of the continuum outside themselves, of the mystery bodied over against them in the created universe, which they fail to experience with any degree of sharpness or to embody with any instress or sensuous depth . . . They seldom for a moment escape beyond the suburban mental ratio which they impose on experience'.[9] But it is difficult to escape the impression that the word 'suburban' carries a note of social distaste, an impression reinforced by Tomlinson's conclusion:

> I shall conclude by suggesting that *New Lines*, with its 'move-ment' bias, is one of the many signs of the relativity of what passes currently for literature and literary criticism. This relativity is grounded in an attitude to life, and that attitude is both widely established and rarely questioned. Its philosophy – if one can call it that – begins with a debased form of humanism which associated itself only too readily with the natural right to 'get on' and to stay on as long as possible. The 'movement' was in the first place a journalist's convenient generalisation. It is only our total relativity of standards, our want of high and objective criteria that can cause us to mistake it for significant literary fact.[10]

It is easy to detect here an anxious anti-democratic bias, a contempt for 'suburbanism' and 'relativism' which characterised some of the first hostile reactions to the Movement (and which was in fact incipient in Larkin and Amis themselves). Writing a few years later, Tomlinson used the same vocabulary. 'Instead of the conscious for-mulation of a position, one has a provincial laziness of mind adopted as a public attitude and as the framework for an equally provincial verse' and he warned against 'the provincializing effects of our suburban culture'.[11] 'Middlebrow', 'provincial', 'suburban': Tomlinson's vocabulary recurs throughout the criticism of Larkin. In the end, for all its apparent class-consciousness, Tomlinson's 'provincialism' is ultimately an aesthetic judgement, as his more recent retrospective account makes clear: 'Hadn't the deliberate narrowing . . . been merely an excuse, one asked oneself, for the British philistine . . . ? England seemed, in all senses, to be becoming an island, adrift from Europe and the past'.[12]

For a long time, the view of Larkin as empirical, sceptical, middlebrow, accessible, unpretentious and debunkingly philistine prevailed. It was precisely the image Larkin wanted to cultivate, a mask behind which he could protect the disappointed ambitions of the aesthete. Tomlinson could not know the buried history of Larkin's romantic aspirations now evident in the posthumously published poems and newly available manuscripts and private material. But the consequence was a slow recognition of the romantically aspiring nature of Larkin's poetry which he allowed to surface only sporadically in the years following *The Less Deceived*.

In 1962, the critic Al Alvarez published *The New Poetry*, a popular anthology introduced by another anti-Movement, and this time more specifically anti-Larkin, polemic. Alvarez wanted to argue that English poetry needed to return to an earlier spirit of challenge and experimentation by absorbing the examples of the most exciting Americans: Lowell, Plath and Berryman. Modern poetry had been virtually stifled by a series of 'negative feed-backs', each one a defensive rejection of what had gone before. Alvarez tended to see literary history as a series of reversals (rather than, for example, a muddled process of absorptions) and his account takes little precise regard of the social and historical circumstances in which these 'feed-backs' happened. Nevertheless, his description of Larkin's work vividly caught its contemporary appeal:

> The pieties of the Movement were as predictable as the politics of the thirties' poets. They are summed up at the beginning of Philip Larkin's 'Church-going' [*sic*] . . . This, in concentrated form, is the image of the post-war Welfare State Englishman: shabby and not concerned with his appearance; poor – he has a bike, not a car; gauche but full of agnostic piety; underfed, underpaid, overtaxed, hopeless, bored, wry. This is the third negative feed-back: an attempt to show that the poet is not a strange creature inspired; on the contrary, he is just like the man next door – in fact, he probably *is* the man next door.[13]

The problem here is the simplistic identification of some aspects of the personae in Larkin's poems with the poet himself. When he saw the anthology, Larkin joked with Conquest: 'Says I'm badly dressed, too, which I take a bit hard',[14] which makes the same point. In fact, Alvarez's target was wider than Larkin, or the Movement. The series of 'negative feed-backs' had preserved, in his view, a complacent idea 'that life in England goes on much as it always has, give or take a few minor changes in the class system'. From here, Alvarez identified the abiding limitation amongst English poets since 1930:

> . . . the concept of gentility still reigns supreme. And gentility is a belief that life is always more or less orderly, people always more or less polite, their emotions and habits more or less

decent and more or less controllable; that God, in short, is more or less good.[15]

It is worth recalling at this point that Alvarez was later to write a study of suicide called *The Savage God*. In applying his 'gentility principle' to Larkin, he is forced to overlook the disruptive elements in his work, the disturbing psychological complexity of 'Deceptions', for example, or the existential anxieties of 'Wants', 'Wires' and 'Absences' (all available to Alvarez in *The Less Deceived*). What Alvarez's description of 'gentility' (and other critics' subsequent use of it) misses is the anger in Larkin's work, the far from genteel rage that he never became the writer he wanted to be. This would have been less evident to Alvarez in 1962, but there is nothing in Larkin to support the reading of a God who is 'in short, more or less good'.

So when Alvarez offers an account of 'At Grass' to show its inferiority to Ted Hughes's 'A Dream of Horses', he does so by ignoring the metaphysical status of the horses. 'His horses are *social* creatures of fashionable race meetings and high style; emotionally, they belong to the world of the R.S.P.C.A.'[16] By contrast, 'Hughes's horses have a violent, impending presence'. Quite so: this is because Larkin wants to honour the *otherness* of the horses, their non-human anonymity, their chastening unknowability, whereas Hughes and Alvarez want to appropriate them as psychologically expressive symbols: 'they reach back, as in a dream, into a nexus of fear and sensation'.[17]

In the end, Alvarez's attack is much like Tomlinson's: Larkin's poetry is unadventurous, aesthetically and experientially timid. These were the terms in which hostility was expressed until quite recently. Colin Falck's review of *The Whitsun Weddings* in 1964 offers one of the most thoughtful criticisms of Larkin, although its basic point is the same as Tomlinson's and Alvarez's. Larkin's sense of futility, argued Falck, is posited as a necessity in most of his poems at the expense of a more humanising ambitiousness. His consolatoriness is based on the assumption that we must remain unfulfilled, an assumption which is ultimately anti-poetic. Falck goes on:

> So that by identifying himself with the drab, fantasy-haunted world of the waste land Larkin has not only downgraded the whole of real existence against an impossible absolute standard,

but has also cut the ground from under the poet's feet. The fantasy-world which he has elected to share has little to do with romanticism, because it destroys the very bridge which romanticism would construct between the ideal and the world which actually exists: the poet can no longer do anything to bring our dreams into relation with reality. The ideal, for Larkin, has become inaccessible, and being inaccessible it can only throw the real world into shadow instead of lighting it up from within. In the typical landscape of Larkin's poems the whole chiaroscuro of meaning, all polarities of life and death, good and evil, are levelled away. Farms, canals, building-plots and dismantled cars jostle one another indiscriminately – the view from the train window, with its complete randomness and detachment, is at the heart of Larkin's vision – and all of them are bathed in the same general wistfulness. There are no epiphanies.[18]

This last sentence is meant to suggest that whilst Larkin's poems might look beyond the actual, there is no access in his work to the ideal, which remains 'out of reach'. For Falck (and, for different reasons, Donald Davie after him), this remains a selling short of the poetic vocation. Falck's view depends on an absolute disjunction in Larkin's work between desire and its objects. But the actual and the ideal exist in a more symbiotic relationship, for it is the very unattainability of desire that renders it desirable. The remoteness is part of the structure of longing: the dream is precisely that which will not be brought into relation with reality. This is not so much a matter of Larkin's willed resignation and defeatism as an acknowledgement of an existential condition: the 'other' must, by definition, remain beyond us. The 'other', for Larkin, was a kind of non-being, or a state of being-other-than-himself. John Bayley has identified in Larkin a romantic tradition of non-fulfilment: 'Disillusion is a working part of the dream . . . For Larkin, dis-illusionment actually intensifies the enchanted comforts of elsewhere and becomes part of them.'[19]

Another questionable aspect of Falck's point of view was identified by Donald Davie in the course of a scrupulously troubled account of Larkin as an heir to Thomas Hardy. Like Falck, Davie notes the levelling tone with which, for example in 'The Whitsun Weddings', Larkin describes contemporary English landscapes. 'There is no meaning, no "placing," in the way preindustrial things like farms, cattle, hedges, and grass are interspersed with industrial things like chemical froth and dismantled cars. And for Larkin indeed this seems to be one of the rules of the game; there is to be no historical perspective, no measuring of present against past . . . Betjeman is the most nostalgic of poets, Larkin the least'.[20] But with the evidence of other poems of Larkin's which do celebrate natural presences (and Davie was probably writing his account before the publication of 'Going, Going'), Davie reckons that Larkin chose to make himself 'numb to the nonhuman creation in order to stay compassionate towards the human'.[21] Davie draws the political implication: Larkin tolerates the squalor of the human scene for the sake of a democratic humanism. Like Hardy, Larkin 'settles for parliamentary democracy as a shabby, unavoidable second-best'.[22] This is what Falck cannot have the poet do, for on his showing the poet must aspire to the ideal. Falck wrote, 'In rejecting Larkin's particular brand of "humanism" I may seem to be asking for the kind of "right wing" violence to which D. H. Lawrence was sometimes led. I think perhaps I am'.[23] Davie's point is that however appealing Falck's élitism, the cost is too great in human terms. 'Hardy and Larkin may have sold poetry short; but at least neither of them sold it so short as to make the poet less than a human being. And part of being human is being a citizen of some commonwealth. I can sympathize with Falck's outraged refusal of the diminished world which Larkin's poetry proffers as the only one available to him; but he cannot escape that world as easily as he thinks.'[24]

Yet Davie cannot so easily accept Larkin's patiently diminished expectations when the non-human is devalued for the sake of the human. His reading of 'Here' emphasises how 'every nonurban thing comes along with a negating or cancelling epithet', that the ultimate pastoral 'shall be among the cut-price stores, and nowhere else'. From this, Davie concludes that Larkin seems '*determined* not to be helped nor instructed by things that plainly he responds to keenly'.[25] But those negating and cancelling epithets are part of Larkin's vocabulary of assent. They signify the restorative otherness of the natural and elemental world. 'Unnoticed' leaves, 'Hidden' flowers, 'neglected' waters and 'neutral' distance represent a life consolingly beyond the human, unmolested, existentially 'out of reach'.

Davie's honouring of Larkin's democratic fair-mindedness is a useful corrective to the portrait of himself Larkin sometimes chose to proffer in his letters. But Davie's uneasy tolerance of Larkin's selling poetry short lasted only until the appearance of Larkin's *Oxford Book of Twentieth Century English Verse* in 1973. To Davie 'This volume is a calamity, and it's very painful that it falls to me to say so'. Davie found himself 'Recoiling aghast from page after page of the anthology' in the face of Larkin's evident philistinism:

> To be, as Philip Larkin is, the author of many poems generally esteemed and loved brings with it certain responsibilities. And in this anthology Larkin shirks those responsibilities quite shamefully. The poems that we have loved, that we love and cherish still, turn out to have been written by a man who thinks that poetry is a private indulgence or a professional entertainer's patter or, at most, a symptom for social historians to brood over. It is a grievous misfortune that in him an exquisite talent for poetry seems to go along with a mocking scepticism about the possibility of critical discrimination among poems.

Davie concluded: 'No one who has read Larkin's poems attentively need be surprised to know that he is as sceptical about poetry as about most other values'.[26] Here Davie touches on the creative and, in the end, self-destructive polarities in Larkin. Davie was right: Larkin should not have undertaken to compile the anthology, not just because it drew him into personal controversy (as he gloomily predicted in his letters to Barbara Pym) but because, committed in public to wearing the philistine mask, the delicate negotiation with the aesthete in him was disrupted irrevocably. There were not many poems after 1973.

The most loyal of Larkin's admirers, however, rescued the anthology in the same terms they used to praise Larkin himself. The orthodox view of Larkin is as the representative of an authentic English tradition all but buried by modernism but recoverable through Housman, Hardy, Edward Thomas and Larkin. Anthony Thwaite has aptly summarised the virtues Larkin is thought pre-eminently to possess:

> His themes – love, change, disenchantment, the mystery and inexplicableness of the past's survival and death's finality – are unshakably major. So too, I think, are the assurance of his cadences and the inevitable rightness of his language at their best . . . And those haunting closing lines to many poems . . . have an authentic gravity, a memorable persistence.[27]

The critical literature on Larkin has been thoroughly summarised, from different perspectives, by Guido Latré and Stephen Regan.

Regan offers a historicist reading of the poems (though in fact Davie's remarks on Larkin already referred to constitute a kind of proto-historicist reading). Regan argues that the thematic approach leads to 'a reductive reading of the poems by concentrating on a monotonous range of topics' and 'also responds to ideas in a patently unhistorical way'.[28] Similarly, practical criticism is hermetically sealed within its own undisclosed ideological prejudices. 'In application, practical criticism claims to be neutral and disinterested in its view of the world, and yet its preoccupation with "order" in the modern world clearly suggests an important social and political purpose'.[29] Above all, these traditional approaches pay little regard to 'the relationship between the poems and a rapidly changing social context'.[30] Linguistic approaches, what Regan calls the study of 'language in use', mostly fail to get 'very close to issues of interpretation' and similarly 'show very little regard for the social and historical contexts in which poetry is written and read'.[31] Historicism offers, says Regan, a contextual approach which recognises the formal and stylistic devices by which a poem mediates a particular image of society. 'Historicist criticism tends to regard "literature" as *social discourse*, a language activity within a particular social structure. The varieties of language found in different literary texts "constitute" different world views or interpretations of "reality"'.[32] Whilst Regan's rigour usefully uncovers some of the vague or hidden assumptions in the work of both admirers and critics of Larkin, it runs the risk of rendering literature, in Davie's words, 'a symptom for social historians to brood over'.

Guido Latré's approach is structuralist. He divides Larkin criticism into two broad categories: one dealing with Larkin's 'énoncé' and the other his 'enunciation' – which seem to mean just the same as 'theme' and 'style'. Each category is sub-divided into 'monistic' and 'dualistic' interpretations. 'Monistic' interpretations 'emphasise mainly one pole in the opposition, whereas the latter determine the essence of Larkin's poetry as a tension between two equally strong antagonistic forces'.[33] Thus, monistic writing on Larkin's themes might interpret Larkin as fundamentally empirical, 'unillusioned, with a metaphysical zero in his bones' (Calvin Bedient) and practising 'The Art of the Real' (the title of a study of modern poetry by Eric Homberger, in which Larkin is described as having the 'saddest heart in the post-war supermarket'). On the other side is a criticism which sees Larkin as metaphysically yearning, epiphanic, searching for another reality to supplant the one he so obviously debunks. Dualistic criticism is concerned to accept these polarities in Larkin and to describe his work in terms of the tensions in it between the 'real' and the 'ideal'.

Both Latré and Regan note how the more recent criticism of Larkin has been anxious to see him variously as a romantic, a symbolist, even a post-modernist. John Bayley has consistently made an impressive case for Larkin's essential romanticism. 'Larkin by temperament is a straightforward romantic of the older school – the school that includes both Housman and Keats – who has introduced it in a later kind of feeling for words and for poetic effect, "the imagination of silence" as a disciple of Mallarmé called it. It is the silence of elsewhere, the place we cannot live in, as the poem "Days" tells us, but which the words of this poetry continually and unobtrusively suggest'.[34] According to Bayley, the poet whom Larkin most resembles is Keats. For both, 'romanticism is the most intense aspect of a common reality, an elsewhere conjured up by the soberly precise insistence on the banality of the here and now'.[35] Where earlier critics read Larkin as lamenting the impossibility of fulfilment, Bayley recognises that in Larkin the impossibility is part of the desire. As for Keats's figures on the Grecian Urn, so for Larkin: unfulfilment is both the pain and pleasure of desire. Hence the romantic charge in Larkin's poems of the vocabulary of nothingness. 'For Larkin romance is not just still bringing up the 9.15; it beckons at the end of every human vista in the shape of death, sex, or just emptiness, the comfort of absence'.[36]

Other critics have noted the transcendental yearnings in Larkin's poetry. Like Seamus Heaney before him, M. W. Rowe, for example, suggests that 'beneath the cautious empirical surface of his work there is a cluster of primordial images – of sunlight, space and water – which gives us a clue as to the true centre of his poetic personality'.[37] Rowe identifies one of the major paradoxes in Larkin's work. 'In one sense, emptiness and absence of self is Larkin's supreme vision of happiness, liberation and transcendence, in another it is his overwhelming dread'.[38]

The most ambitiously symbolist reading of Larkin has come from Barbara Everett. In 'Philip Larkin: After Symbolism' she places Larkin as an ambivalent inheritor of modernism. 'His poems appear to have profited from a kind of heroic struggle *not* to be modernistic, not to be mere derivative footnotes to a Symbolism as much disapproved of as admired; they have wished to be, not merely after, but *well* after Eliot.'[39] This is to make Larkin's well-known anti-modernist pronouncements the obverse of a more complicit sympathy. Rather than seeing Larkin as a recidivist to a native tradition unspoiled by modernist influences, as many of Larkin's admirers do, his being well *after* Eliot makes him the inheritor of modernism's aspirations and dislocations. Everett locates for 'Sympathy in White Major', for example, a complex history of borrowings and allusions amongst French sources in Baudelaire, Mallarmé and Gautier. And in 'Larkin's Edens', she unearths from beneath the 'realistic reporter whose detachment from what he sees . . . is explained as the writer's disaffiliation of mood' a strangely 'secret poet': 'Larkin's great art is to appear to achieve the literal while in fact doing something altogether other; his three volumes of major verse are the odd reticent triumph of a self-undercutting artist . . . And the results in Larkin's case are so far from the sociological, and so other than the dreary, that the poet might be described as creating the most potent contemporary images of Eden'.[40]

The performative element of Larkin's work, its construction of a particular kind of poetic 'personality', offers material for reading Larkin as a 'post-modernist'. Peter MacDonald Smith isolates the element of 'display' in the poems and the way they work to create distance between the 'poet' and the characters in the poems who are disapproved of. He concludes:

> . . . it is uncanny how often Larkin's themes strike one as also the themes of postmodernism: the prominence of the individual and the conversion of his life into art; the division between the poet and 'the poet' – that degree of detachment that leaves the reader unsure whether to curse or bless, to sympathise or to condemn; the reader's more general uncertainty whether to put faith in the poet, and then which attitude or course of action the poet is in sympathy with; the poet's own unease here, and the sense of one course of action cancelling out another, and neither being obviously for the best; the contraction into frustration, silence and nihilism . . .[41]

The construction of identities was noted by Andrew Motion's 1982 study of Larkin, a book which consolidated the effort over twenty-five years to answer Tomlinson's criticism of Larkin. Larkin's 'tenderly nursed sense of defeat' represents one side of the argument with himself about his own artistic aspirations. 'As a young man, this determination to shed all traces of illusion was the outward and social sign of his inward and literary intentions: it was the expression of his attempts to destroy his original Yeatsian mask. Now, in his maturity, the attitudes themselves have become a mask – one that is intensely self-knowing, as well as protective.'[42] For Motion, Larkin achieved

> more than any other living poet to solve the crisis that beset British poetry after the modernists had entered its bloodstream. He has not only made evident what Edna Longley called 'a significant coincidence and continuity of effort' with the interrupted English tradition; he has revitalized existing strengths by introducing them to elements of the poetic revolution by which they were challenged.[43]

In Motion's view, Larkin re-invigorates a 'native' tradition by marrying it to some aspects of an 'alien' modernism, which is perhaps a way of allowing Larkin to have the best of both worlds. More to the point, in the earlier quotation Motion isolates the protean nature of Larkin's 'masks', the self-protective pose of iconoclasm which also looks inward and becomes 'intensely self-knowing'. In returning to 'Posterity', we can see Larkin once again exploring fundamental questions about individual identity.

'Posterity' is an Englishman's view of an American's view of an Englishman. It collides attitudes by dealing in stereotypes: the American's jeans and sneakers; the Coke machine; the Englishman's periphrastic irony ('Some slight impatience with his destiny') compared with the American's frank colloquialisms ('I'm stuck with this old fart' – but not as stuck as the old fart himself is). At the centre of Larkin's poetry is the pursuit of self-definition, a self which feels threatened by the proximity of others but which fears that without relationship with otherness the self has no validity. Though the argument often takes the form of solitariness and selfishness set against sociability and selflessness, it is not really an argument about the profit and pains of loneliness. Fundamentally, Larkin's is an existential argument about the nature of individual identity, about the existential authority of choice and chance, about the articulation of an absolute self. Larkin approached these issues through the vocabulary of separateness, of exclusion and difference, establishing a kind of negative self-definition. His sense of identity is often expressed in the vocabulary of nullity and anonymity, suggesting both the ultimate desire for oblivion and an absolute terror of death. In the face of these teasing negatives and the vocabulary of denial, critics have been happier to construct a national identity for Larkin, perceiving in him a defining voice of Englishness.

In 'Englands of the Mind', Seamus Heaney adduced Larkin as representing a national attitude. 'The loss of imperial power, the failure of economic nerve, the diminished influence of Britain inside Europe, all this has led to a new sense of the shires, a new valuing of the native English experience'.[44] The particular 'England' represented in Larkin is identified in the ancestry of Larkin's language:

> What we hear is a stripped standard English voice, a voice indeed with a unique break and remorseful tone, but a voice that leads back neither to the thumping beat of Anglo–Saxon nor to the Gregorian chant of the Middle Ages. Its ancestry begins, in fact, when the Middle Ages are turning secular, and plays begin to take their place beside the Mass as a form of communal telling and knowing.[45]

Heaney goes on to identify Larkin's social representativeness and tolerance in terms reminiscent of Donald Davie, and certainly more generously and disinterestedly than some other recent critics. 'He is a poet, indeed, of composed and tempered English nationalism, and his voice is the not untrue, not unkind voice of post-war England . . .'[46]

But the nationalism Heaney has in mind is the 'defensive love of their territory which was once shared only by those poets whom we might call colonial',[47] for Larkin committed himself to a provincial identity which is the paradigm of the insider/outsider figure so common in his poetry. Like Terry Whalen, Robert Crawford has located features of modernism in Larkin, especially in his use of demotic language: '. . . so often Larkin achieves his lyricism by an aggressively anti-literary opening that deploys the demotic which Modernism had brought into high art'.[48] Furthermore, 'Larkin, like so many of the Modernist writers, is a "provincial", rather than simply a poet of the English cultural centre'.[49] Living on the margins was not only a geographical fact for Larkin, but an imaginative site as well, where 'here' met 'elsewhere' and beyond the margin lay endlessness. Tomlinson's old charge of 'parochialism' actually begins to identify one of Larkin's most aspiring situations: at the limit, exposed to the beyond.

One of the most intelligent analyses of Larkin's national identity has come from Neil Corcoran, who finds in Larkin's poems about social ritual and national culture not only the obviously displaced feelings of religious devotion but a much more problematic assent than at first appears. 'The Importance of Elsewhere', as we have noted, laments the loss of a self-validating sense of difference on the poet's return from Belfast to England. Corcoran suggests that the imperialistic militarism of the band in 'The March Past' which brings 'a blind// Astonishing remorse for things now ended' belongs to 'a conception of an Englishness as the repository of value and identity for this poet who could find precious little of either anywhere else'. Corcoran translates this, and the unironic treatment of 'The differently-dressed servants' in 'MCMXIV', into a kind of willed nostalgia: 'the compulsions of nostalgia betray Larkin himself into an odd kind of historical "innocence" '.[50] On the other hand, Corcoran (and Tom Paulin too) might note that 'The March Past' is written as a swirl of confused and intense visions – the 'blind' remorse is also blinded – of which the poem can make little sense, and which are just as likely to relate to Larkin's having parted from his former fiancée as anything else. Corcoran is in danger of forcing an assumptive reading on to a poem which takes care to deal in an indefinite experience.

Corcoran argues that nostalgia overwhelms historical accuracy in such poems as 'To the Sea', 'Show Saturday' and 'The Explosion'. He emphasises the disjunction between the speaker and the community in the first two poems, and notes their creation of a pastoral 'no-time'. Of 'The Explosion', he asks: 'Did miners ever engage in this kind of activity on the way *to* work?' Thus, these poems represent 'fantasies of an impossibly idealised community',[51] idealised because the speaker separates himself from them. That separation, as we have seen, is not necessarily a fictionalising, artificial de-historicising of England, but part of a wider argument about separateness and communality, about the individual self as a perpetual outsider. (Of Larkin's nationalism, Corcoran could not have known what Andrew Motion's biography parenthetically revealed. One of the best known photographs of Larkin shows him sitting demurely on the large sign which says 'England' at Coldstream on the English/Scottish border; 'immediately before posing he had urinated copiously just behind the word'.[52])

As language becomes more multivocal in Larkin's poems, so they become more rhetorically devious in portraying versions of himself.

Anxiously preoccupied with marriage and death, with solitude and communality, the poems pursue the nature of identity by nurturing a precious reticence. 'Something to do with violence/ A long way back, and wrong rewards,/ And arrogant eternity'('Love Again'): disclosure gratefully evaporates in the frustrated vagueness of 'Something to do with'. Tom Paulin has perceived in Larkin's reticence a quintessentially English strategy and emotional woundedness.

> Larkin speaks not for the imperial male – too transcendental a subject that – but for the English male, middle-class, professional, outwardly confident, controlled and in control. The history of that distinctive personality has yet to be written, but anyone who has observed it as a phenomenon, as a distinctive pattern of behaviour and attitude, is bound to see Larkin as a secret witness to what it feels like to be imprisoned in a personality that 'something hidden from us chose'. Thus Larkin's favourite romantic value, 'solitude', designates the consciousness of the autonomous English male professional. It refers not to physical isolation, but to a consciousness which has been moulded by upbringing and education to manage and govern. Such personalities . . . are seldom attractive, but what is so lovable about Larkin's persona is the evident discomfort he feels with the shape of the personality he has been given. Angry at not being allowed to show emotion, he writhes with anxiety inside that sealed bunker which is the English ethic of privacy. He journeys into the interior, into the unknown heart – the maybe missing centre – of Englishness.[53]

For Paulin, part of Larkin's Englishness is an imperialist nostalgia. At this point, he comes close to caricaturing the poems. Larkin's lyricism persuades us 'to miss Larkin's real theme – national decline'. Thus, the falling autumn leaves in 'Afternoons' are 'rather like colonies dropping out of the empire' and the young mothers' sense of having been pushed to the side of their own lives is a metaphor for 'fading imperial power'. From this perspective, 'The March Past' is an English Protestant royalist's fiercely pro-imperial lament, and 'At Grass' tells of the threat felt by an imagination nostalgically Edwardian in the face of modern social democracy. The argument against marriage thus becomes a plea for an autonomy equivalent to national sovereignty. By thus identifying Larkin with a set of

English nationalistic nostalgias, Paulin can use one stick to beat the other: Larkin represents a damaging sort of English culture, and a particular element of the English Establishment has taken Larkin to its heart as one of its own.

Paulin's interpretation rests on a deteminedly ideological view of language and on a questionable allegorising: 'The autumn leaves fall in ones and twos, rather like colonies dropping out of the empire'. 'Rather like' begs a good deal of indulgence. For Paulin, the lyric voice 'promises an exit from history into personal emotion', but his argument turns on there being no escape from 'social experience'.[54] So for Paulin, Larkin's imagined sites of solitude, the 'padlocked cube of light', the isolated fortress of the lighthouse, the high windows of the bachelor flat and library office, are versions of Yeats's mystic symbol of the platonic poet in his ancient tower. But English reticence cannot reveal that kind of romanticism, and so Larkin conceals his innermost sense of himself behind masks of pretended disclosure and self-disgust. The poems protect an ultimate privacy, 'his commitment to what Coleridge in his poem to Wordsworth terms "the dread watch-tower of man's absolute self" '.[55] So Paulin concludes that 'In that distinctively embarrassed English manner he had to bury his pride in his artistic creations under several sackfuls of ugly prejudices'.

Paulin's powerful argument returns us again to the struggle between the aesthete and the philistine in Larkin, the aesthete secretly committed to a solitary Yeatsian vocation, the philistine having to be reticently sociable, speaking for 'that gnarled and angry puritanism which is so deeply ingrained in the culture'.[56] Paulin wants to use Larkin to attack a certain kind of Englishness and, in turn, a certain kind of Englishness to attack Larkin, so that he sees behind the poems 'the very cunning and very wounded personality of a poet whose sometimes rancid prejudices are part of his condition, part of the wound'.[57] The 'padlocked cube of light' is the Englishman's fastness, the ultimate privacy to which he can retreat in solitude. Paulin thus says that for Larkin, solitude has a 'romantic value'. But the poem from which this image comes, 'Dry-Point', in truth offers no such romanticism. The cube of light is not only padlocked, but allows 'no right of entry'. It is inviolable, because existentially beyond us. It does not protect the costive Englishman from 'the other'; it *is* the other. It is that condition of desirelessness, of emptiness, of anonymity, of sentient oblivion which in Larkin's work is felt as an existential absolute. It is Paulin who romanticises Larkin's yearnings into the the reflexes of a national identity. For Larkin, the attempt to define himself, whether by relating the 'self' to marriage, or other people, or death, was a more purely existential problem. It meant asking what about the self was unique or universal, contingent or absolute, isolated or connected.

The ending of Larkin's 'Love Again', which characteristically reveals by withdrawing, carries something else hidden too. The manuscript draft ended:

> Something to do with difference
> A long way back . . .

with 'difference' amended to 'violence'.[58] 'Violence' is more mysterious and apparently disclosing; but the erased 'difference' tells a truer story. Larkin's poetry is the pursuit of difference, the thing just out of reach, the being different from yourself. In demarcating difference, in remaining the privileged outsider, Larkin was tracing, in Richard Rorty's words, 'what made his I different from all the other I's'.[59] His outsiderness was an outsiderness to language as well, manipulating it as a dialogic negotiation with otherness: personae, caricatures, the reader. Ultimately, his poems create a community of difference: uncles shouting smut, mothers loud and fat, girls marked off unreally from the rest, grim head-scarved wives, young mothers at swing and sandpit, the men you meet of an afternoon, Dockery and son, and, fundamentally, writer and reader. They pay tribute to the universality of uniqueness, expressing a tender regard for the other individual selves in relation to which his own self is defined. When his poetry turns away from society, it is to confront those abiding elemental presences which clarify loneliness as 'oneness'. Its yearning for 'nowhere', 'unfenced existence', the annihilation of self in an infinity of vacancy, is the expression of a desire to merge difference in an absolute unity. In an early poem called 'Continuing to Live', Larkin wondered about the value of defining his own identity:

> And what's the profit? Only that, in time,
> We half-identify the blind impress
> All our behavings bear, may trace it home.
>   But to confess,

> On that green evening when our death begins,
> Just what it was, is hardly satisfying,
> Since it applied only to one man once,
>   And that one dying.[60]

Hence, the effort in Larkin's poems is to find continuities, the something rather than the nothing to be said. Finding continuities becomes a way of defining the self not in terms of separateness, but in its sensitiveness to otherness. Thus, Larkin's poems speak to us and for us in their unique and representative individuality, in their need to define 'the blind impress which chance has given him, to make a self for himself by redescribing that impress in terms which are, if only marginally, his own'.[61]

Notes

References to material held in the Philip Larkin Archive lodged in the Brynmor Jones Library, University of Hull (BJL), are given as file numbers preceded by 'DPL'.

1. PHILIP LARKIN

1. Harry Chambers, 'Meeting Philip Larkin', in *Larkin at Sixty*, ed. Anthony Thwaite (London: Faber and Faber, 1982) p. 62.
2. John Haffenden, *Viewpoints: Poets in Conversation* (London, Faber and Faber, 1981) p. 127.
3. Christopher Ricks, *Beckett's Dying Words* (Oxford: Oxford University Press, 1993).
4. D. J. Enright, 'Down Cemetery Road: the Poetry of Philip Larkin', in *Conspirators and Poets* (London: Chatto & Windus, 1966) p. 142.
5. Hugo Roeffaers, 'Schriven tegen de Verbeelding', *Streven*, vol. 47 (December 1979) pp. 209–22.
6. Andrew Motion, *Philip Larkin: A Writer's Life* (London: Faber and Faber, 1993).
7. Philip Larkin, *Required Writing* (London: Faber and Faber, 1983) p. 48.
8. See *Selected Letters of Philip Larkin 1940–1985*, ed. Anthony Thwaite (London: Faber and Faber, 1992) pp. 648–9.
9. DPL 2 (in BJL).
10. DPL 5 (in BJL).
11. Kingsley Amis, *Memoirs* (London: Hutchinson, 1991) p. 52.
12. Philip Larkin, Introduction to *Jill* (London: The Fortune Press, 1946; rev. edn. Faber and Faber, 1975) p. 12.
13. Donald Davie, *Thomas Hardy and British Poetry* (London: Routledge & Kegan Paul, 1973) p. 64.
14. *Required Writing*, p. 297.
15. Blake Morrison, 'In the grip of darkness', *The Times Literary Supplement*, 14–20 October 1988, p. 1152.
16. Lisa Jardine, 'Saxon violence', *Guardian*, 8 December 1992.
17. Bryan Appleyard, 'The dreary laureate of our provincialism', *Independent*, 18 March 1993.
18. Ian Hamilton, 'Self's the man', *The Times Literary Supplement*, 2 April 1993, p. 3.
19. DPL 13 (in BJL). Quoted by Motion, *A Writer's Life*, p. 56.
20. See Stephen Regan, *Philip Larkin* (Basingstoke: Macmillan, 1992).
21. DPL 13 (in BJL).
22. DPL 14 (in BJL).
23. DPL 13 (in BJL).

24. DPL 23 (in BJL).
25. DPL 23 (in BJL).
26. DPL 5 (in BJL).
27. DPL 28 (in BJL).
28. Philip Larkin, *Collected Poems*, ed. Anthony Thwaite (London: The Marvell Press and Faber and Faber, 1988; rev. edn. 1990) p. xvii.
29. DPL 7 (in BJL).
30. DPL 7 (in BJL).
31. DPL 4 (in BJL).
32. DPL 3 (in BJL).
33. DPL 7 (in BJL).

2. THE EARLY POEMS

1. 'Not Like Larkin', *Listener*, 17 August 1972, p. 209.
2. Larkin, *Collected Poems*, p. 221.
3. See, for example, Noel Hughes, 'The Young Mr Larkin', in *Larkin at Sixty*, pp. 17–22 and Kingsley Amis, *Memoirs*, pp. 51–64.
4. *Selected Letters*, p. 11. As Thwaite notes, the reference misquotes Isherwood: 'my fatal facility for pastiche'.
5. Philip Larkin, Introduction to *The North Ship* (London: The Fortune Press, 1945; rev. edn. Faber and Faber, 1966) p. 8.
6. Ibid., p. 9.
7. Ibid., p. 10.
8. 'Not The Place's Fault', in *An Enormous Yes: in memoriam Philip Larkin (1922–1985)*, ed. Harry Chambers (Calstock: Peterloo Poets, 1986) p. 53.
9. Edward Mendelson, Preface to *W. H. Auden: Selected Poems* (London: Faber and Faber, 1979) p. ix.
10. From an unpublished autobiographical essay written in 1943, quoted in Motion, *A Writer's Life*, pp. 43–4.
11. *Required Writing*, p. 123.
12. Mendelson, *Preface to W. H. Auden: Selected Poems*, p. xiii.
13. See A. T. Tolley, *My Proper Ground: A Study of the Work of Philip Larkin and its Development* (Edinburgh: Edinburgh University Press, 1991) p. 5.
14. Larkin, *Collected Poems*, p. 235.
15. Ibid., p. 263.
16. Ibid., p. 247.
17. *Selected Letters*, pp. 5–6.
18. Ibid., pp. 34–5.
19. Quoted in Janice Rossen, *Philip Larkin: His Life's Work* (Hemel Hempstead: Harvester Wheatsheaf, 1989) p. 7.
20. Quoted in Terry Whalen, *Philip Larkin and English Poetry* (Basingstoke: Macmillan, 1986; rev. edn. 1990) p. 71. Larkin's later poem, 'Solar', bears revealing similarities to this passage.
21. Quoted in Motion, *A Writer's Life*, p. 57.

22. For further connections between Larkin and Lawrence, see Whalen, *Philip Larkin and English Poetry.*

23. Interview with Ian Hamilton, *London Magazine*, vol. 4, no. 8 (November 1964) p. 72.

24. Regan, *Philip Larkin*, p. 67. See also Bernard Bergonzi, *Wartime and Aftermath: English Literature and its Background 1939–1960* (Oxford: Oxford University Press, 1993) pp. 54–80.

25. Regan, *Philip Larkin*, pp. 71 and 77.

26. *Selected Letters*, p. 55.

27. See Larkin's retrospective essay, 'Vernon Watkins: an Encounter and a Re–encounter', in *Required Writing*, pp. 40–4.

28. *Selected Letters*, p. 56.

29. Ibid., p. 93.

30. Ibid., p. 59.

31. Quoted in Motion, *A Writer's Life*, p. 85. Years later, Larkin spoke of 'That shit Yeats, farting out his histrionic rubbish'. See R. J. C. Watt, '"Scragged by embryo–Leavises": Larkin reading his poems', *Critical Survey*, vol. 1, no. 2 (1989) pp. 172–5.

32. For specific echoes of Yeats in Larkin's work, see Edna Longley, 'Larkin, Edward Thomas and the Tradition', in *Phoenix*, nos. 11/12 (Autumn & Winter 1973/4) pp. 63–89.

33. Introduction to *The North Ship*, p. 10.

34. See Motion, *A Writer's Life*, p. 81.

35. *Selected Letters*, p. 374.

36. Introduction to *The North Ship*, p. 8.

37. Andrew Motion, *Philip Larkin* (London: Methuen, 1982) p. 33.

38. Interview with Ian Hamilton, *London Magazine*, vol. 4, no. 8 (November 1964) p. 72.

39. Motion, *Philip Larkin*, p. 15.

40. Quoted in Rossen, *Philip Larkin: His Life's Work*, p. 2.

41. Quoted in James Booth, *Philip Larkin: Writer* (Hemel Hempstead: Harvester Wheatsheaf, 1992) p. 15.

42. Ibid.

43. *Selected Letters*, p. 110.

44. Ibid., p. 147.

45. Ibid., p. 152.

46. Quoted in Booth, *Philip Larkin: Writer*, p. 21.

47. *Selected Letters*, p. 116.

48. *Jill*, pp. 242–3.

49. Philip Larkin, *A Girl in Winter* (London: Faber and Faber, 1947; re-issued, 1975) p. 248.

50. Larkin, *Collected Poems*, pp. 270–1.

51. Motion, *A Writer's Life*, p. 101.

52. *Required Writing*, p. 68.

53. Larkin, *Collected Poems*, p. 19.

54. *Selected Letters*, p. 144.

55. Ibid., p. 115.

56. Larkin, *Collected Poems*, pp. 8–9, 12 and 20 respectively.

57. Introduction to *The North Ship*, p. 10.

58. Motion, *A Writer's Life*, p. 359.
59. *Required Writing*, p. 172.
60. Ibid., p. 147.
61. Hardy's notebook, 1 July 1879.
62. *Required Writing*, pp. 175–6.
63. Larkin, *Collected Poems*, p. 21.
64. For a discussion of Larkin's use of metonymy, see David Lodge, 'Philip Larkin: the Metonymic Muse', in *Philip Larkin: The Man and His Work*, ed. Dale Salwak (Basingstoke: Macmillan, 1989) pp. 118–28.
65. Larkin, *Collected Poems*, pp. 23, 22, 24–5, 28, and 26 respectively.
66. Quoted in Peter Ferguson, 'Philip Larkin's *XX Poems*: The Missing Link', in *Philip Larkin 1922–1985: A Tribute*, ed. George Hartley (London: The Marvell Press, 1988) p. 156.
67. *Required Writing*, p. 47.
68. *Selected Letters*, p. 164.
69. *Required Writing*, p. 62.
70. See Motion, *A Writer's Life*, pp. 196–7.
71. Larkin, *Collected Poems*, pp. 45, 50, and 64 respectively.
72. Ibid., pp. 38 and 34.
73. Ibid., p. 46.
74. Ibid., pp. 62, 58, and 59 respectively.
75. Ibid., p. 40.
76. Ibid., p. 51.
77. Ibid., p. 55.
78. Ibid., pp. 56–7.

3.   *THE LESS DECEIVED*

1. See Booth, *Philip Larkin: Writer*, p. 112.
2. Quoted in George Hartley, 'Nothing To Be Said', in *Philip Larkin 1922–1985: A Tribute*, p. 299.
3. Ibid., p. 300.
4. Booth, *Philip Larkin: Writer*, p. 127.
5. *Selected Letters*, p. 110.
6. Quoted in Haffenden, *Viewpoints*, p. 123.
7. Quoted in Booth, *Philip Larkin: Writer*, p. 21.
8. DPL 3 (in BJL).
9. Quoted in David Lodge, *After Bakhtin: Essays on Criticism and Fiction* (London: Routledge, 1990) p. 98.
10. DPL 5 (in BJL).
11. *Selected Letters*, p. 154.
12. Ibid.
13. Ibid., p. 156.
14. Ibid., p. 157.
15. George Hartley, 'No Right Of Entry', in *Philip Larkin 1922–1985: A Tribute*, pp. 136–7.
16. Larkin, *Collected Poems*, p. 36.

17. See, for example, Regan, *Philip Larkin*, p. 64; J. Goode, 'The More Deceived: A Reading Of Deceptions', in *Philip Larkin 1922–1985: A Tribute*, pp. 126–34; Graham Holderness, 'Reading "Deceptions" – a dramatic conversation', *Critical Survey*, vol. 1, no. 2 (1989) pp. 122–30.

18. Rossen, *Philip Larkin: His Life's Work*, pp. 89–90.

19. All quotations from Mayhew in Goode, 'The More Deceived'.

20. For a discussion of the significance of light imagery in Larkin's poetry, see Seamus Heaney, 'The Main of Light', in *Larkin at Sixty*, pp. 131–8.

21. Goode, 'The More Deceived', p. 133.

22. Booth, *Philip Larkin: Writer*, p. 160.

23. Andrew Motion identifies the phrase as one Larkin 'dreaded hearing as a child whenever he reached the head of a queue at school or in shops: it meant he would shortly have to speak, which would be embarrassing because of his stammer'. See *A Writer's Life*, p. 208. The phrase also carries a note of black comedy as a deathly 'next to go . . .'.

24. See Rossen, *Philip Larkin: His Life's Work*, p. 17.

25. Worksheets of 'At Grass' in *Phoenix*, nos 11/12 (Autumn & Winter, 1973/4) p. 93.

26. Simon Petch, *The Art of Philip Larkin* (Sydney: Sydney University Press, 1981) p. 60.

27. Booth, *Philip Larkin: Writer*, p. 99.

28. Tolley, *My Proper Ground*, p. 180.

29. See, for example, Tolley, *My Proper Ground*, p. 120, and Petch, *The Art of Philip Larkin*, p. 60.

30. Larkin in *Poet's Choice*, ed. Paul Engle and Joseph Langland (New York: Dial Press, 1962) p. 202.

31. Booth, *Philip Larkin: Writer*, p. 161.

32. *Poet's Choice*, p. 202.

33. Booth, *Philip Larkin: Writer*, p. 162.

4.   LARKIN IN THE MOVEMENT

1. Quoted in Tolley, *My Proper Ground*, p. 85.

2. *Required Writing*, p. 20.

3. Ibid., p. 22.

4. Amis, *Memoirs*, p. 52.

5. Introduction to *Jill*, p. 12. See also *Required Writing*, p. 18.

6. Tolley, *My Proper Ground*, p. 138.

7. Introduction to *Anthology of Modern Poetry*, ed. John Wain (London: Hutchinson, 1963) pp. 34–5.

8. Donald Davie, *Purity of Diction in English Verse and Articulate Energy* (Harmondsworth: Penguin, 1992) pp. x–xi.

9. 'Towards a new poetic diction', *Prospect*, vol. 2, no. 2 (Summer 1949) pp. 7–8.

10. Regan, *Philip Larkin*, p. 23. For the historical context of the Movement, see Blake Morrison, *The Movement: English Poetry and Fiction of the 1950s* (Oxford: Oxford University Press, 1980) and Bernard Bergonzi,

Wartime and Aftermath: English Literature and its Background 1939–1960. For a provocative account of Movement poetry, see Andrew Crozier, 'Thrills and frills: poetry as figures of empirical lyricism', in *Society and Literature 1945–1970*, ed. Alan Sinfield (London: Methuen, 1983) pp. 199–233.

11. Robert Hewison, quoted in Regan, *Philip Larkin*, p. 23.
12. Quoted in John Press, *A Map of Modern English Verse* (London: Oxford University Press, 1969) p. 230.
13. Ibid., pp. 232–3.
14. *Selected Letters*, p. 392.
15. Davie, 'A Postscript: 1966' in *Purity of Diction in English Verse* (London: Routledge & Kegan Paul, 1967) p. 198.
16. Quoted in Morrison, *The Movement*, p. 21.
17. Davie, *Purity of Diction* (1967) p. 5.
18. Ibid., p. 2. The Augustan connection was made again by F. W. Bateson in his review of *The Less Deceived* and Davie's *Brides of Reason*. See 'Auden's (and Empson's) Heirs', *Essays in Criticism*, Vol. VII, no. 1 (January 1957) pp. 76–80.
19. Ibid., p. 107.
20. Ibid., p. 197.
21. Interview with Ian Hamilton, *London Magazine*, vol. 4, no. 8 (November 1964) p. 72.
22. Quoted in Morrison, *The Movement*, p. 47.
23. An account of Larkin's association with *Listen* and The Marvell Press is given by Jean Hartley in *Philip Larkin, The Marvell Press, And Me* (Manchester: Carcanet, 1989).
24. Anthony Hartley, 'Poets of the Fifties', *Spectator*, 27 August 1954 (vol. 193) pp. 260–1.
25. Quoted in Morrison, *The Movement*, p. 51.
26. J. D. Scott, 'In the Movement', *Spectator*, 1 October 1954 (vol. 193) pp. 399–400.
27. Introduction to *Poets of the 1950s*, ed. D. J. Enright (Tokyo: Kenkyusha, 1955) pp. 1–15.
28. Introduction to *New Lines*, ed. Robert Conquest (London: Macmillan, 1956) pp. xi–xviii.
29. See Morrison, *The Movement*, pp. 56–7.
30. See, for example, Bernard Bergonzi, *Exploding English* (Oxford: Clarendon Press, 1990) pp. 1–9.
31. Morrison, *The Movement*, p. 100.
32   Larkin, *Collected Poems*, p. 34.
33. Regan, *Philip Larkin*, p. 18.
34. Interview with Hamilton, *London Magazine*, vol. 4, no 8 (November 1964) p. 72.
35. *Required Writing*, p. 79.
36. Ibid., pp. 80–2.
37. *Selected Letters*, pp. 241–2.
38. Interview with Ian Hamilton, *London Magazine*, vol. 4, no. 8 (November 1964) pp. 74–5.
39. *Selected Letters*, p. 230.

40. Davie, 'The Earnest and the Smart: Provincialism in Letters', *Twentieth Century*, November 1953 (vol. 154) pp. 387–94.
41. Charles Tomlinson, 'The Middlebrow Muse', *Essays in Criticism*, vol. 7, no. 2 (April 1957) p. 215.
42. *Poets of the 1950s*, pp. 17–18.
43. Quoted in Morrison, *The Movement*, p. 58.
44. Quoted in Press, *A Map of Modern English Verse*, p. 257. MacNeice's sarcastic reference to 'the ascent of C3' is a playful allusion to the verse play *The Ascent of F6* by Auden and Isherwood, substituting F6 with the class indicator C3.
45. Quoted in Morrison, *The Movement*, p. 59.
46. Ibid., p. 58.
47. Davie, *The Poet in the Imaginary Museum*, ed. Barry Alpert (Manchester: Carcanet, 1977) pp. 43–4.
48. Ibid., pp. 72–5.
49. Morrison, *The Movement*, pp. 134–5.
50. Philip Oakes, quoted in Morrison, *The Movement*, p. 56.

5. *THE WHITSUN WEDDINGS*

1. These terms are taken from the Russian literary theorist Mikhail Bakhtin. For a brief description of his work, see Terry Eagleton, *Literary Theory: An Introduction* (Oxford: Blackwell, 1983) pp. 116–18. Extended discussion can be found in David Lodge, *After Bakhtin: Essays in Fiction and Criticism*.
2. See Motion, *A Writer's Life*, p. 189.
3. Ibid., p. 270.
4. Booth, *Philip Larkin: Writer*, pp. 85–6.
5. Ibid., p. 86.
6. Larkin, *Collected Poems*, p. 208.
7. Quoted in Motion, *A Writer's Life*, p. 247.
8. *Required Writing*, pp. 68 and 58.
9. Larkin, *Collected Poems*, pp. 56–7.
10. John Goodby, '"The importance of elsewhere", or "No man is an Ireland": self, selves and social consensus in the poetry of Philip Larkin', *Critical Survey*, vol. 1, no. 2 (1989) p. 134.
11. Michael O'Neill, 'The Importance of Difference: Larkin's *The Whitsun Weddings*', in *Philip Larkin 1922–1985: A Tribute*, p. 196. Amongst the most interesting discussions of 'The Importance of Elsewhere' is John Bayley, 'Too Good For This World', in *Philip Larkin 1922–1985: A Tribute*, pp. 198–212.
12. He can be found on p. 73.
13. J. R. Watson, 'The other Larkin', *Critical Quarterly*, vol. 17, no. 4 (Winter 1975) p. 348.
14. Haffenden, *Viewpoints*, p. 126.
15. H. G. Widdowson, 'The Conditional Presence of Mr Bleaney', in *Language and Literature: An Introductory Reader in Stylistics*, ed. Ronald Carter (London: George Allen & Unwin, 1982) pp. 24–5.

16. *Selected Letters*, p. 313.
17. DPL 5 (in BJL).
18. Seamus Heaney, 'The Main of Light', in *Larkin at Sixty*, p. 133.
19. Ibid., p. 136.
20. Motion, *Philip Larkin*, p. 77.
21. Ibid., p. 78.
22. Neil Powell, *Carpenters of Light* (Manchester: Carcanet, 1979) p. 101.
23. Interview with Ian Hamilton, *London Magazine*, vol. 4, no. 8 (November 1964) p. 76.
24. *Selected Letters*, p. 330.
25. John Bayley, 'Too Good For This World', in *Philip Larkin 1922–1985: A Tribute*, p. 211.
26. Haffenden, *Viewpoints*, p. 129.
27. Motion, *A Writer's Life*, p. 298.
28. Ibid., p. 301.
29. Stan Smith, quoted in Regan, *Philip Larkin*, p. 116.
30. Haffenden, *Viewpoints*, p. 125.
31. Motion, *A Writer's Life*, p. 288.
32. *Required Writing*, p. 135.
33. Motion, *A Writer's Life*, p. 290.
34. Larkin, *Collected Poems*, p. 54.
35. Ibid., pp. 63–4.
36. Ibid., p. 150.
37. Motion, *A Writer's Life*, p. 334.
38. Regan, *Philip Larkin*, p. 113.
39. Motion, *A Writer's Life*, p. 274.
40. Booth, *Philip Larkin: Writer*, p. 144.
41. Regan, *Philip Larkin*, p. 120.
42. Motion, *A Writer's Life*, p. 321.
43. Rossen, *Philip Larkin: His Life's Work*, p. 72. In fact, the final image seems to have originated in an earlier, unfinished poem as an explicit image of death. Headed 'When women die', the manuscript draft reads:

    > At last they see out of the finishing light
    > Walking towards them Death. He is far off,
    > Treading the gentle gradient like water. . .
    > (DPL 5 (in BJL))

44. Motion, *A Writer's Life*, p. 234.
45. Steven Clark, 'Get Out As Early As You Can: Larkin's Sexual Politics', in *Philip Larkin 1922–1985: A Tribute*, p. 265.
46. Ibid.
47. Petch, quoted in Clark, 'Get Out As Early As You Can', p. 266.
48. Ibid., p. 265.
49. DPL 7 (in BJL).
50. Clark, 'Get Out As Early As You Can', pp. 265–6.
51. Matt Simpson, 'Never such innocence – a reading of Larkin's "Sunny Prestatyn"', *Critical Survey*, vol. 1, no. 2 (1989) p. 180.
52. Larkin's introductory comment on the recorded reading of *The Whitsun Weddings*.

53. Booth, *Philip Larkin: Writer*, p. 73.
54. *Selected Letters*, p. 344.
55. Booth, *Philip Larkin: Writer*, p. 90.
56. Hartley, 'Nothing To Be Said', in *Philip Larkin 1922–1985: A Tribute*, p. 299.

6.   *HIGH WINDOWS*

1. Motion, *A Writer's Life*, p. 446.
2. Ibid., p. 342.
3. Postcard to Barbara Pym, postmarked 12 May 1965. See MS Pym 151/36 in the Bodleian Library.
4. Al Alvarez, review of *The Whitsun Weddings*, *Observer*, 1 March 1964, p. 27.
5. Motion, *A Writer's Life*, p. 445.
6. Interview with Ian Hamilton, *London Magazine*, vol. 4, no. 8 (November 1964) p. 77.
7. *Selected Letters*, p. 521. Clive James, in his review of *High Windows*, emphasised its note of desperation: 'The total impression of *High Windows* is of despair made beautiful . . . Apart from an outright cry for help, he has sent every distress signal a shy man can'. *At the Pillar of Hercules* (London: Faber and Faber, 1979) pp. 51 and 57.
8. 'Not Like Larkin', *Listener*, 17 August 1972, p. 209.
9. David Trotter, *The Making of the Reader* (London and Basingstoke: Macmillan, 1984) p. 179.
10. Ibid., p. 181.
11. See, for example, Regan, *Philip Larkin*, pp. 123–42.
12. Trotter, *The Making of the Reader*, pp. 184 and 186.
13. Stan Smith, *Inviolable Voice: History and Twentieth–Century Poetry* (Dublin: Gill and Macmillan, 1982) p. 176.
14. Rossen, *Philip Larkin: His Life's Work*, p. 131.
15. *Selected Letters*, p. 386.
16. Ibid., p. 387.
17. Ibid., p. 460.
18. Ibid., p. 696.
19. Haffenden, *Viewpoints*, p. 116.
20. Ibid., p. 127.
21. Barbara Everett, 'Art and Larkin', in *Philip Larkin: The Man and His Work*, p. 131.
22. R. P. Draper, *Lyric Tragedy* (Basingstoke: Macmillan, 1985), p. 205.
23. Booth, *Philip Larkin: Writer*, p. 157.
24. Whalen, *Philip Larkin and English Poetry*, p. 24.
25. Motion, *A Writer's Life*, p. 427.
26. Trotter, *The Making of the Reader*, p. 186.
27. DPL 11 (in BJL).
28. Ibid.
29. Haffenden, *Viewpoints*, p. 124.

30. Everett, 'Art and Larkin', in *Philip Larkin: The Man and His Work*, p. 134.
31. Ibid., p. 132.
32. Barbara Everett, *Poets in Their Time* (London: Faber and Faber, 1986) p. 243.
33. Everett, 'Art and Larkin', in *Philip Larkin: The Man and His Work*, p. 131.
34. *Selected Letters*, p. 453.
35. Ibid., p. 653.
36. Everett, 'Art and Larkin', in *Philip Larkin: The Man and His Work*, p. 135.
37. Haffenden, *Viewpoints*, p. 128.
38. Steven Clark, 'Get Out As Early As You Can: Larkin's Sexual Politics', in *Philip Larkin 1922–1985: A Tribute*, p. 241.
39. Booth, *Philip Larkin: Writer*, p. 168.
40. Ibid.
41. Motion, *A Writer's Life*, p. 355.
42. Ibid.
43. Petch, *The Art of Philip Larkin*, p. 101.
44. In fact, the relationship between Hood's poem and Larkin's is rather less ironic. Hood's poem, for all its sentimental drooping, is essentially as fatalistic as anything in Larkin.
45. Haffenden, *Viewpoints*, pp. 128–9.
46. Rossen, *Philip Larkin: His Life's Work*, p. 126.
47. Larkin, *Collected Poems*, p. 214.
48. See Regan, *Philip Larkin*, pp. 123–42.
49. *Required Writing*, p. 52.
50. *Selected Letters*, p. 452.
51. Motion, *A Writer's Life*, pp. 419 and 418.
52. Roger Day, *Larkin* (Milton Keynes: Open University Press, 1987) p. 66.
53. Motion, *A Writer's Life*, p. 395.
54. DPL 9 (in BJL).
55. Larkin, *Collected Poems*, pp. 154–8.
56. Motion, *A Writer's Life*, p. 338.
57. Larkin, *Collected Poems*, p. 202.
58. Booth, *Philip Larkin: Writer*, p. 101.
59. Motion, *A Writer's Life*, p. 372.
60. Donald Davie, *Czeslaw Milosz and the Insufficiency of Lyric* (Cambridge: Cambridge University Press, 1986) p. 42.
61. Motion, *A Writer's Life*, p. 411.
62. Seamus Heaney, 'The Main of Light', in *Larkin at Sixty*, p. 133.
63. Ibid.
64. Regan, *Philip Larkin*, p. 129.
65. Ibid., p. 127.
66. Everett, *Poets in Their Time*, pp. 254–5.
67. Peter Hollindale, 'Philip Larkin's "The Explosion"', *Critical Survey*, vol. 1, no. 2 (1989) p. 139.
68. Motion, *A Writer's Life*, p. 394.

69. Hollindale, 'Philip Larkin's "The Explosion"', p. 141.
70. Ibid, p. 144.
71. Ibid.
72. Tolley, *My Proper Ground*, p. 135.
73. See Motion, *A Writer's Life*, p. 468.
74. Larkin, *Collected Poems*, p. 209.
75. DPL 11 (in BJL).
76. Larkin, *Collected Poems*, p. 215.
77. Motion, *A Writer's Life*, p. 477.
78. Larkin, *Collected Poems*, p. 211.

7. LARKIN'S IDENTITIES

1. Eagleton, *Literary Theory*, p. 118.
2. George Watson, *British Literature since 1945* (Basingstoke: Macmillan, 1991) p. 132.
3. Haffenden, *Viewpoints*, p. 129.
4. Quoted by David Lodge, in *After Bakhtin*, p. 90.
5. Ibid., p. 91.
6. Ibid., pp. 92–3.
7. Ibid., pp. 97–8.
8. Charles Tomlinson, 'The Middlebrow Muse', *Essays in Criticism*, vol. VII, no. ii (1957) p. 214.
9. Ibid., p. 215.
10. Ibid., p. 216.
11. Charles Tomlinson, 'Poetry Today', in *The Pelican Guide to English Literature, Vol. 7: The Modern Age*, ed. Boris Ford (Harmondsworth: Penguin, 1961; rev. edn. 1964) pp. 458–9.
12. Charles Tomlinson, 'Some Aspects of Poetry since the War', in *The New Pelican Guide to English Literature, vol. 8: The Present*, ed Boris Ford (Harmondsworth: Penguin, 1983) pp. 450–1.
13. Al Alvarez, *The New Poetry* (Harmondsworth: Penguin, 1962; rev. edn. 1966) pp. 24–5.
14. *Selected Letters*, p. 341.
15. *The New Poetry*, p. 25.
16. Ibid., p. 30.
17. Ibid., p. 31.
18. Colin Falck, 'Philip Larkin', in *British Poetry since 1970: a critical survey*, ed. Peter Jones and Michael Schmidt (Manchester: Carcanet, 1980) p. 410.
19. John Bayley, 'The Last Romantic', *London Review of Books*, vol. 5, no. 8 (5–18 May 1983) p. 11.
20. Donald Davie, *Thomas Hardy and British Poetry*, p. 65.
21. Ibid., p. 66.
22. Ibid., p. 74.
23. Falck, 'Philip Larkin', p. 411.

24. Davie, *Thomas Hardy and British Poetry*, p. 75.
25. Ibid., p. 81.
26. Donald Davie, 'Larkin's Choice', *The Listener*, vol. 89 (29 March 1973) pp. 420–1.
27. Anthony Thwaite, 'The Poetry of Philip Larkin', in *The Survival of Poetry: A Contemporary Survey*, ed. Martin Dodsworth (London: Faber and Faber, 1970) pp. 54–5.
28. Regan, *Philip Larkin*, p. 34.
29. Ibid., p. 36
30. Ibid., p. 39.
31. Ibid., p. 48.
32. Ibid., p. 63.
33. Guido Latré, *Locking Earth to Sky: A Structuralist Approach to Philip Larkin's Poetry* (Frankfurt am Maine: Peter Lang, 1985) p. 100.
34. John Bayley, 'Larkin and the romantic tradition', *Critical Quarterly*, vol. 26, nos. 1–2 (Spring & Summer 1984) p. 65.
35. Ibid., p. 62.
36. Ibid., p. 63.
37. M. W. Rowe, 'The Transcendental Larkin', *English*, vol. XXXVIII, no. 161 (Summer 1989) p. 143.
38. Ibid., p. 149.
39. Barbara Everett, 'Philip Larkin: After Symbolism', in *Poets in Their Time*, p. 232.
40. Barbara Everett, 'Larkin's Edens', in *Poets in Their Time*, p. 245.
41. Peter MacDonald Smith, 'The Postmodernist Larkin', *English*, vol. XXXVIII, no. 161 (Summer 1989) pp. 159–60.
42. Motion, *Philip Larkin*, p. 28.
43. Ibid., p. 20.
44. Seamus Heaney, *Preoccupations: Selected Prose 1968–78* (London: Faber and Faber, 1980) p. 169.
45. Ibid., p. 165.
46. Ibid., p. 167.
47. Ibid., pp. 150–1.
48. Robert Crawford, *Devolving English Literature* (Oxford: Clarendon Press, 1992) p. 275.
49. Ibid., p. 276.
50. Neil Corcoran, *English Poetry Since 1940* (Harlow: Longman, 1993) p. 92.
51. Ibid., p. 94.
52. Motion, *A Writer's Life*, p. 372.
53. Tom Paulin, *Minotaur: Poetry and the Nation State* (London: Faber and Faber, 1992) pp. 239–40.
54. Ibid., p. 233–4.
55. Ibid., p. 248.
56. Ibid., p. 250.
57. Ibid., p. 251.
58. DPL 11 (in BJL).

59. Richard Rorty, *Contingency, irony and solidarity* (Cambridge: Cambridge University Press, 1989) p. 23.
60. Larkin, *Collected Poems*, p. 94.
61. Rorty, *Contingency, irony and solidarity*, p. 43.

Select Bibliography

The standard bibliography is B. C. Bloomfield, *Philip Larkin: A Bibliography (1933–1976)* (London: Faber and Faber, 1979). The selection below lists mainly UK publications; Terry Whalen's *Philip Larkin and English Poetry* (Basingstoke: Macmillan, 1986; Vancouver: University of British Columbia, 1986; rev. edn. 1990) gives some items published in the USA.

PRIMARY SOURCES

Major Works by Larkin

The North Ship (London: The Fortune Press, 1945; rev. edn. London: Faber and Faber, 1966).

Jill (London: The Fortune Press, 1946; rev. edn. London: Faber and Faber, 1975).

A Girl in Winter (London: Faber and Faber, 1947; re-issued 1975).

XX Poems (Belfast: privately printed, 1951).

The Less Deceived (Hessle: The Marvell Press, 1955).

The Whitsun Weddings (London: Faber and Faber, 1964).

All What Jazz: A Record Diary 1961–68 (London: Faber and Faber, 1970; rev. edn. 1985).

The Oxford Book of Twentieth Century English Verse (Ed.) (Oxford: Clarendon Press, 1973).

High Windows (London: Faber and Faber, 1974).

Required Writing: Miscellaneous Pieces 1955–1982 (London: Faber and Faber, 1983).

Collected Poems, ed. Anthony Thwaite (London: The Marvell Press and Faber and Faber, 1988; rev. edn. 1990).

Selected Letters of Philip Larkin 1940–85, ed. Anthony Thwaite (London: Faber and Faber, 1992).

Significant Anthologies

Oxford Poetry 1942–1943, ed. Ian Davie (Oxford: Blackwell, 1943).

Poetry from Oxford in Wartime, ed. William Bell (London: The Fortune Press, 1945).

Springtime, ed. G. S. Fraser and Iain Fletcher (London: Peter Owen, 1953).

Poets of the 1950s, ed. D. J. Enright (Tokyo: Kenkyusha, 1955).

New Lines, ed. Robert Conquest (London: Macmillan, 1956).

The New Poetry, ed A. Alvarez (Harmondsworth: Penguin, 1962; rev. edn. 1966).

SECONDARY SOURCES

Monograph Studies

Booth, James, *Philip Larkin: Writer* (Hemel Hempstead: Harvester Wheat-sheaf, 1992).

Brownjohn, Alan, *Philip Larkin* (Harlow: Longman, 1975).

Day, Roger, *Larkin* (Milton Keynes: Open University Press, 1987).

Dunn, Douglas, *Under the Influence: Douglas Dunn on Philip Larkin* (Edinburgh: Edinburgh University Library, 1987).

Hassan, Salem K., *Philip Larkin and his Contemporaries* (Basingstoke: Macmillan, 1988).

Kuby, Lolette, *An Uncommon Poet for the Common Man* (The Hague: Mouton, 1974).

Latré, Guido, *Locking Earth to Sky: A Structuralist Approach to Philip Larkin's Poetry* (Frankfurt am Maine: Peter Lang, 1985).

Martin, Bruce K., *Philip Larkin* (Boston: Twayne, 1978).

Motion, Andrew, *Philip Larkin* (London: Methuen, 1982).

——, *Philip Larkin: A Writer's Life* (London: Faber and Faber, 1993).

Petch, Simon, *The Art of Philip Larkin* (Sydney: Sydney University Press, 1981).

Regan, Stephen, *Philip Larkin* (Basingstoke: Macmillan, 1992).

Rossen, Janice, *Philip Larkin: His Life's Work* (Hemel Hempstead: Harvester Wheatsheaf, 1989).

Swarbrick, Andrew, *The Whitsun Weddings and The Less Deceived* (Basingstoke: Macmillan, 1986).

Tolley, A. T., *My Proper Ground: A Study of the Work of Philip Larkin and its Development* (Edinburgh: Edinburgh University Press, 1991).

Timms, David, *Philip Larkin* (Edinburgh: Oliver & Boyd, 1973).

Whalen, Terry, *Philip Larkin and English Poetry* (Basingstoke: Macmillan 1986; rev. edn. 1990).

Collections of Essays on Larkin by Various Hands

Chambers, Harry (ed.), *An Enormous Yes: in memoriam Philip Larkin (1922–1985)* (Calstock: Peterloo Poets, 1986).

Cookson, Linda, and Brian Loughrey, (eds), *Philip Larkin: The Poems* (Harlow: Longman, 1989).

Hartley, George (ed.), *Philip Larkin 1922–1985: A Tribute* (London: The Marvell Press, 1988).

Salwak, Dale (ed.), *Philip Larkin: The Man and His Work* (Basingstoke: Macmillan, 1989).

Thwaite, Anthony (ed.), *Larkin at Sixty* (London: Faber and Faber, 1982).

Phoenix, nos. 11/12 (Autumn & Winter 1973/4): Philip Larkin Issue.

Critical Survey, vol 1, no. 2 (1989): Larkin.

Other Books and Essays

Alvarez, A., Review of *The Whitsun Weddings*, *Observer*, 1 March 1964, p. 27.

Amis, Kingsley, 'Oxford and After', in Anthony Thwaite (ed.), *Larkin at Sixty* (London: Faber and Faber,1982) pp. 23–30.

——, 'Farewell to a Friend', in Dale Salwak (ed.), *Philip Larkin: The Man and His Work* (Basingstoke: Macmillan, 1989) pp. 3–6.

——, *Memoirs* (London: Hutchinson, 1991).

Amis, Martin, 'A poetic injustice', *Guardian Weekend*, 21 August 1993.

Appleyard, Bryan, 'The dreary laureate of our provincialism', *Independent*, 18 March 1993.

Augustine, John H., 'Tentative Initiation in the Poetry', in Dale Salwak (ed.), *Philip Larkin: The Man and His Work* (Basingstoke: Macmillan, 1989) pp. 112–7.

Barnes, Julian, 'When He Sat Down His Tongue Came Out', *Literary Review*, November 1992, pp. 4–6.

Bateson, F. W., 'Auden's (and Empson's) Heirs', *Essays in Criticism*, vol. VII, no. 1 (January 1957) pp. 76–80.

Bayley, John, *The Uses of Division: Unity and Disharmony in Literature* (London: Chatto & Windus, 1976).

——, 'The Last Romantic', *London Review of Books*, 5–18 May 1983, pp. 11–13.

——, 'Larkin and the romantic tradition', *Critical Quarterly*, vol. 26, nos. 1–2 (Spring & Summer 1984) pp. 61–6.

——, 'Too Good For This World', in George Hartley (ed.), *Philip Larkin 1922–1985: A Tribute* (London: The Marvell Press, 1988) pp. 198–212.

——, 'Larkin's Short Story Poems', in George Hartley (ed.), *Philip Larkin 1922–1985: A Tribute* (London: The Marvell Press, 1988) pp. 272–83.

——, 'Philip Larkin's Inner World', in Dale Salwak (ed.), *Philip Larkin: The Man and His Work* (Basingstoke: Macmillan, 1989) pp. 158–61.

——, 'Becoming a girl', *London Review of Books*, 25 March 1993, p. 10.

Bedient, Calvin, *Eight Contemporary Poets* (London: Oxford University Press, 1974).

Bennett, Alan, 'Instead of a Present', in Anthony Thwaite (ed.), *Larkin at Sixty* (London: Faber and Faber,1982) pp. 69–74.

——, 'Alas! Deceived', *London Review of Books*, 25 March 1993, pp. 3–9.

Bergonzi, Bernard, *The Myth of Modernism and Twentieth Century Literature* (Brighton: Harvester Press, 1986).

——, *Exploding English: Criticism, Theory and Culture* (Oxford: Clarendon Press, 1990).

——, *Wartime and Aftermath: English Literature and its Background 1939–1960* (Oxford: Oxford University Press, 1993).

Bloomfield, B. C., 'Larkin the Librarian', in Anthony Thwaite (ed.), *Larkin at Sixty* (London: Faber and Faber, 1982) pp. 48–52.

Brennan, Maeve M., '"I Remember, I Remember", 1955–1985', in Dale Salwak (ed.), *Philip Larkin: The Man and His Work* (Basingstoke: Macmillan, 1989) pp. 27–37.

Brett, R. L., 'Philip Larkin In Hull', in George Hartley (ed.), *Philip Larkin 1922–1985: A Tribute* (London: The Marvell Press, 1988) pp. 100–14.

Brown, Merle, *Double Lyric: Divisiveness and Communal Creativity in Recent English Poetry* (London: Routledge & Kegan Paul, 1980).

Brownjohn, Alan, 'Novels into Poems', in Anthony Thwaite (ed.), *Larkin at Sixty* (London: Faber and Faber, 1982) pp. 109–19.

Carey, John, 'Mail chauvinism', *The Sunday Times*, 25 October 1992, p. 5.

——, 'Not a hope in Hull', *The Sunday Times*, 4 April 1993, p. 3.

Chambers, Harry, 'Some Light Views of A Serious Poem: a footnote to the misreading of Philip Larkin's "Naturally The Foundation Will Bear Your Expenses"', *Phoenix* (1973/4) pp. 110–14.

——, 'Meeting Philip Larkin', in Anthony Thwaite (ed.), *Larkin at Sixty* (London: Faber and Faber, 1982) pp. 61–4.

Clark, Steve, 'Get Out As Early As You Can: Larkin's Sexual Politics', in George Hartley (ed.), *Philip Larkin 1922–1985: A Tribute* (London: The Marvell Press, 1988) pp. 237–71.

Conquest, Robert, 'A Proper Sport', in Anthony Thwaite (ed.), *Larkin at Sixty* (London: Faber and Faber, 1982) pp. 31–7.

Conrad, Peter, 'The laureate of our failure', *Observer*, 28 March 1993.

Corcoran, Neil, *English Poetry Since 1940* (Harlow: Longman, 1993).

Crawford, Robert, *Devolving English Literature* (Oxford: Clarendon Press, 1992).

Crozier, Andrew, 'Thrills and frills: poetry as figures of empirical lyricism', in Alan Sinfield (ed.), *Society and Literature 1945–1970* (London: Methuen, 1983) pp. 199–233.

Curtis, Anthony, 'Larkin's Oxford', in Dale Salwak (ed.), *Philip Larkin: The Man and His Work* (Basingstoke: Macmillan, 1989) pp. 7–17.

Davie, Donald, *Thomas Hardy and British Poetry* (London: Routledge & Kegan Paul, 1973).

——, 'Larkin's Choice', *Listener*, vol. 89 (29 March 1973) pp. 420–21.

——, 'Remembering the Movement', in Barry Alpert (ed.), *The Poet in the Imaginary Museum* (Manchester: Carcanet, 1977) pp. 72–5.

——, *Under Briggflatts: A History of Poetry in Great Britain 1960–1980* (Manchester: Carcanet, 1989).

——, *Purity of Diction in English Verse and Articulate Energy* (Harmondsworth: Penguin, 1992).

——, 'Letters from Hull', *PN Review*, vol. 19, no. 3 (January/February 1993) pp. 4–5.

Dawes, Edwin A., 'Larkin Around in the Library', in Dale Salwak (ed.), *Philip Larkin: The Man and His Work* (Basingstoke: Macmillan, 1989) pp. 18–26.

Dawson, S. W., 'On Re–Reading *The Less Deceived*', in George Hartley (ed.) *Philip Larkin 1922–1985: A Tribute* (London: The Marvell Press, 1988) pp. 178–83.

Day, Roger, '"That vast moth-eaten musical brocade": Larkin and religion', in Cookson and Loughrey (eds), *Philip Larkin: The Poems* (Harlow: Longman, 1989) pp. 81–92.

Dodsworth, Martin, 'Pain and Recent Poetry', *London Magazine*, vol. 4, no. 8 (November 1964) pp. 86–95.

Draper, R. P., *Lyric Tragedy* (Basingstoke: Macmillan, 1985).

——, 'The Positive Larkin', in Cookson and Loughrey (eds), *Philip Larkin: The Poems* (Harlow: Longman, 1989) pp. 94–104.

Dunn, Douglas, 'Memoirs of the Brynmor Jones Library', in Anthony Thwaite (ed.), *Larkin at Sixty* (London: Faber and Faber, 1982) pp. 53–60.

Eagleton, Terry, *Literary Theory: An Introduction* (Oxford: Blackwell, 1983).

Enright, D. J., *Conspirators and Poets* (London: Chatto & Windus, 1966).

Everett, Barbara, *Poets in Their Time* (London: Faber and Faber, 1986).

——, 'Larkin And Dockery: The Limits Of The Social', in George Hartley (ed.), *Philip Larkin 1922–1985: A Tribute* (London: The Marvell Press, 1988) pp. 140–52.

——, 'Art and Larkin', in Dale Salwak (ed.), *Philip Larkin: The Man and His Work* (Basingstoke: Macmillan, 1989) pp. 129–39.

Ewart, Gavin, 'Larkin About (One Reader's Guide)', in George Hartley (ed.), *Philip Larkin 1922–1985: A Tribute* (London: The Marvell Press, 1988) pp. 115–8.

Falck, Colin, 'Philip Larkin', in *British Poetry since 1970: a critical survey*, ed. Peter Jones and Michael Schmidt (Manchester: Carcanet, 1980) pp. 403–11.

Ferguson, Peter, 'Philip Larkin's *XX Poems*: The Missing Link', in George Hartley (ed.), *Philip Larkin 1922–1985: A Tribute* (London: The Marvell Press, 1988) pp. 153–65.

Finch, G. J., 'Larkin, nature, and Romanticism', *Critical Survey*, vol. 3, no. 1 (1991) pp. 53–60.

Gardiner, Alan, 'Larkin's England', in Cookson and Loughrey (eds), *Philip Larkin: The Poems* (Harlow: Longman, 1989) pp. 62–70.

Gardner, Philip, 'The Wintry Drum', *Phoenix* (1973/4) pp. 27–39.

——, '"One does one's best": Larkin's posthumous', *Critical Survey*, vol. 1, no. 2 (1989) pp. 194–200.

Gervais, David, *Literary Englands: Versions of Englishness in modern writing* (Cambridge: Cambridge University Press, 1993).

Gearin-Tosh, Michael, 'Deprivation and love in Larkin's poetry', in Cookson and Loughrey (eds), *Philip Larkin: The Poems* (Harlow: Longman, 1989) pp. 29–37.

Gibson, Andrew, 'Larkin and ordinariness', in Cookson and Loughrey (eds), *Philip Larkin: The Poems* (Harlow: Longman, 1989) pp. 9–18.

Goodby, John, '"The importance of elsewhere", or "No man is an Ireland": self, selves and social consensus in the poetry of Philip Larkin', *Critical Survey*, vol. 1, no. 2 (1989) pp. 131–8.

Goode, J., 'The More Deceived: A Reading Of Deceptions', in George Hartley (ed.), *Philip Larkin 1922–1985: A Tribute* (London: The Marvell Press, 1988) pp. 126–34.

Gross, John, 'The Anthologist', in Anthony Thwaite (ed.), *Larkin at Sixty* (London: Faber and Faber, 1982) pp. 81–6.

Grubb, Frederick A., *A Vision of Reality: A Study of Liberalism in Twentieth Century Verse* (London: Chatto & Windus, 1965).

——, 'Dragons', *Phoenix* (1973/4), pp. 119–36.

Haffenden, John, *Viewpoints: Poets in Conversation* (London: Faber and Faber, 1981).

Hall, Donald, 'Philip Larkin, 1922–85', in Dale Salwak (ed.), *Philip Larkin: The Man and His Work* (Basingstoke: Macmillan, 1989) pp. 165–8.

Hallsmith, Harvey, 'The "I" in Larkin', in Cookson and Loughrey (eds), *Philip Larkin: The Poems* (Harlow: Longman, 1989) pp. 72–9.

Hamilton, Ian, Review of *The Whitsun Weddings*, *London Magazine*, vol. 24, no. 2 (May 1964) pp. 70–73.

——, 'Four Conversations' [interview with Larkin], *London Magazine*, vol. 4, no. 8 (November 1964) pp. 71–7.

——, 'Bugger me blue', *London Review of Books*, 16 October 1992, pp. 3–4.

——, 'Self's the man', *The Times Literary Supplement*, 2 April 1993, pp. 3–4.

Hartley, George, 'No Right Of Entry', *Phoenix* (1973/4), pp. 105–9; reprinted in George Hartley (ed.), *Philip Larkin 1922–1985: A Tribute* (London: The Marvell Press, 1988) pp. 135–9.

——, 'Nothing To Be Said', in Anthony Thwaite (ed.), *Larkin at Sixty* (London: Faber and Faber, 1982) pp. 87–97; reprinted in George Hartley (ed.), *Philip Larkin 1922–1985: A Tribute* (London: The Marvell Press, 1988) pp. 298–308.

——, 'Not Like Us', in George Hartley (ed.), *Philip Larkin 1922–1985: A Tribute* (London: The Marvell Press, 1988) pp. 213–9.

Hartley, Jean, *Philip Larkin, The Marvell Press, and Me* (Manchester: Carcanet, 1989).

Harvey, Geoffrey, *The Romantic Tradition in Modern English Poetry* (Basingstoke: Macmillan, 1986).

Heaney, Seamus, 'Englands of the Mind', in *Preoccupations: Selected Prose 1968–78* (London: Faber and Faber, 1980) pp. 150–69.

——, 'The Main of Light', in Anthony Thwaite (ed.), *Larkin at Sixty* (London: Faber and Faber, 1982) pp. 131–8.

Hendon, Paul, 'Larkin and the logic of replacement', *Critical Survey*, vol. 1, no. 2 (1989), pp. 164–71.

Hobsbaum, Philip, 'Larkin's Singing Line', in George Hartley (ed.), *Philip Larkin 1922–1985: A Tribute* (London: The Marvell Press, 1988) pp. 284–92.

Holbrook, David, *Lost Bearings in English Poetry* (London: Vision Press, 1977).

Holderness, Graham, 'Philip Larkin: the limitations of experience', in Cookson and Loughrey (eds), *Philip Larkin: The Poems* (Harlow: Longman, 1989) pp. 106–14.

——, 'Reading "Deceptions" – a dramatic conversation', *Critical Survey*, vol. 1, no. 2 (1989) pp. 122–30.

Hollindale, Peter, 'The long perspectives', in Cookson and Loughrey (eds), *Philip Larkin: The Poems* (Harlow: Longman, 1989) pp. 50–60.

——, 'Philip Larkin's "The Explosion"', *Critical Survey*, vol. 1, no. 2 (1989) pp. 139–48.

Holt, Hazel, 'Philip Larkin and Barbara Pym: Two Quiet People', in Dale Salwak (ed.), *Philip Larkin: The Man and His Work* (Basingstoke: Macmillan, 1989) pp. 59–68.

Homberger, Eric, *The Art of the Real* (London: Dent, 1977).

Hughes, Noel, 'The Young Mr Larkin', in Anthony Thwaite (ed.), *Larkin at Sixty* (London: Faber and Faber, 1982) pp. 17–22.

——, 'An Innocent at Home', in Dale Salwak (ed.), *Philip Larkin: The Man and His Work* (Basingstoke: Macmillan, 1989) pp. 54–8.

Imlah, Mick, 'Selfishly yours, Philip', *The Times Literary Supplement*, 23 October 1992, p. 13.

James, Clive, 'Don Juan in Hull: Philip Larkin', in *At the Pillars of Hercules* (London: Faber and Faber, 1979) pp. 51–72.

——, 'On His Wit', in Anthony Thwaite (ed.), *Larkin at Sixty* (London: Faber and Faber, 1982) pp. 98–108.

——, 'Somewhere becoming rain', in *The Dreaming Swimmer* (London: Jonathan Cape, 1992) pp. 9–20.

——, 'Authority of sadness', *Independent on Sunday*, 4 April 1993, p. 34.

Jardine, Lisa, 'Saxon violence', *Guardian*, 8 December 1992.

Jones, Alun R., 'The Poetry of Philip Larkin: A Note On Transatlantic Culture', *Phoenix* (1973/4) pp. 139–51.

Joseph, Jenny, 'Larkin The Poet: The Old Fools', in George Hartley (ed.), *Philip Larkin 1922–1985: A Tribute* (London: The Marvell Press, 1988) pp. 119–25.

Kennedy, X. J., 'Larkin's Voice', in Dale Salwak (ed.), *Philip Larkin: The Man and His Work* (Basingstoke: Macmillan, 1989) pp. 162–4.

Kilmarnock, Hilary, 'A Personal Memoir', in Dale Salwak (ed.), *Philip Larkin: The Man and His Work* (Basingstoke: Macmillan, 1989) pp. 153–7.

King, P. R., *Nine Contemporary Poets* (London: Methuen, 1979).

Kirkham, Michael, 'Philip Larkin and Charles Tomlinson', in Boris Ford (ed.), *The New Pelican Guide to English Literature, vol. 8: The Present* (Harmondsworth: Penguin, 1983) pp. 294–313.

——, 'No Hokum', in George Hartley (ed.), *Philip Larkin 1922–1985: A Tribute* (London: The Marvell Press, 1988) pp. 293–7.

Lane, Anthony, 'Lonesome Larks and the Fabulous Rosina', *Independent*, 17 October 1992.

Lerner, Laurence, 'Larkin's strategies', *Critical Survey*, vol. 1, no. 2 (1989) pp. 113–21.

Levi, Peter, 'The English Wisdom Of A Master Poet', in Harry Chambers (ed.), *An Enormous Yes: in memoriam Philip Larkin (1922–1985)* (Calstock: Peterloo Poets, 1986) pp. 33–5.

——, *The Art of Poetry* (New Haven and London: Yale University Press 1991).

Lindop, Grevel, 'Being different from yourself: Philip Larkin in the 1970s', in Graham Martin and P. N. Furbank (eds), *Twentieth Century Poetry: Critical Essays & Documents* (Milton Keynes: Open University Press) pp. 46–54.

Lodge, David, 'Philip Larkin: the Metonymic Muse', in Dale Salwak (ed.), *Philip Larkin: The Man and His Work* (Basingstoke: Macmillan, 1989) pp. 118–28.

——, *After Bakhtin: Essays on Fiction and Criticism* (London: Routledge, 1990).

Logan, Stephen, 'Larkin's Half-Secret Self', *PN Review*, vol. 19, no. 4 (March/April 1993) pp. 11–12.

Longley, Edna, 'Larkin, Edward Thomas and the Tradition', *Phoenix* (1973/4) pp. 63–89.

——, 'Poète Maudit Manqué', in George Hartley (ed.), *Philip Larkin 1922–1985: A Tribute* (London: The Marvell Press, 1988) pp. 220–31.

Lucas, John, *Modern English Poetry from Hardy to Hughes* (London: Batsford, 1986).

MacDonald Smith, Peter, 'The Postmodernist Larkin', *English*, vol. XXXVIII, no. 161 (Summer 1989) pp. 153–61.

Martin, Bruce K., 'Larkin's Humanity Viewed from Abroad', in Dale Salwak (ed.), *Philip Larkin: The Man and His Work* (Basingstoke: Macmillan, 1989) pp. 140–49.

Miller, Christopher, 'The Egotistical Banal, or Against Larkitudinising', *Agenda*, vol. 21, no. 3 (Autumn 1983) pp. 69–103.

Mitchell, Donald, 'Larkin's Music', in Anthony Thwaite (ed.), *Larkin at Sixty* (London: Faber and Faber, 1982) pp. 75–80.

Molony, Rowland, 'Philip Larkin and Personal Space', *The English Review*, vol. 3, no. 2 (November 1992) pp. 2–4.

Monteith, Charles, 'Publishing Larkin', in Anthony Thwaite (ed.), *Larkin at Sixty* (London: Faber and Faber, 1982) pp. 38–47.

Morrison, Blake, *The Movement: English Poetry and Fiction of the 1950s* (Oxford: Oxford University Press, 1980).

——, 'In the grip of darkness', *The Times Literary Supplement*, 14–20 October 1988, pp. 1151–2.

——, 'Bigger than his bigoted letters', *Independent on Sunday*, 22 November 1992, p. 24.

Motion, Andrew, 'On the Plain of Holderness', in Anthony Thwaite (ed.), *Larkin at Sixty* (London: Faber and Faber, 1982) pp. 65–8.

O'Neill, Michael, 'The Importance of Difference: Larkin's *The Whitsun Weddings*', in George Hartley (ed.), *Philip Larkin 1922–1985: A Tribute* (London: The Marvell Press, 1988) pp. 184–97.

Paulin, Tom, 'She Did Not Change: Philip Larkin', in *Minotaur: Poetry and the Nation State* (London: Faber and Faber, 1992) pp. 233–51.

Porter, Peter, 'Larkin's philippics', *Sunday Telegraph*, 18 October 1992, p. x.

Powell, Anthony, 'The narrow road to Hull', *Spectator*, 24 October 1992, p. 39.

Powell, Neil, *Carpenters of Light* (Manchester: Carcanet, 1979).

Press, John, *Rule and Energy: Trends in British Poetry Since the Second World War* (London: Oxford University Press, 1963).

——, *A Map of Modern English Verse* (London: Oxford University Press, 1969).

Pritchard, William H., 'Larkin's Presence', in Dale Salwak (ed.), *Philip Larkin: The Man and His Work* (Basingstoke: Macmillan, 1989) pp. 71–89.

Raban, Jonathan, *The Society of the Poem* (London: Harrap, 1971).

——, 'Mr Miseryguts', *Independent on Sunday*, 18 October 1992, pp. 28–9.

Ratcliffe, Michael, 'Friday lunch blues', *Observer*, 15 November 1992.

Raine, Craig, 'Closing Lines On A Life', in Harry Chambers (ed.), *An Enormous Yes: in memoriam Philip Larkin (1922–1985)* (Calstock: Peterloo Poets, 1986) pp. 36–8.

Ricks, Christopher, 'The Whitsun Weddings', *Phoenix* (1973/4) pp. 6–10.

——, 'Like Something Almost Being Said', in Anthony Thwaite (ed.), *Larkin at Sixty* (London: Faber and Faber, 1982) pp. 120–30.

Robson, Bryan, 'Philip Larkin: *The Whitsun Weddings* or The Syllabus with a Hole in It', in Roger Knight (ed.), *English in Practice: Literature at A Level* (Edinburgh: Scottish Academic Press, 1989).

Rorty, Richard, *Contingency, irony and solidarity* (Cambridge: Cambridge University Press, 1989).

Rossen, Janice, 'Philip Larkin Abroad', in Dale Salwak (ed.), *Philip Larkin: The Man and His Work* (Basingstoke: Macmillan, 1989) pp. 48–53.

Rowe, M. W., 'The Transcendental Larkin', *English*, vol. XXXVIII, no. 161 (Summer 1989) pp. 143–52.

Russel, Nick, 'Larkin About At St. John's', in George Hartley (ed.), *Philip Larkin 1922–1985: A Tribute* (London: The Marvell Press, 1988) pp. 82–7.

Saunders, John, 'Beauty and Truth in three poems from *The Whitsun Weddings*', in Cookson and Loughrey (eds), *Philip Larkin: The Poems* (Harlow: Longman, 1989) pp. 39–48.

Scupham, Peter, 'A Caucus-race', *Phoenix* (1973/4) pp. 173–82.

Selzer, David, 'Touchstones', in Harry Chambers (ed.), *An Enormous Yes: in memoriam Philip Larkin (1922–1985)* (Calstock: Peterloo Poets, 1986) pp. 39–42.

Simmons, James, 'The Trouble With Larkin', in George Hartley (ed.), *Philip Larkin 1922–1985: A Tribute* (London: The Marvell Press, 1988) pp. 232–6.

Simpson, Matt, 'Never such innocence – a reading of Larkin's "Sunny Prestatyn"', *Critical Survey*, vol. 1, no. 2 (1989) pp. 176–82.

Smith, Stan, *Inviolable Voice: History and Twentieth-Century Poetry* (Dublin: Gill and Macmillan, 1982).

Snowdon, Peter, 'Larkin's conceit', *Critical Survey*, vol. 3, no. 1 (1991) pp. 61–70.

Sutton, James, 'Early Days', in George Hartley (ed.), *Philip Larkin 1922–1985: A Tribute* (London: The Marvell Press, 1988) pp. 76–81.

Swarbrick, Andrew, 'Larkin: First and Final Drafts', *Poetry Review*, vol. 83, no. 4 (Winter 1993/94) pp. 50–3.

——, Philip Larkin: from Novelist to Poet', *The Use of English*, vol. 46, no. 1 (Autumn 1994) pp. 53–8.

Swinden, Patrick, 'Old Lines, New Lines: The Movement Ten Years After', *Critical Quarterly*, vol. 9, no. 4 (Winter 1967) pp. 347–59.

Terry, Arthur, 'Larkin in Belfast', in George Hartley (ed.), *Philip Larkin 1922–1985: A Tribute* (London: The Marvell Press, 1988) pp. 91–9.

Thurley, Geoffrey, *The Ironic Harvest: English poetry in the twentieth century* (London: Edward Arnold, 1974).

Thwaite, Anthony, *Essays on Contemporary English Poetry* (Tokyo: Kenkyusha, 1957).

——, 'The Poetry of Philip Larkin', in Martin Dodsworth (ed.), *The Survival of Poetry: A Contemporary Survey* (London: Faber and Faber, 1970) pp. 37–55; reprinted in *Phoenix* (1973/4) pp. 41–58.

——, 'Larkin's Recent Uncollected Poems', *Phoenix* (1973/4) pp. 59–61.

——, *Twentieth-Century English Poetry* (London: Heinemann, 1978).

——, *Poetry Today: A Critical Guide to British Poetry 1960–1984* (Harlow: Longman, in association with the British Council, 1985).

Timms, David, '"Church Going" Revisited: "The Building" And The Notion Of Development in Larkin's Poetry', *Phoenix* (1973/4) pp. 13–25.

——, 'Philip Larkin's Novels', *Phoenix* (1973/4) pp. 153–70.

Tolley, A. T., 'Philip Larkin's Unpublished Book: In The Grip Of Light', in George Hartley (ed.), *Philip Larkin 1922–1985: A Tribute* (London: The Marvell Press, 1988) pp. 166–77.

Tomlinson, Charles, 'The Middlebrow Muse', *Essays in Criticism*, vol. VII, no. ii (1957) pp. 208–17.

——, 'Poetry Today', in Boris Ford (ed.), *The Pelican Guide to English Literature, vol 7: The modern age* (Harmondsworth: Penguin, 1961; rev. edn. 1964) pp. 458–74.

——, 'Some Aspects of Poetry since the War', in Boris Ford (ed.), *The New Pelican Guide to English Literature, vol. 8: The Present* (Harmondsworth: Penguin, 1983) pp. 450–70.

Trotter, David, *The Making of the Reader: Language and Subjectivity in Modern American, English and Irish Poetry* (London: Macmillan, 1984).

Underhill, Hugh, 'Poetry of departures: Larkin and the power of choosing', *Critical Survey*, vol. 1, no. 2 (1989) pp. 183–93.

Wain, John, 'Engagement or Withdrawal? Some Notes on the Work of Philip Larkin', *Critical Quarterly*, vol. 6, no. 2 (Summer 1964) pp. 167–78.

Walcott, Derek, 'The Master of the Ordinary', *New York Review of Books*, 1 June 1989, pp. 37–40.

Watson, George, *British Literature since 1945* (Basingstoke: Macmillan, 1991).

Watson, J. R., 'The other Larkin', *Critical Quarterly*, vol. 17, no. 4 (Winter 1975) pp. 347–60.

——, 'Philip Larkin: Voices and Values', in Dale Salwak (ed.), *Philip Larkin: The Man and His Work* (Basingstoke: Macmillan, 1989) pp. 90–111.

——, 'Clichés and common speech in Philip Larkin's poetry', *Critical Survey*, vol. 1, no. 2 (1989) pp. 149–56.

Watt, R. J. C., '"Scragged by embryo-Leavises": Larkin reading his poems', *Critical Survey*, vol. 1, no. 2 (1989) pp. 172–5.

Watts, Cedric, 'Larkin and jazz', in Cookson and Loughrey (eds), *Philip Larkin: The Poems* (Harlow: Longman, 1989) pp. 20–7.

——, 'The poetics of a Larkin poem', *Critical Survey*, vol. 1, no. 2 (1989) pp. 157–63.

Ward, John Powell, *The English Line: Poetry of the Unpoetic from Wordsworth to Larkin* (Basingstoke: Macmillan, 1991).

Whalen, Terry, 'Philip Larkin's imagist bias: his poetry of observation', *Critical Quarterly*, vol. 23, no. 2 (Summer 1981) pp. 29–46.

Whiffen, David, 'A Note On Larkin At Oxford', in George Hartley (ed.), *Philip Larkin 1922–1985: A Tribute* (London: The Marvell Press, 1988) pp. 88–90.

White, John, '"Goodbye, Witherspoon": a Jazz Friendship', in Dale Salwak (ed.), *Philip Larkin: The Man and His Work* (Basingstoke: Macmillan, 1989) pp. 38–47.

Widdowson, H. G., 'The Conditional Presence of Mr Bleaney', in Ronald Carter (ed.), *Language and Literature: An Introductory Reader in Stylistics* (London: George Allen and Unwin, 1982) pp. 19–26.

Index